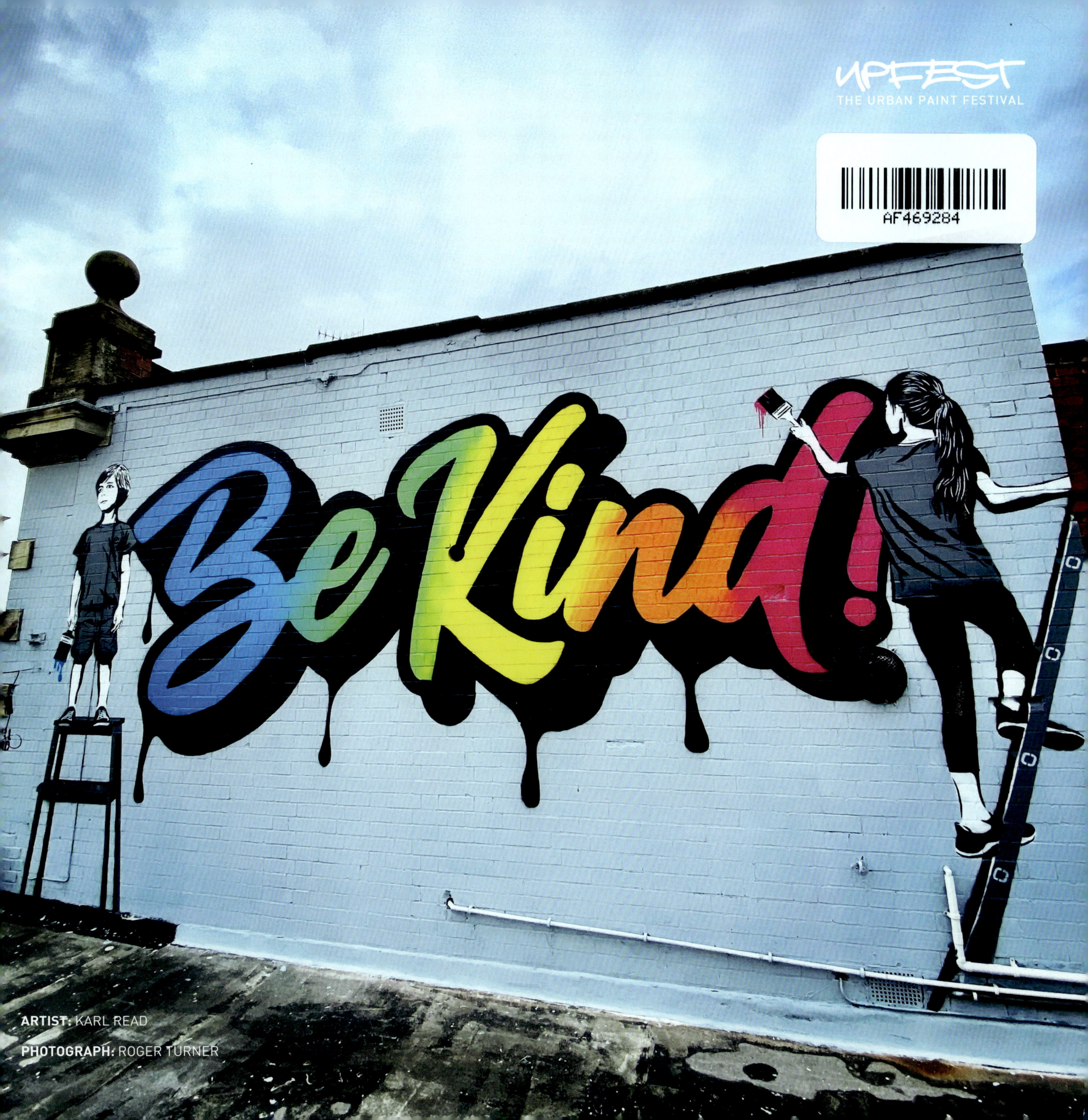
UPFEST
THE URBAN PAINT FESTIVAL
AF469284
Be Kind!
ARTIST: KARL READ
PHOTOGRAPH: ROGER TURNER

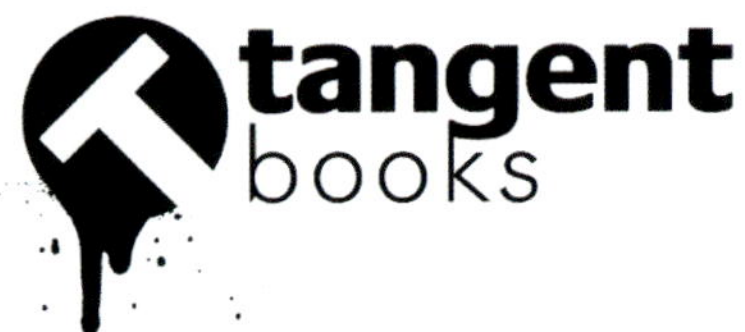

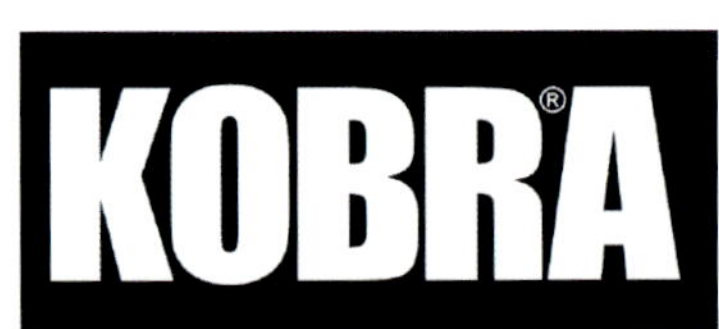

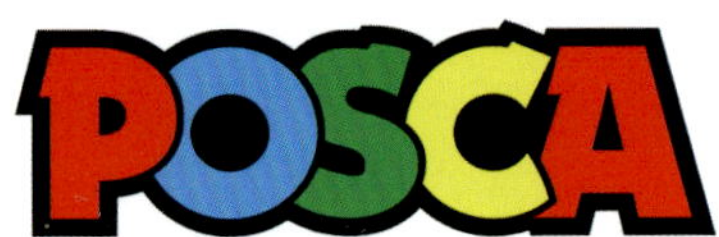

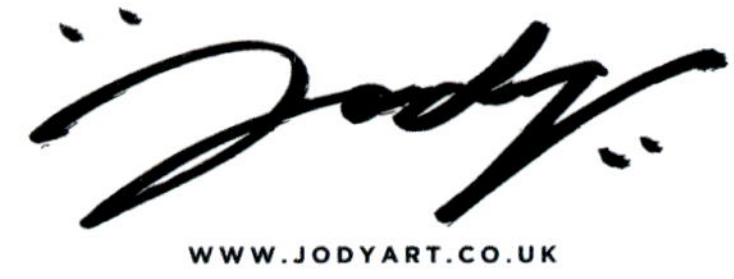

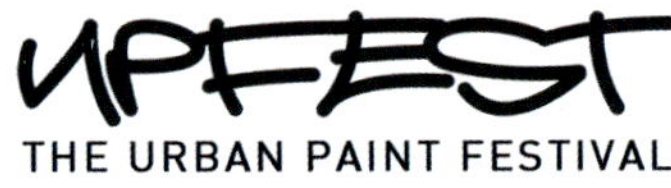

First published 2022 by Tangent Books
Unit 5.16 Paintworks
Arnos Vale
Bristol
BS4 3EH
0117 972 0645

www.tangentbooks.co.uk
Publisher: Richard Jones richard@tangentbooks.co.uk

ISBN 9-978-1914345-21-0

Design & Layout: Jody Thomas hello@jodyart.co.uk / www.jodyart.co.uk

A CIP record for this book is available from the British Library

Printed by Gomer in Wales using paper from a sustainable source

Upfest Gallery,
198 North Street,
Bristol BS3 1JF

www.upfest.co.uk
festival@upfest.co.uk
Tel: 01173305877

FRONT PAGE ARTIST: JODY

PHOTOGRAPH: NEIL JAMES BRAIN

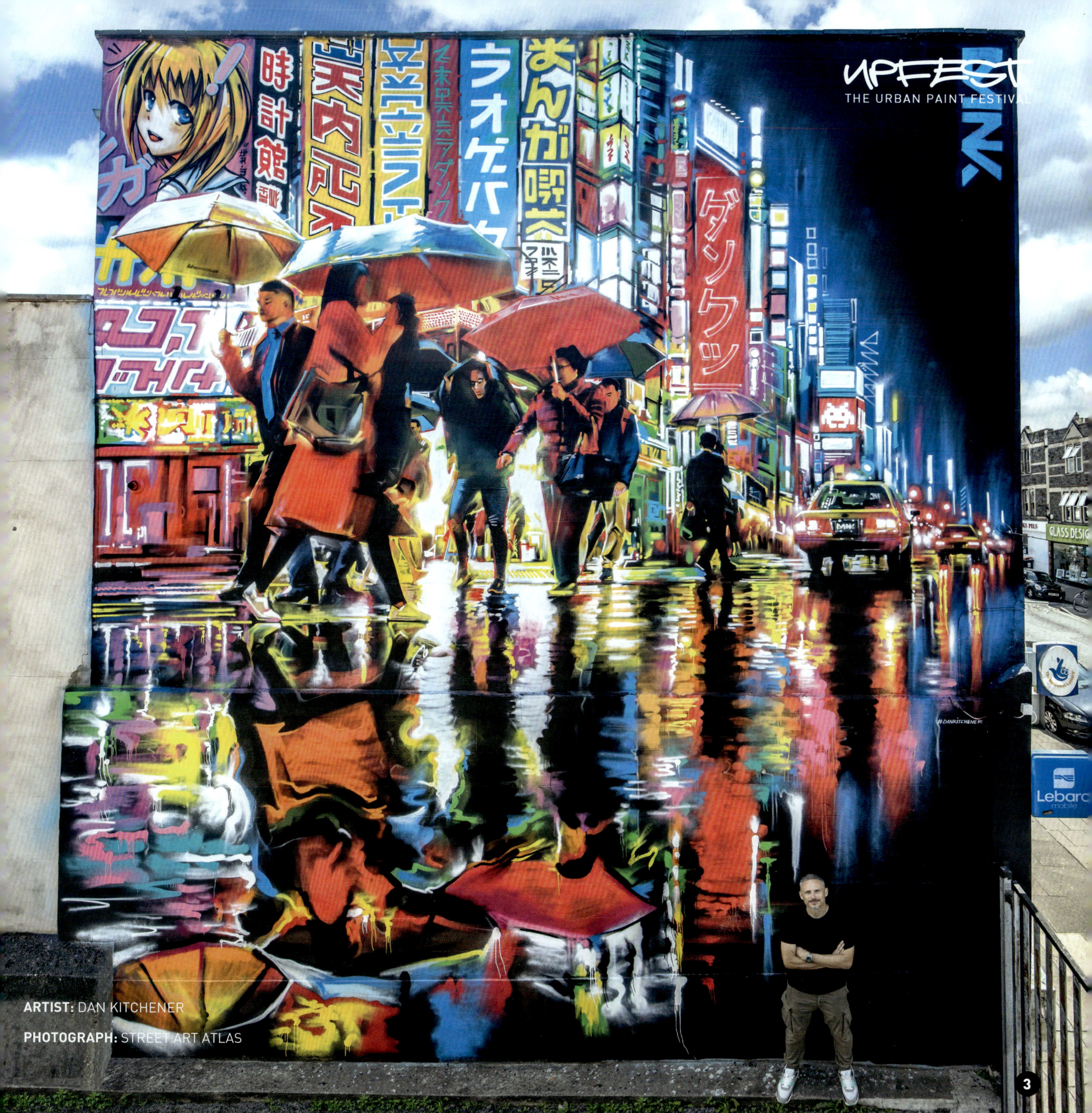

ARTIST: DAN KITCHENER

PHOTOGRAPH: STREET ART ATLAS

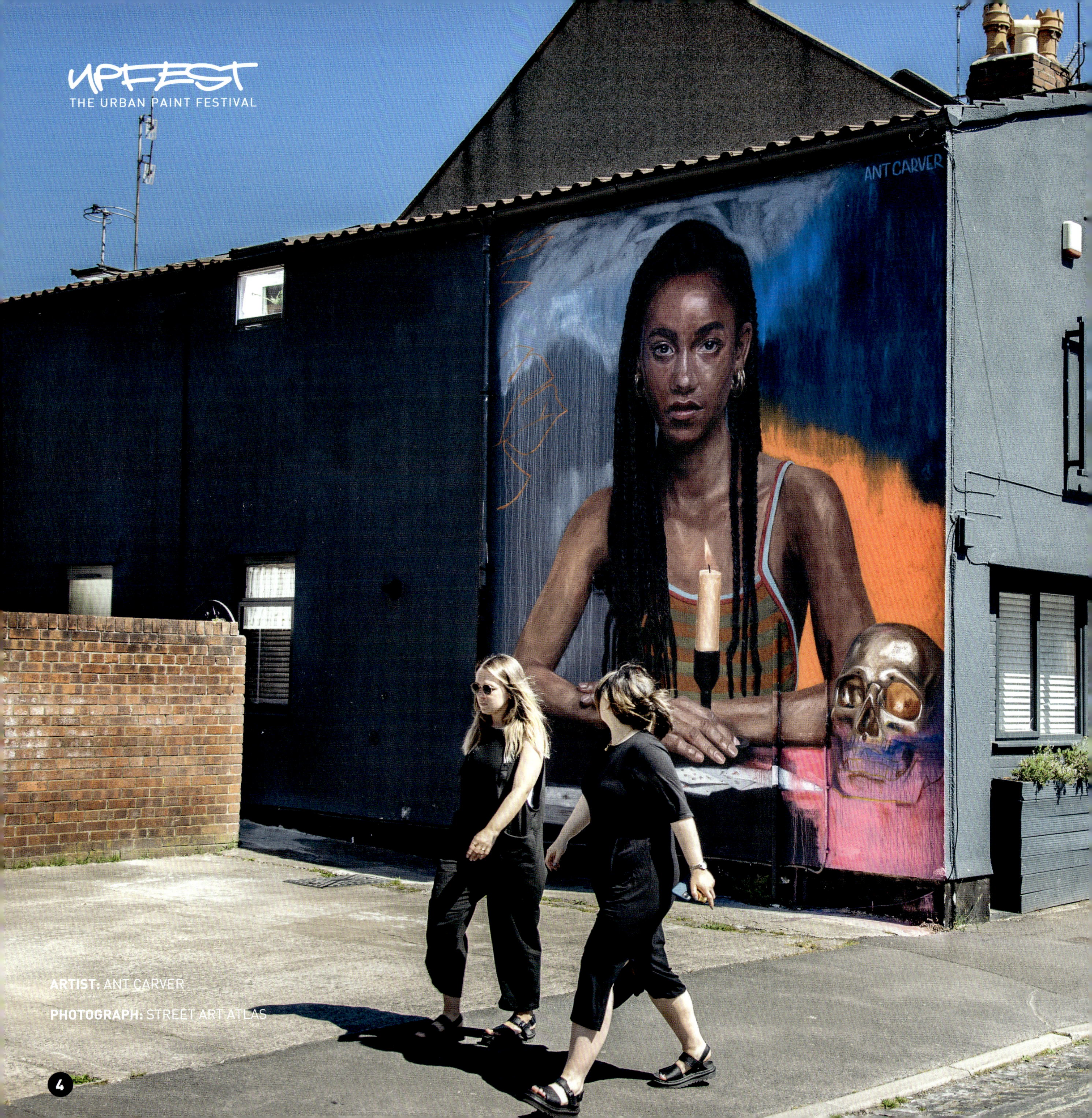

ARTIST: ANT CARVER

PHOTOGRAPH: STREET ART ATLAS

Welcome to our fourth edition of the Upfest Book and what an edition it is! We've all had to adapt over the past few years, and this is our first book that doesn't feature any artwork created at our traditional annual festival, but that's not to say we haven't brought you big walls and lots and lots of colour.

Following a hugely successful run of festivals from 2015 to 2018 the crew needed a break, what we didn't know at the time was that taking 2019 as a fallow year would then lead to a further two years of being unable to gather all our friends, artists and visitors together. After a few head spinning months in early 2020, we gathered our thoughts and creativity to make the most of the very weird situation, plans were afoot on what we could do to bring colour back into people's lives and release the pent-up creativity that was brewing up like a corked champagne bottle.

This book shares with you three of our major projects from the past few years, Upfest Summer Editions, Six Sisters and most recently our 75Walls project from last summer. These projects have definitely kept us going and we hope they've bought smiles to many faces. Huge thanks to all the artists who've contributed to keeping our world and this book awash with colour and the Upfest crew who've kept us all going through these mad times. Big UP to Posca Paint Pens and the Bedminster BID for their continued contribution, Kobra Spraypaint and Arts Council England for their support with the 75Walls project.

Special thanks to Jody for continuing the tradition of designing yet another awesome book, Lindsey for pulling these amazing photos together and of course our happy snapping photographers, Chris Hill, Colin Moody, Hannah Judah, Jon Craig, Lindsey Davis, Neil James Brain, Roger Turner & Street Art Atlas who've allowed the use of these incredible photos.

It's crazy to think that on a damp October afternoon in 2008 the very first Upfest took place, yes we're all a bit older now but we continue our passion of bringing artists together and slapping paint on walls!

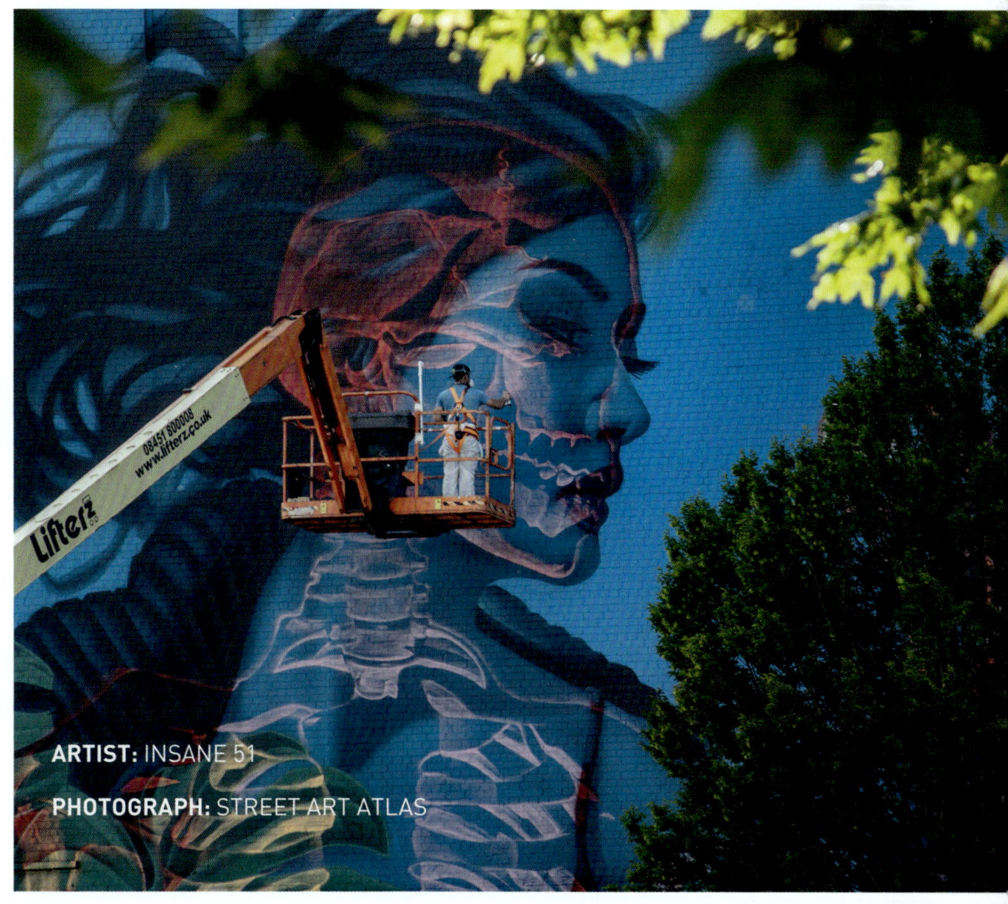

ARTIST: INSANE 51

PHOTOGRAPH: STREET ART ATLAS

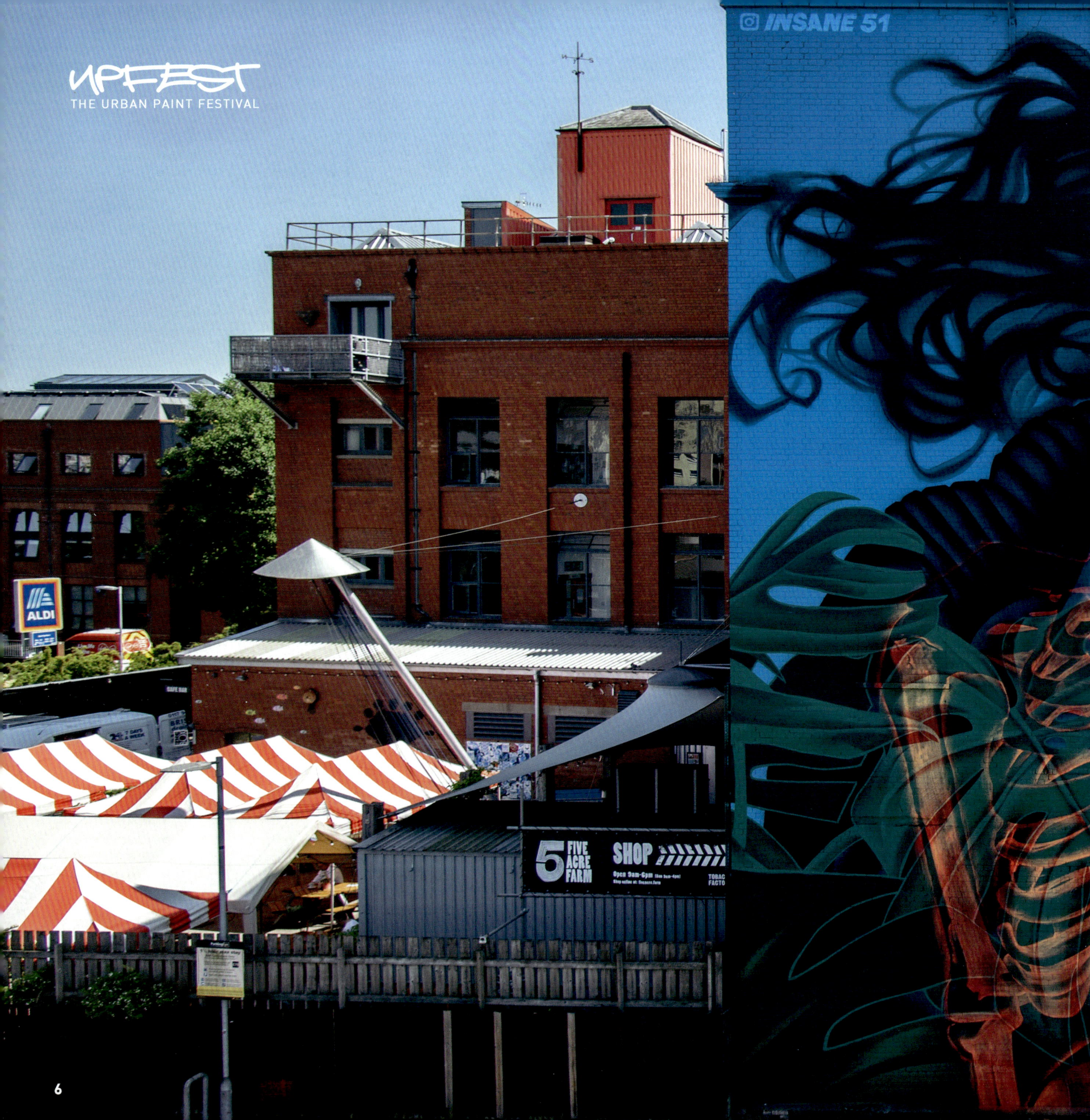

UPFEST
THE URBAN PAINT FESTIVAL
INSANE 51
ALDI
5 FIVE ACRE FARM
SHOP
Open 9am-6pm

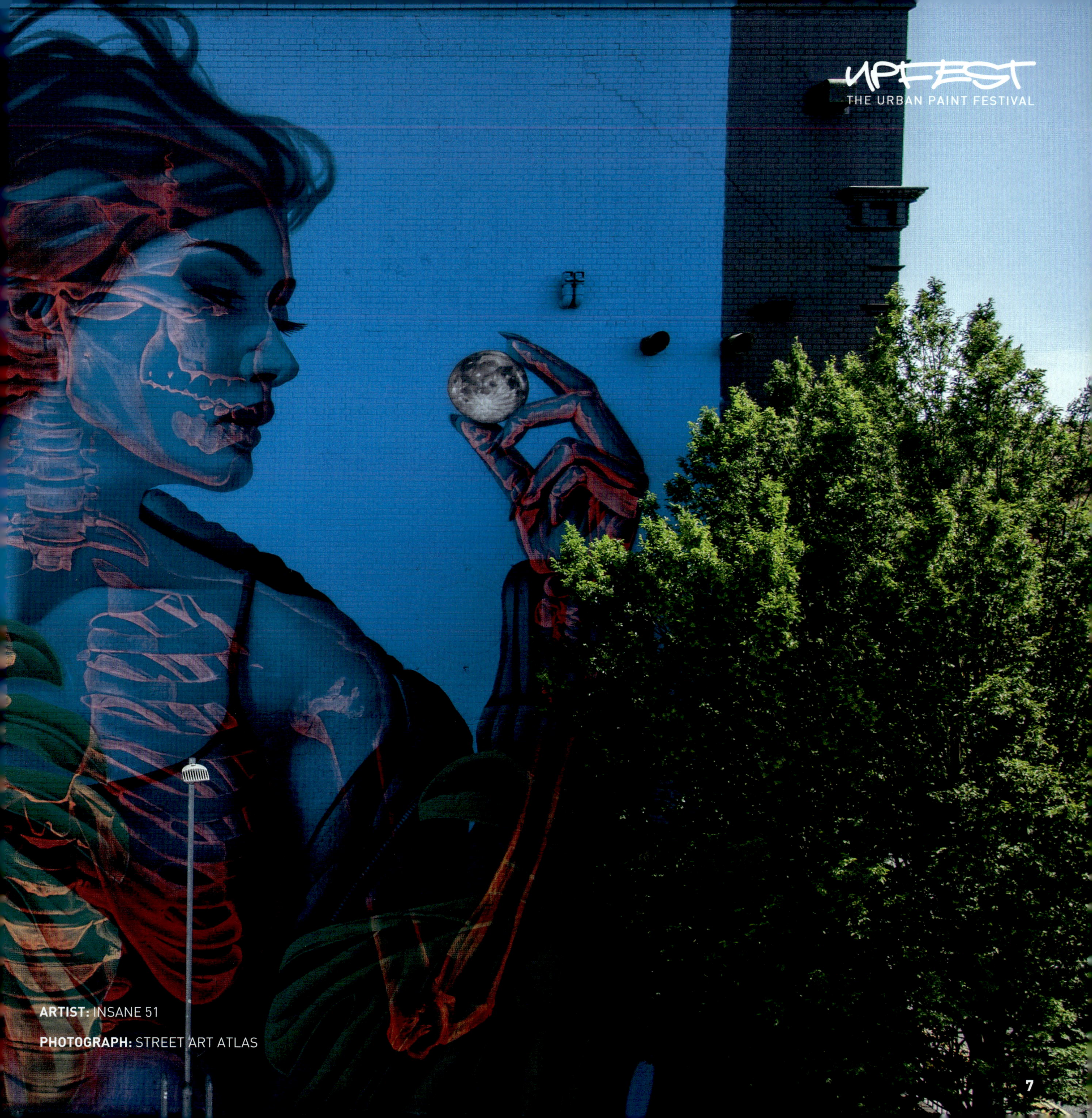

ARTIST: INSANE 51

PHOTOGRAPH: STREET ART ATLAS

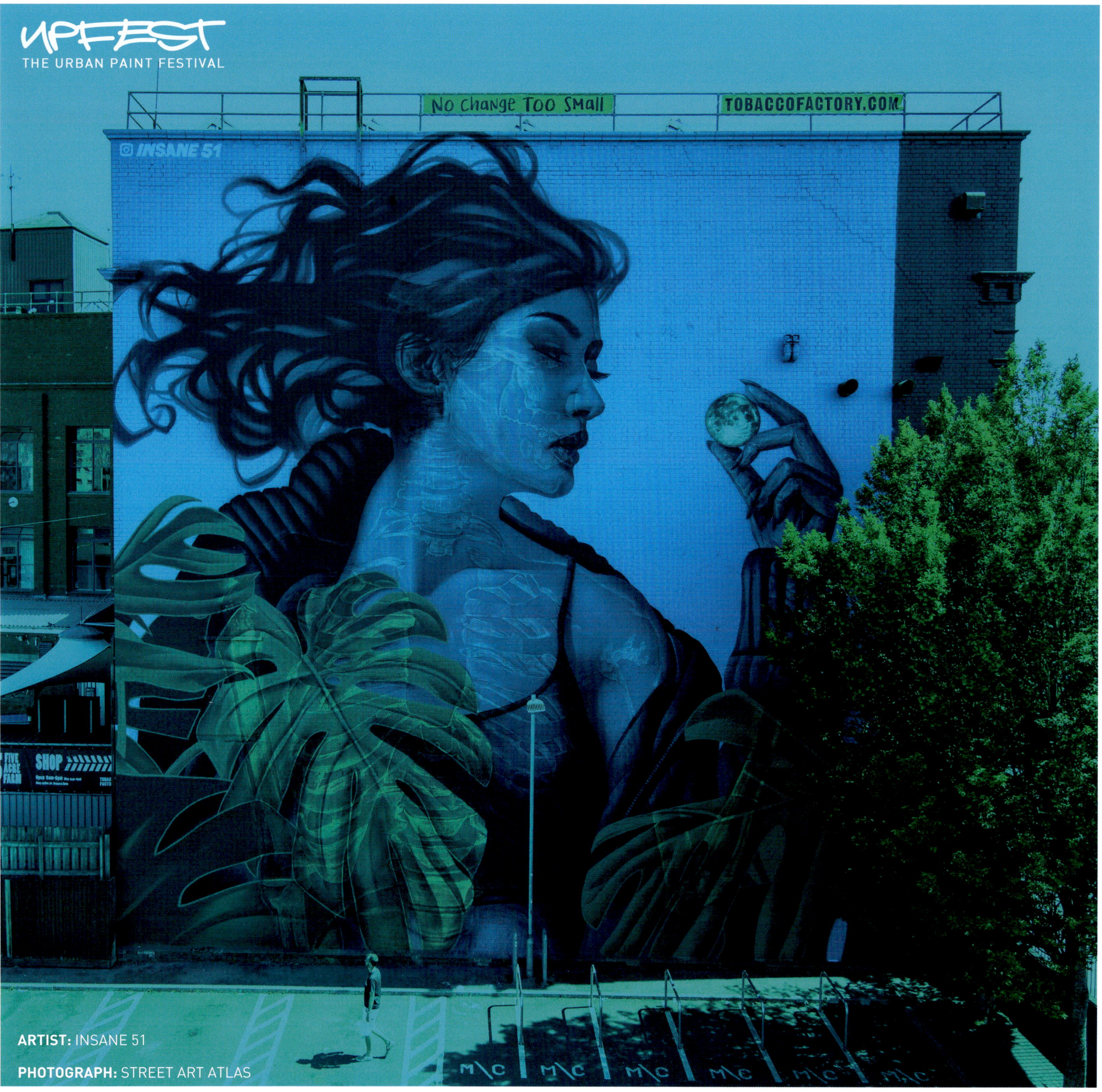

ARTIST: INSANE 51

PHOTOGRAPH: STREET ART ATLAS

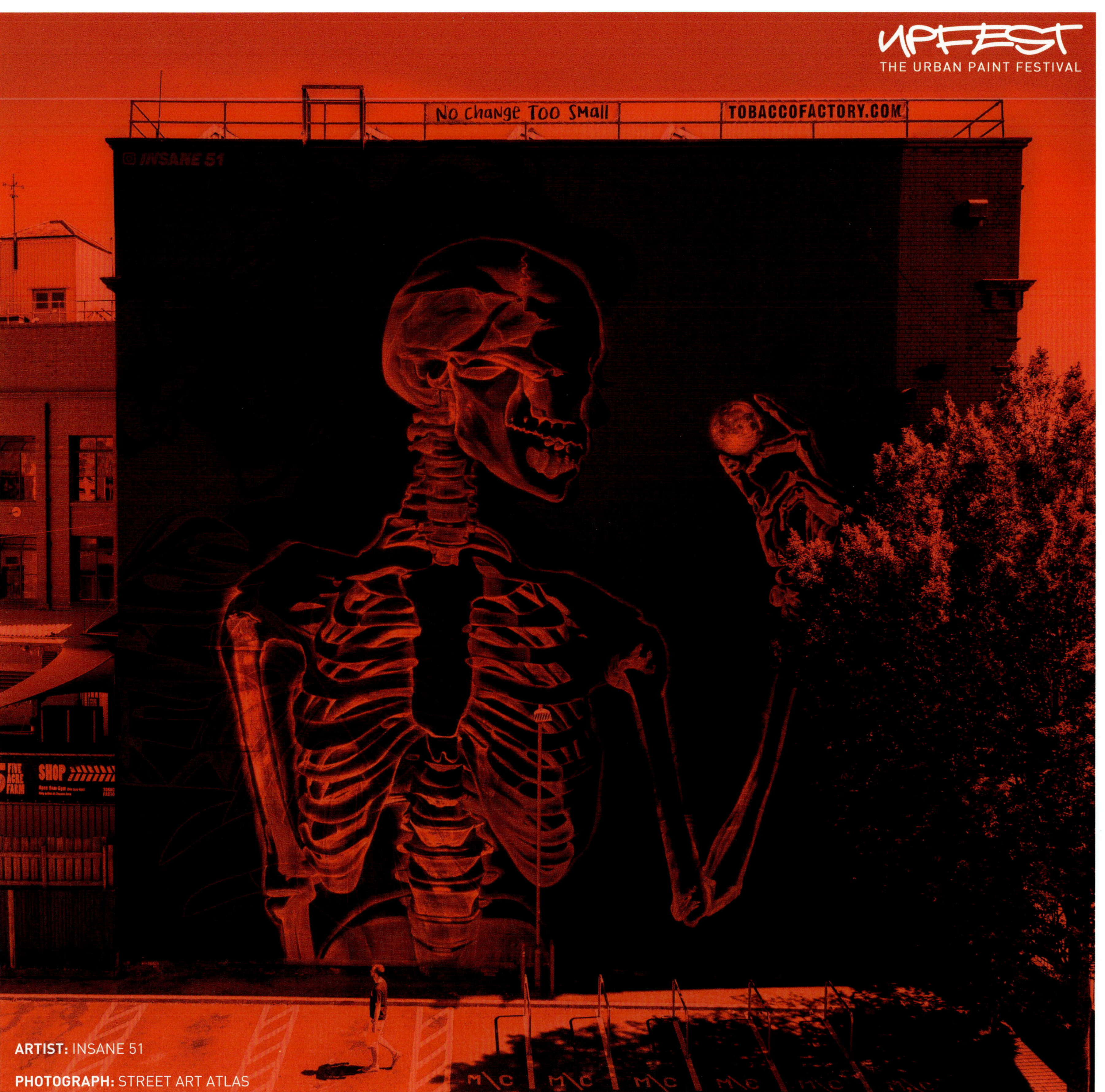

ARTIST: INSANE 51

PHOTOGRAPH: STREET ART ATLAS

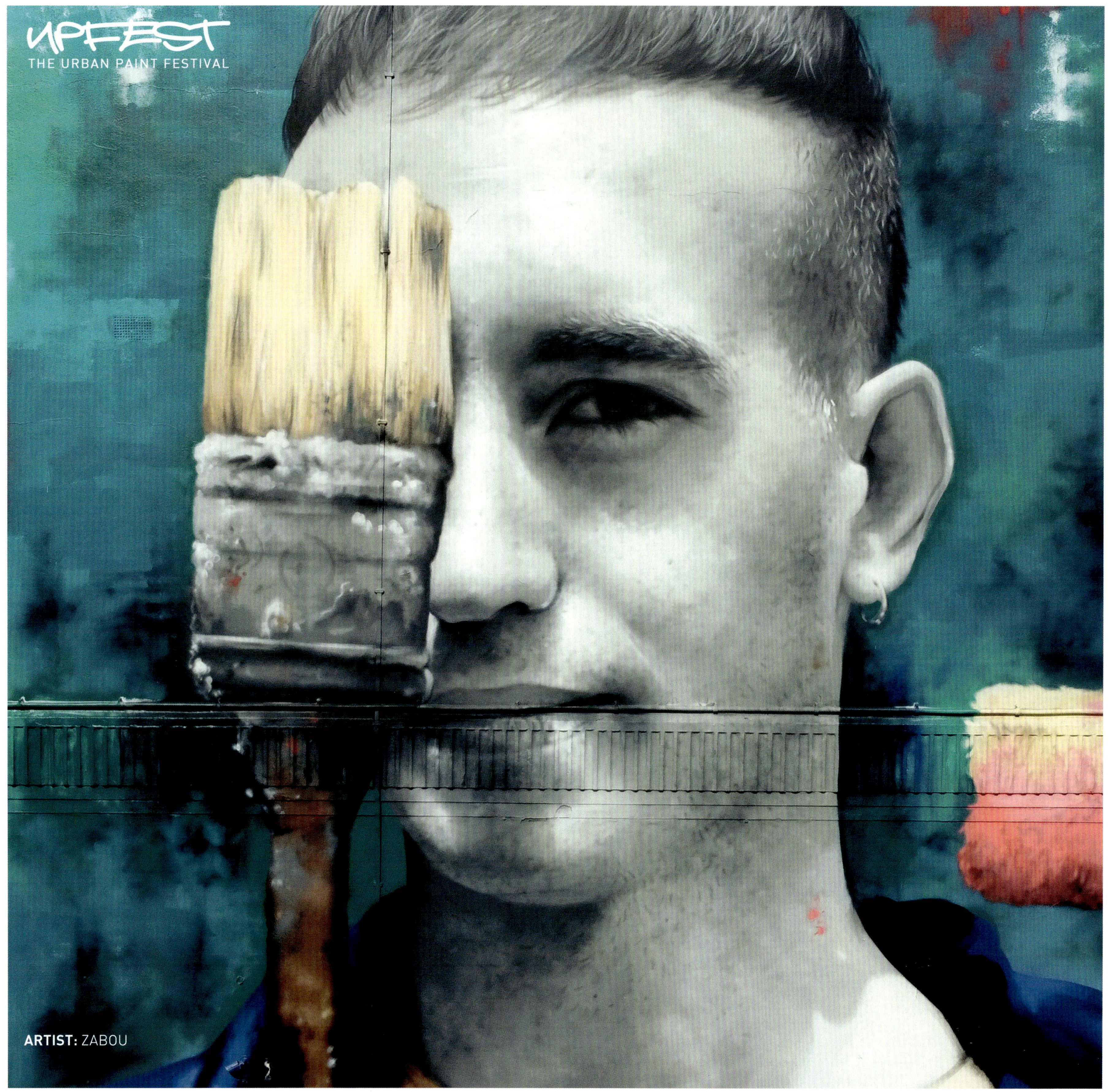
UPFEST
THE URBAN PAINT FESTIVAL
ARTIST: ZABOU

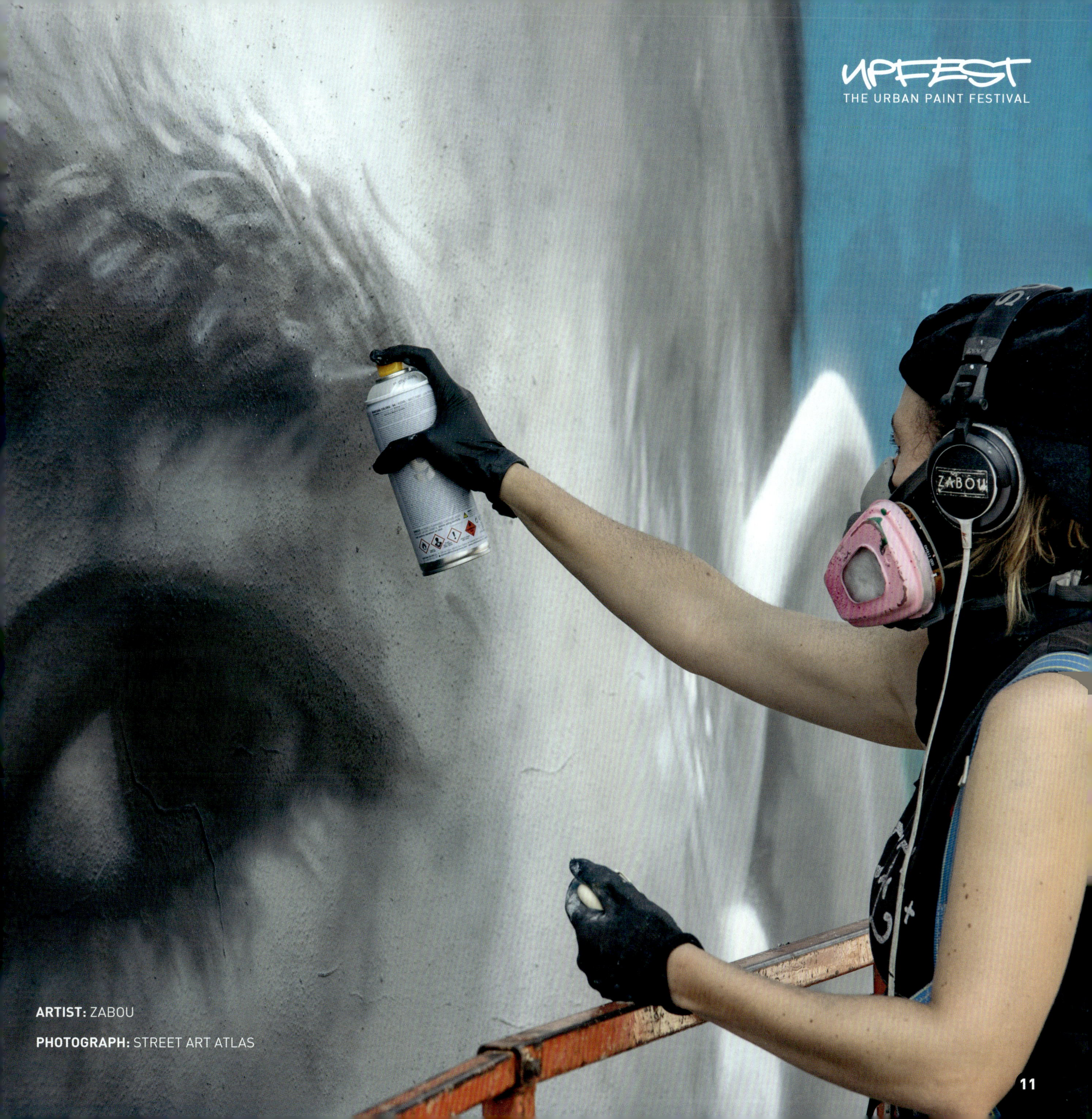

ARTIST: ZABOU

PHOTOGRAPH: STREET ART ATLAS

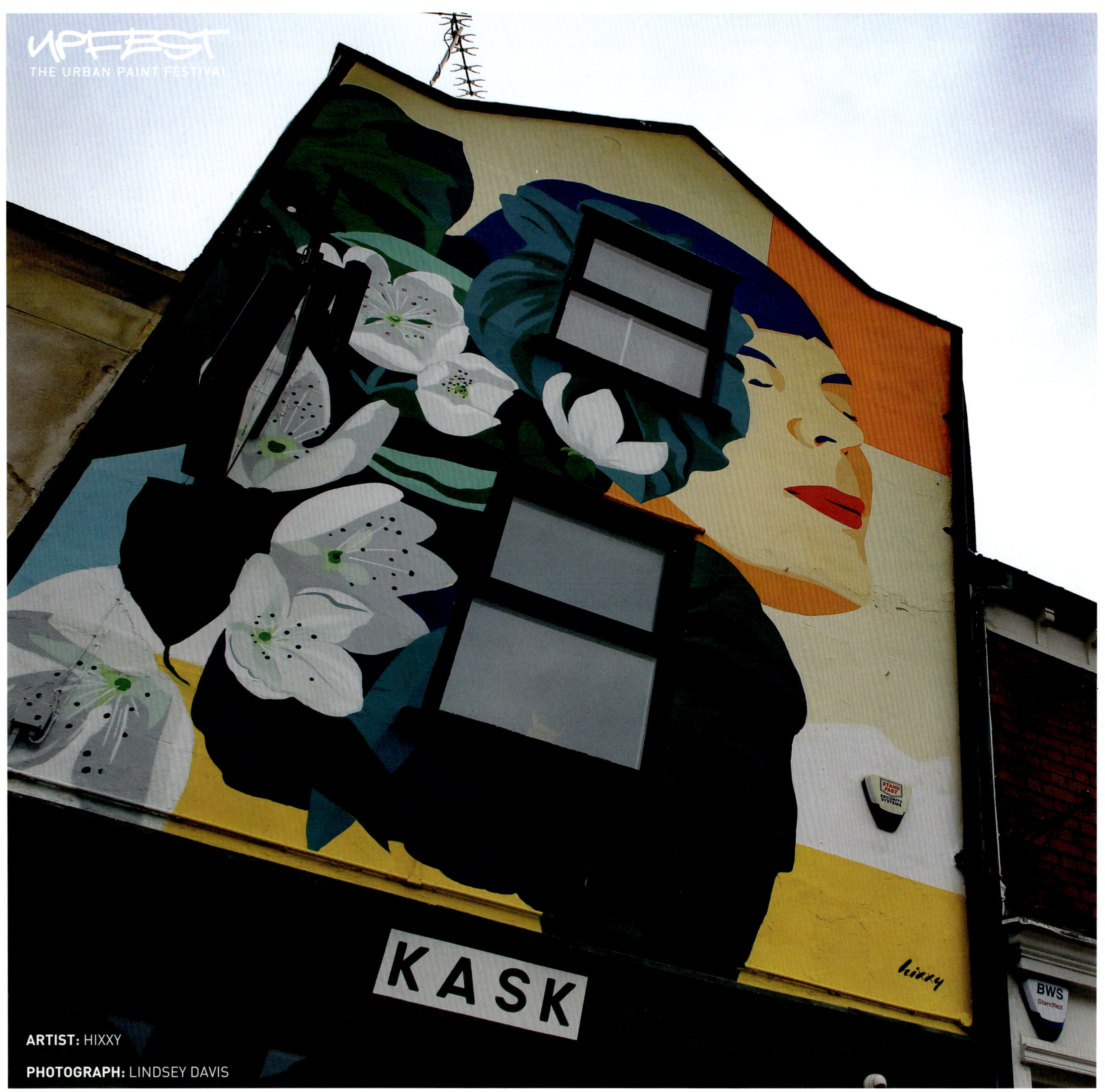

ARTIST: HIXXY

PHOTOGRAPH: LINDSEY DAVIS

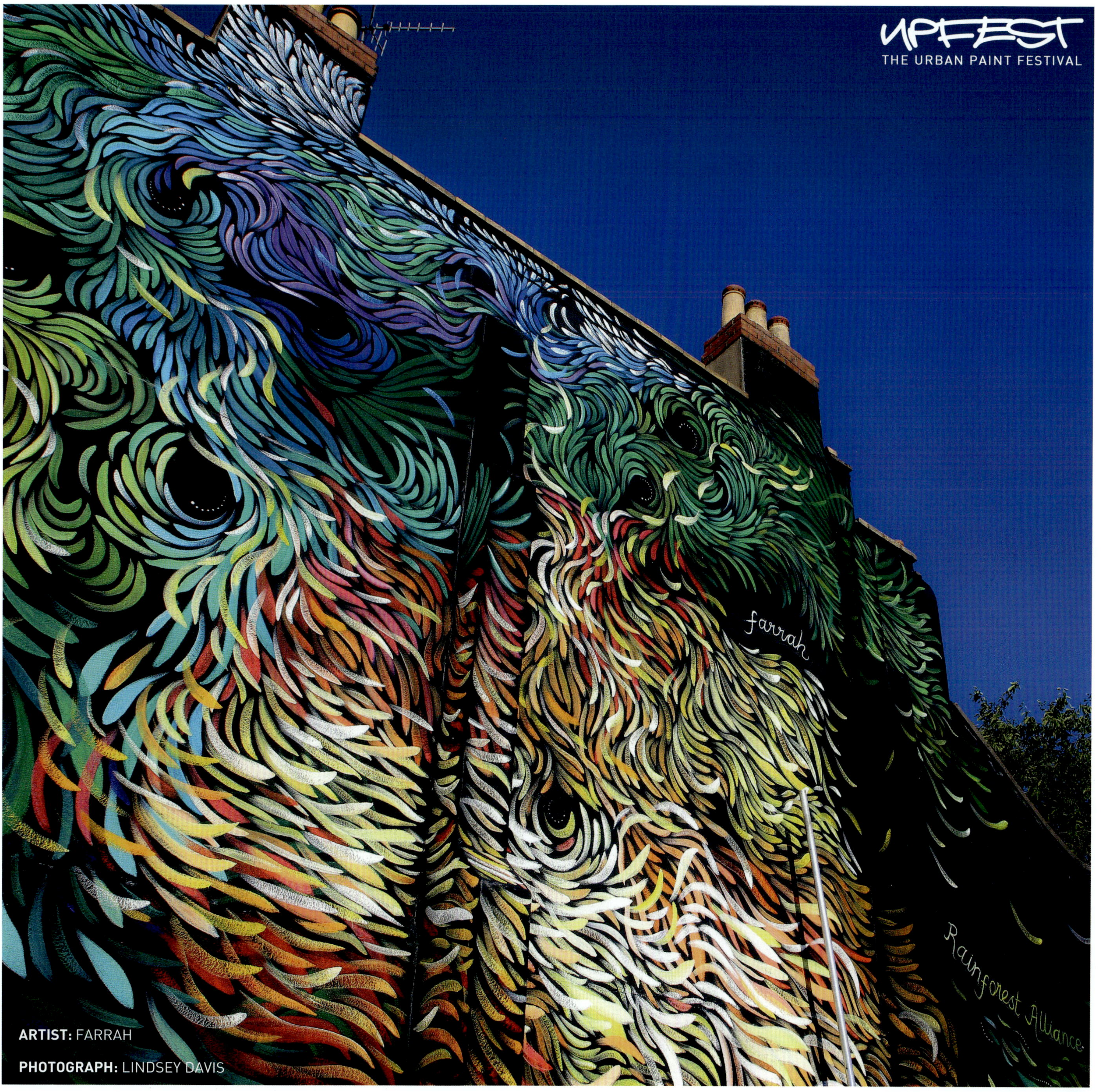

ARTIST: FARRAH

PHOTOGRAPH: LINDSEY DAVIS

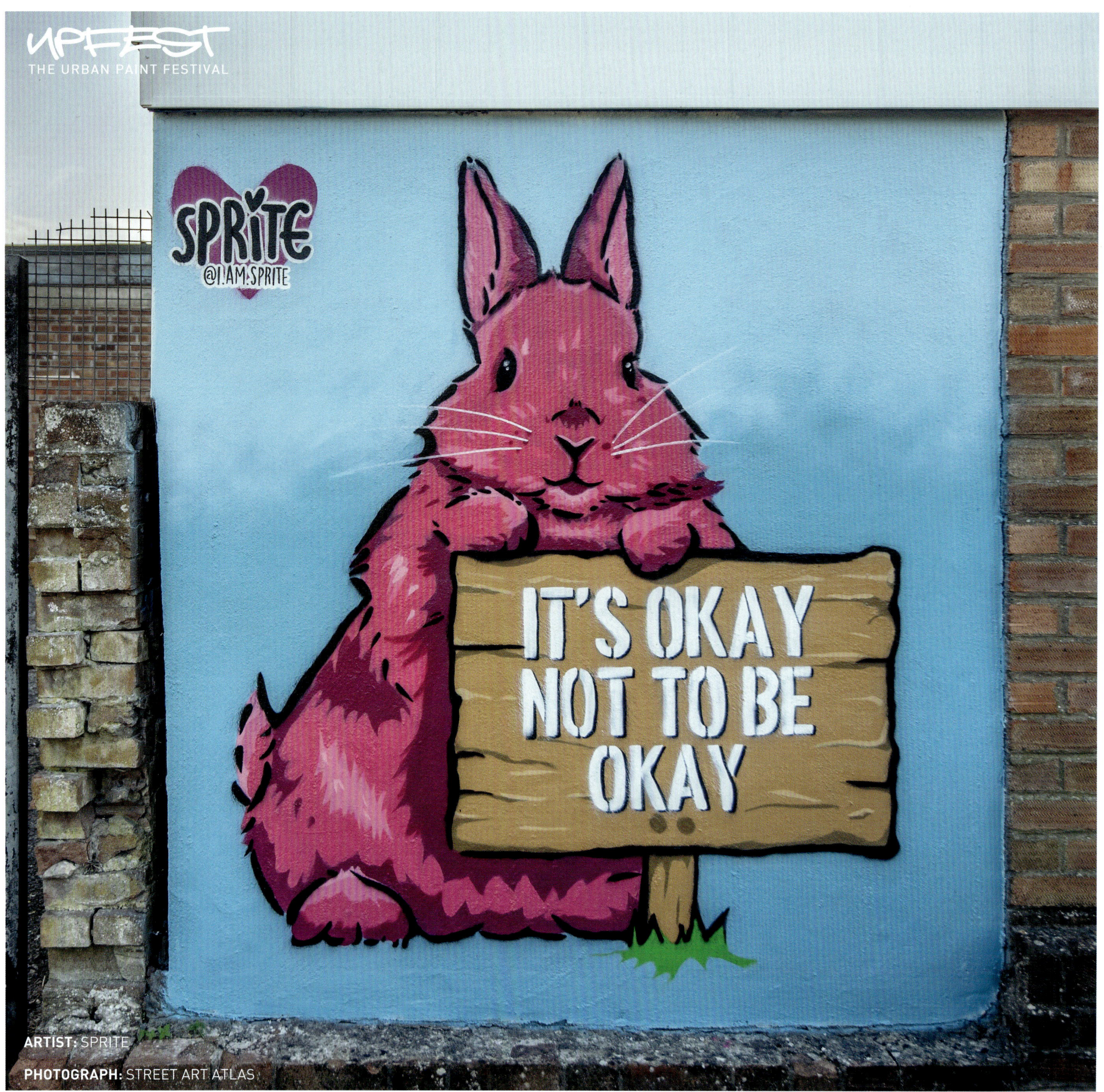

ARTIST: SPRITE

PHOTOGRAPH: STREET ART ATLAS

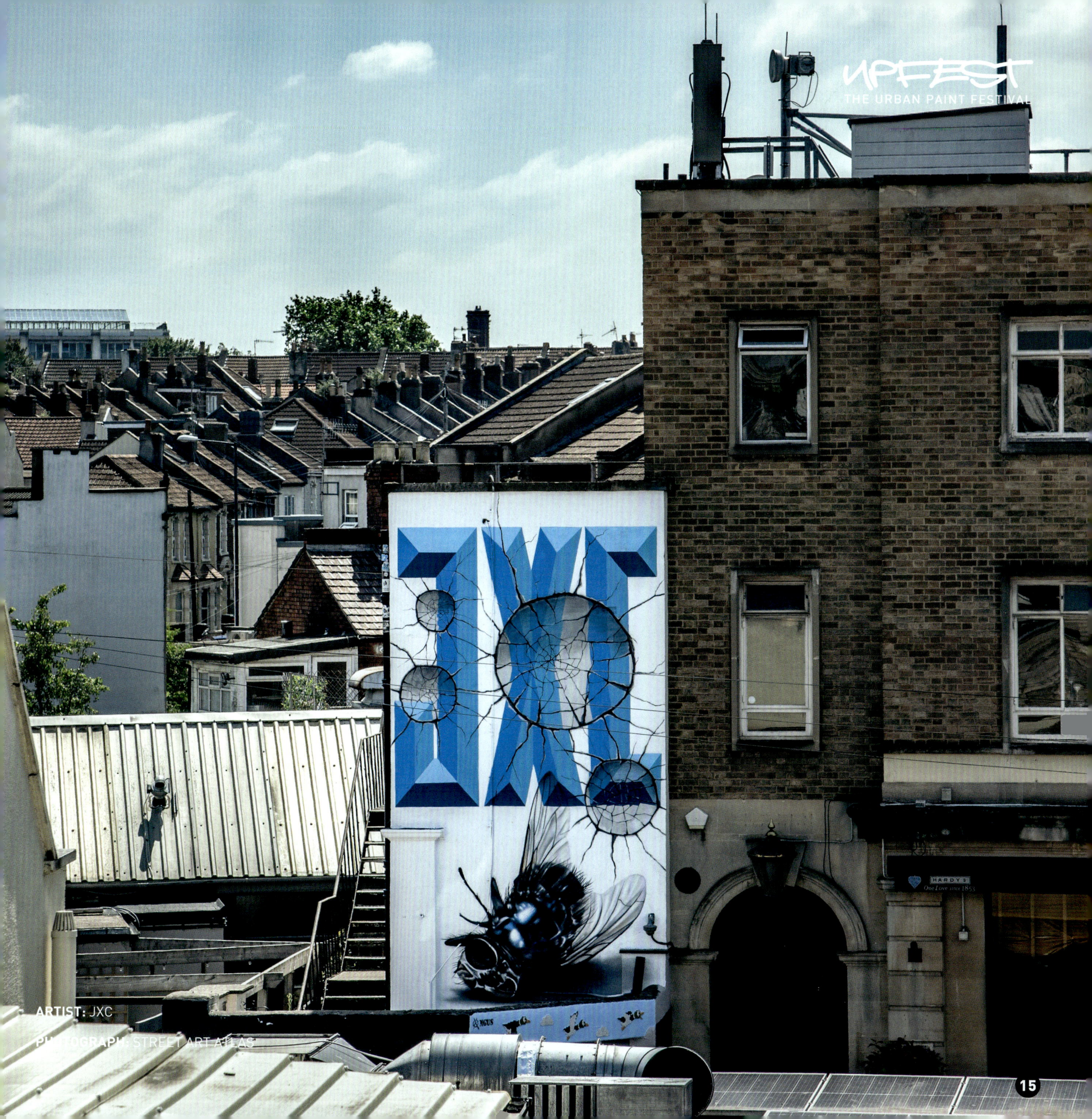

ARTIST: JXC

PHOTOGRAPH: STREET ART ATLAS

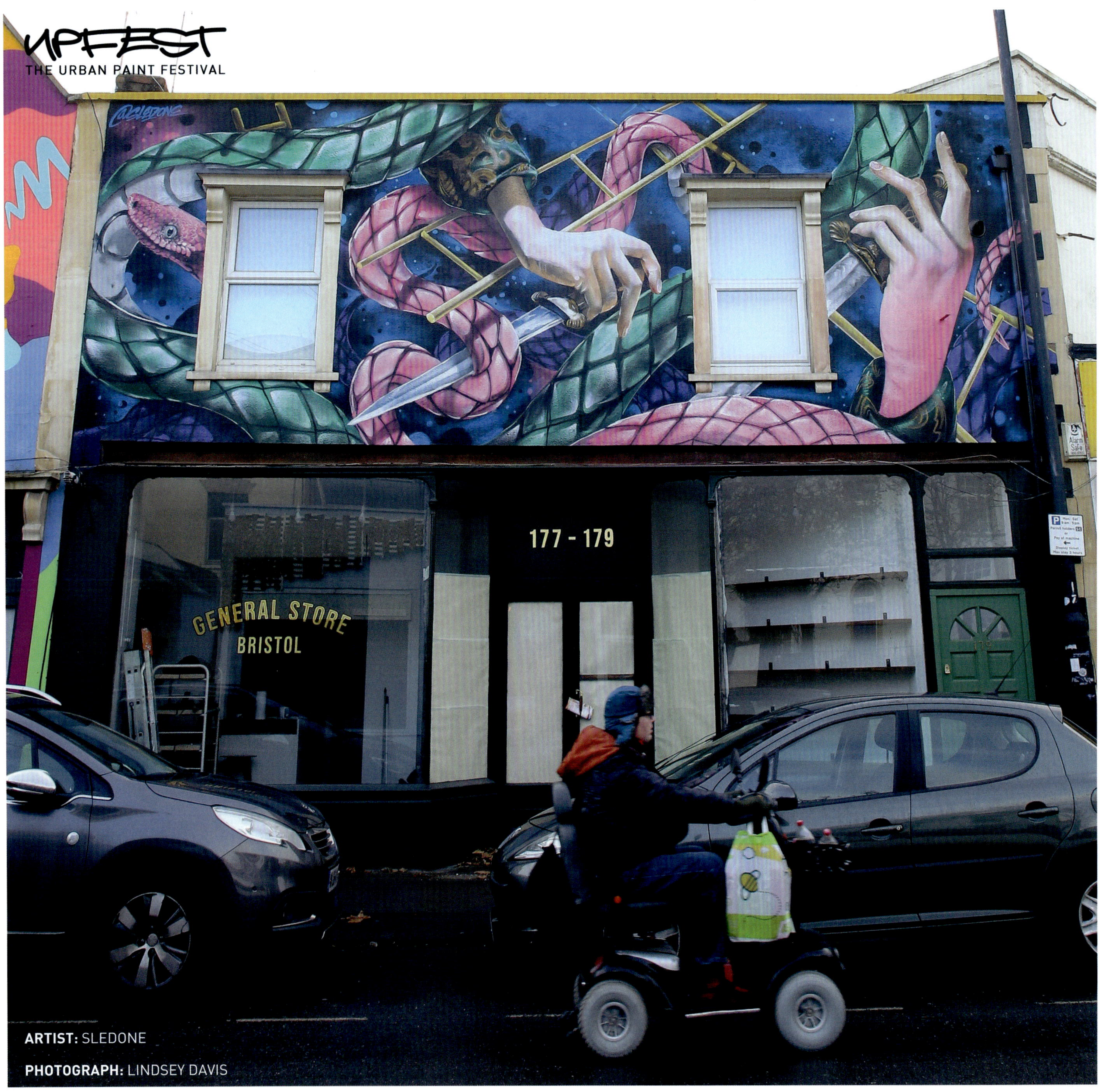

ARTIST: SLEDONE

PHOTOGRAPH: LINDSEY DAVIS

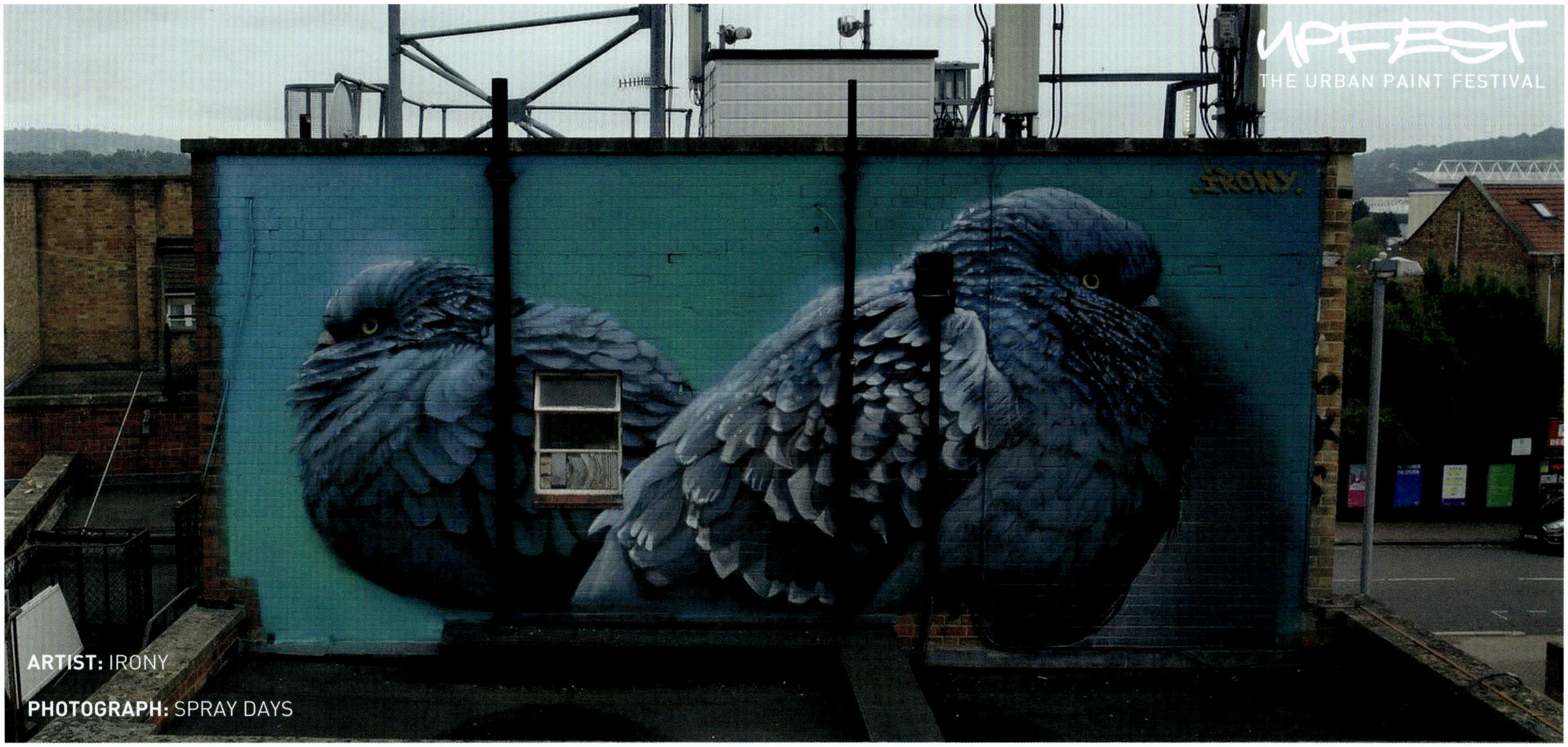

ARTIST: IRONY

PHOTOGRAPH: SPRAY DAYS

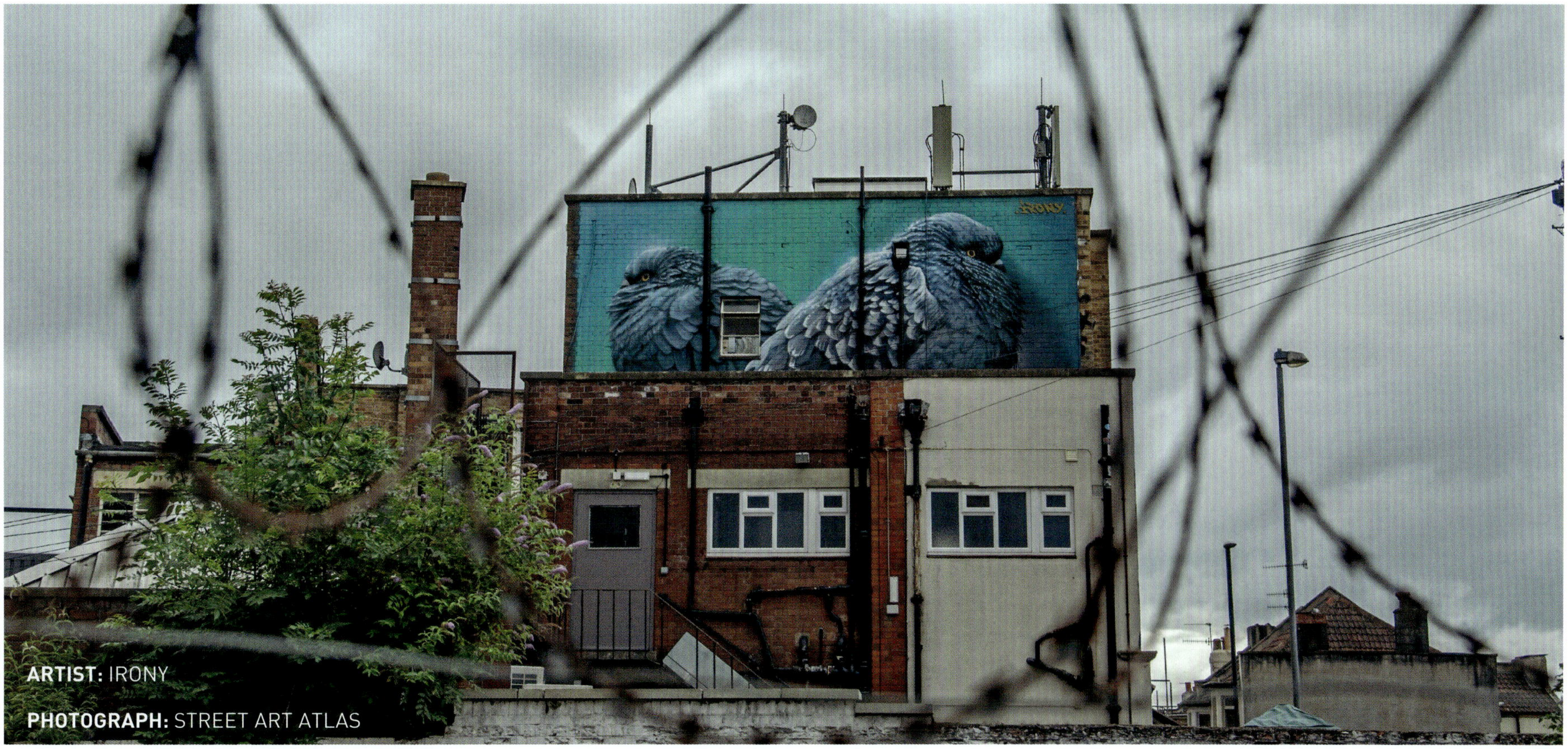

ARTIST: IRONY

PHOTOGRAPH: STREET ART ATLAS

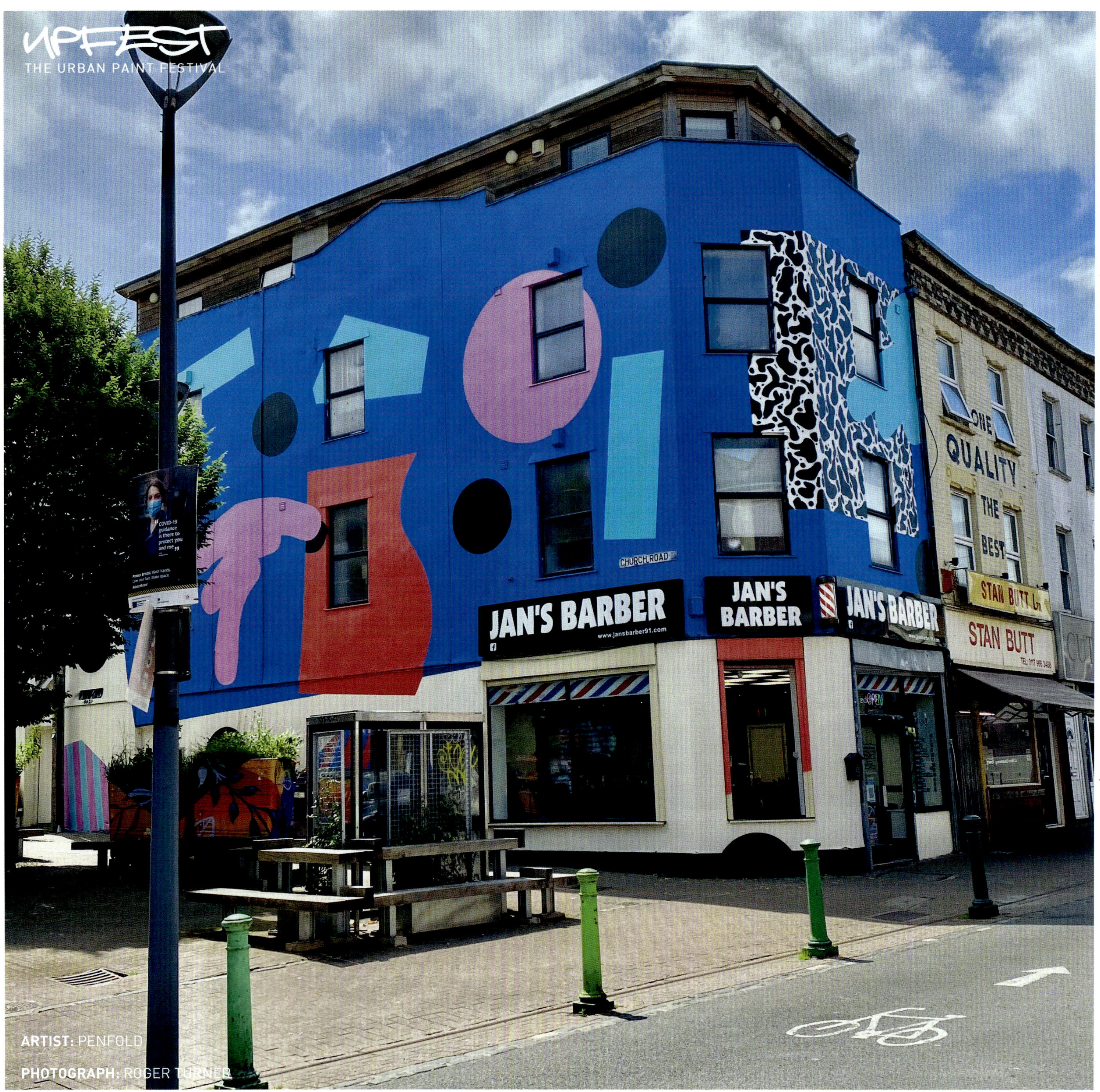

ARTIST: PENFOLD

PHOTOGRAPH: ROGER TURNER

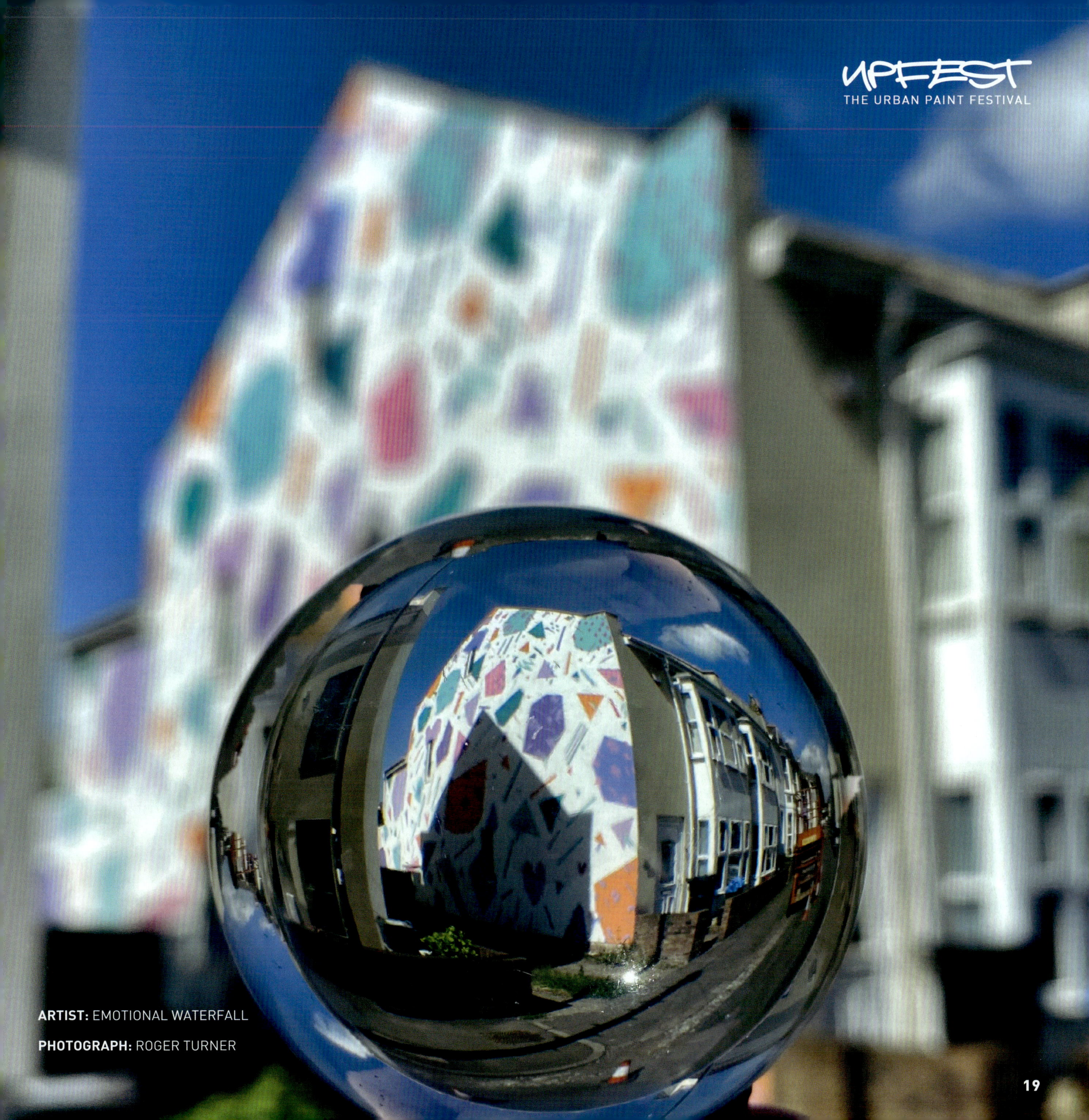

ARTIST: EMOTIONAL WATERFALL

PHOTOGRAPH: ROGER TURNER

ARTIST: PHILTH X N4T4

PHOTOGRAPH: STREET ART ATLAS

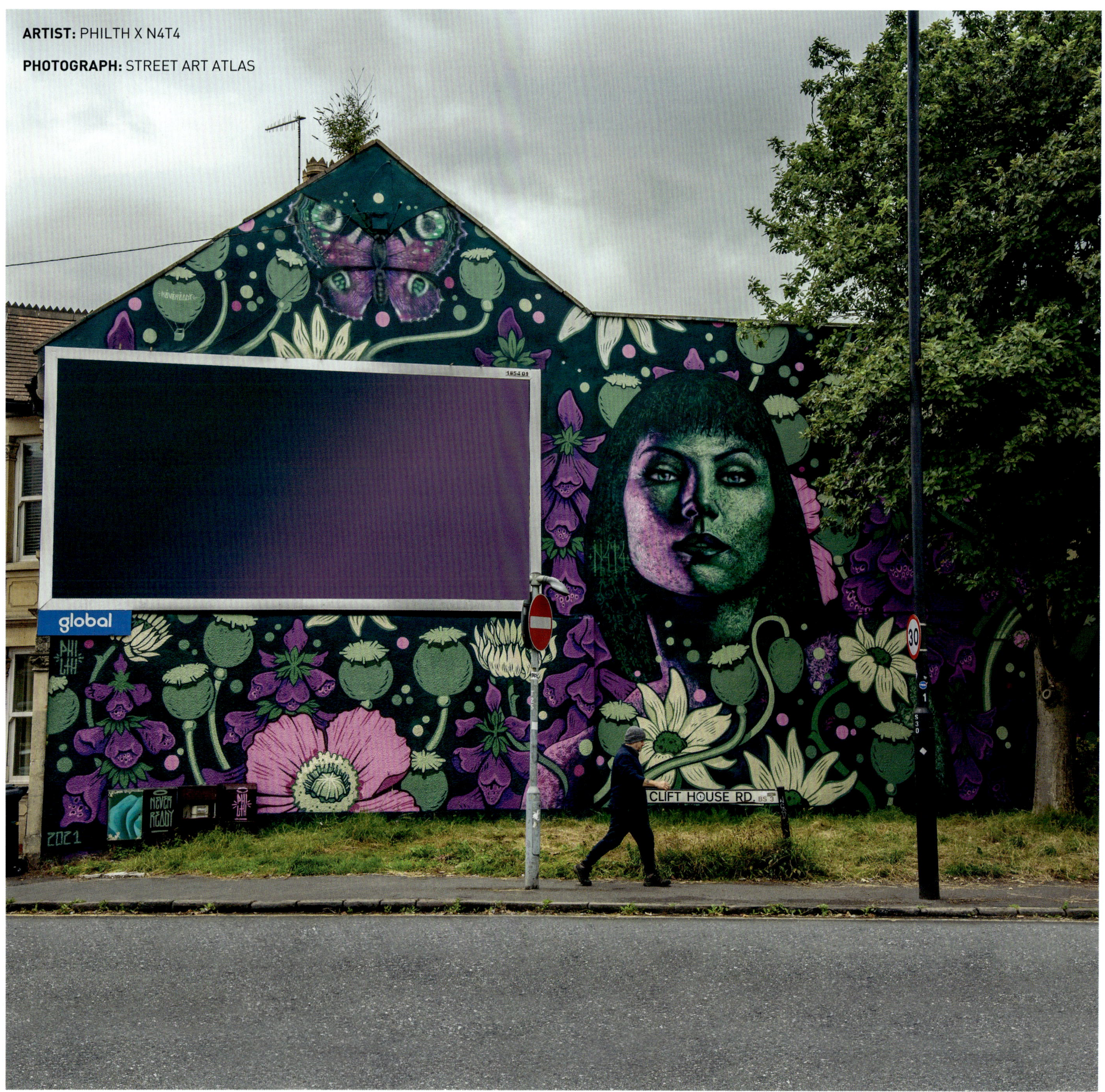

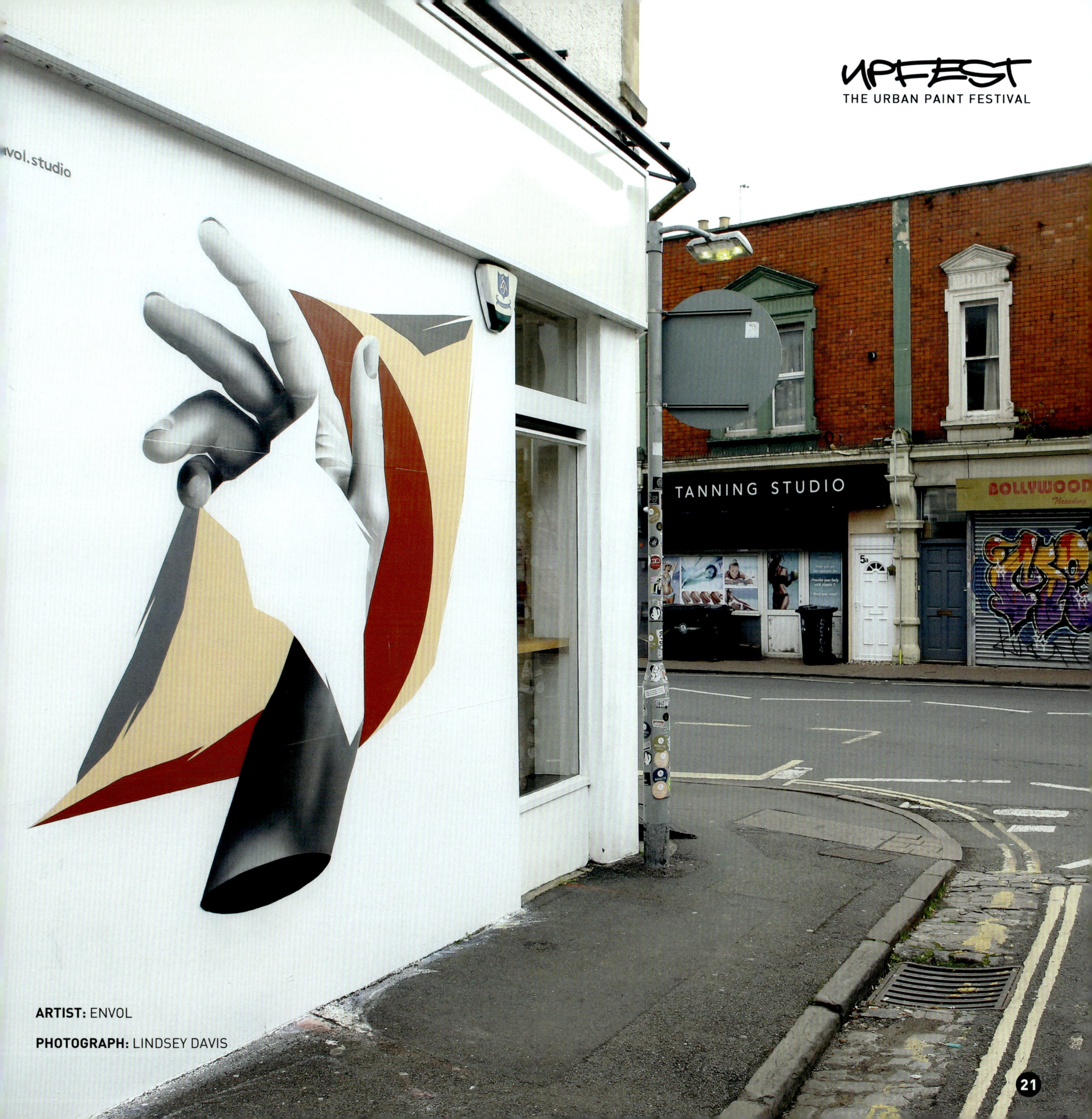

ARTIST: ENVOL

PHOTOGRAPH: LINDSEY DAVIS

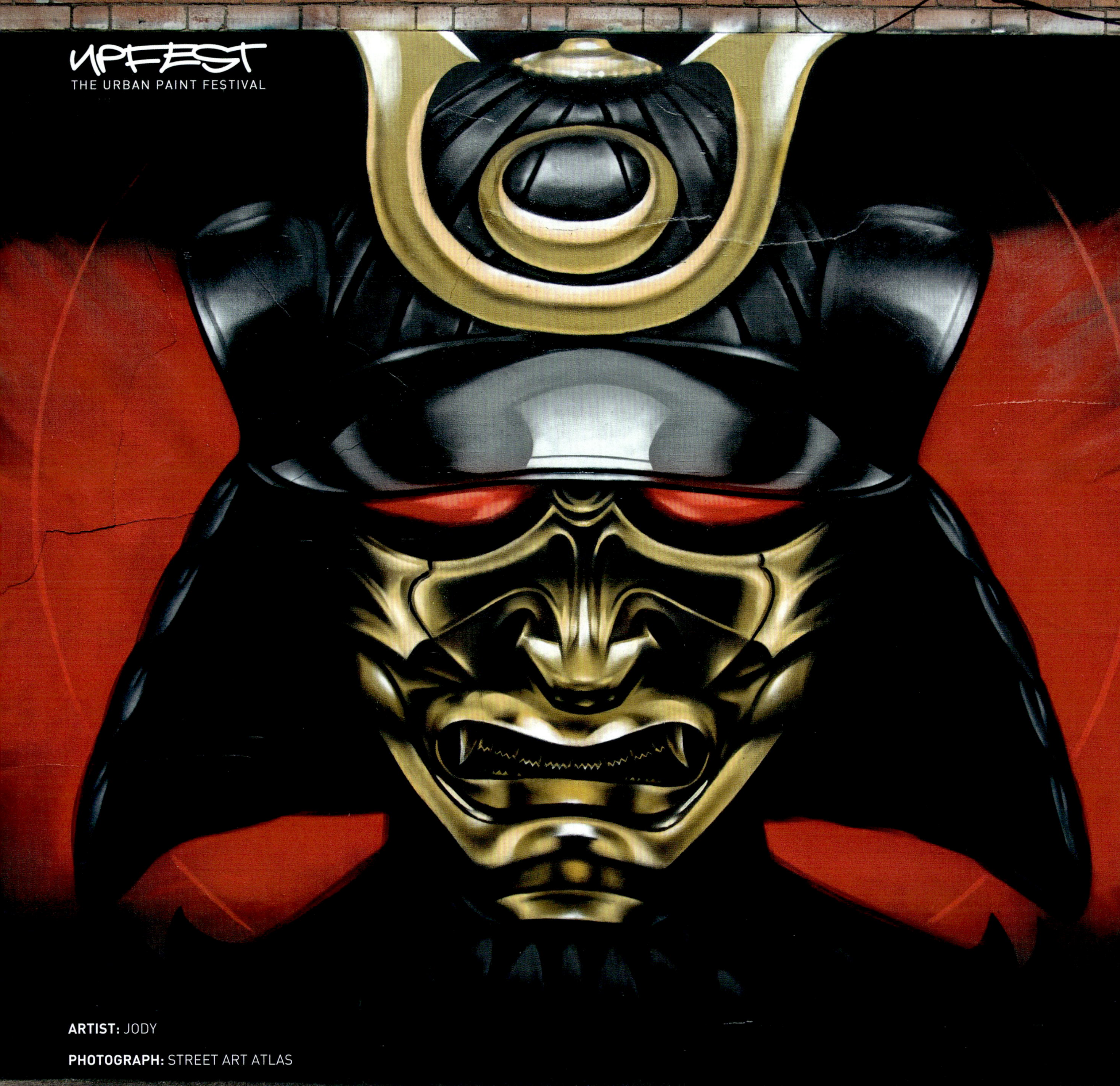

ARTIST: JODY

PHOTOGRAPH: STREET ART ATLAS

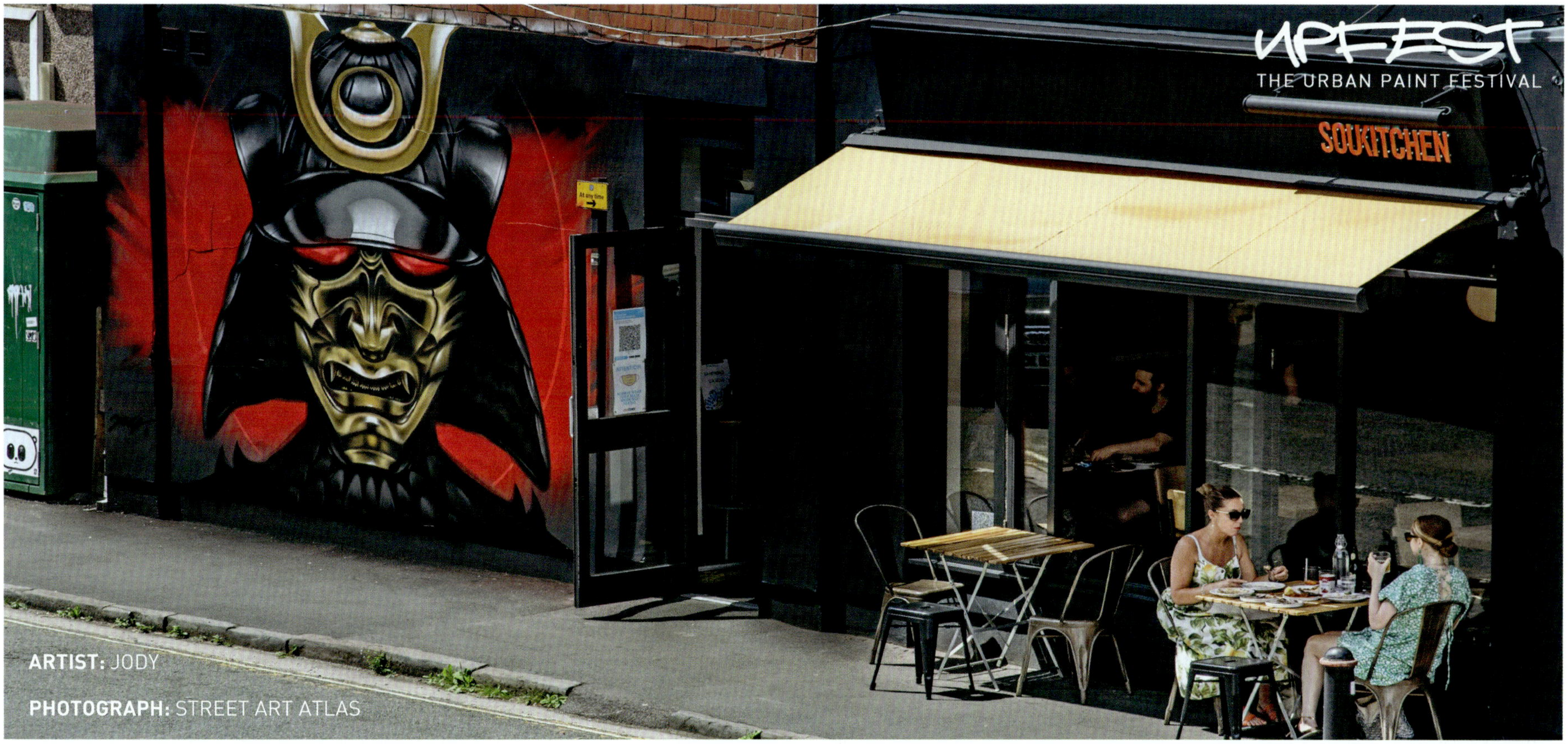

ARTIST: JODY

PHOTOGRAPH: STREET ART ATLAS

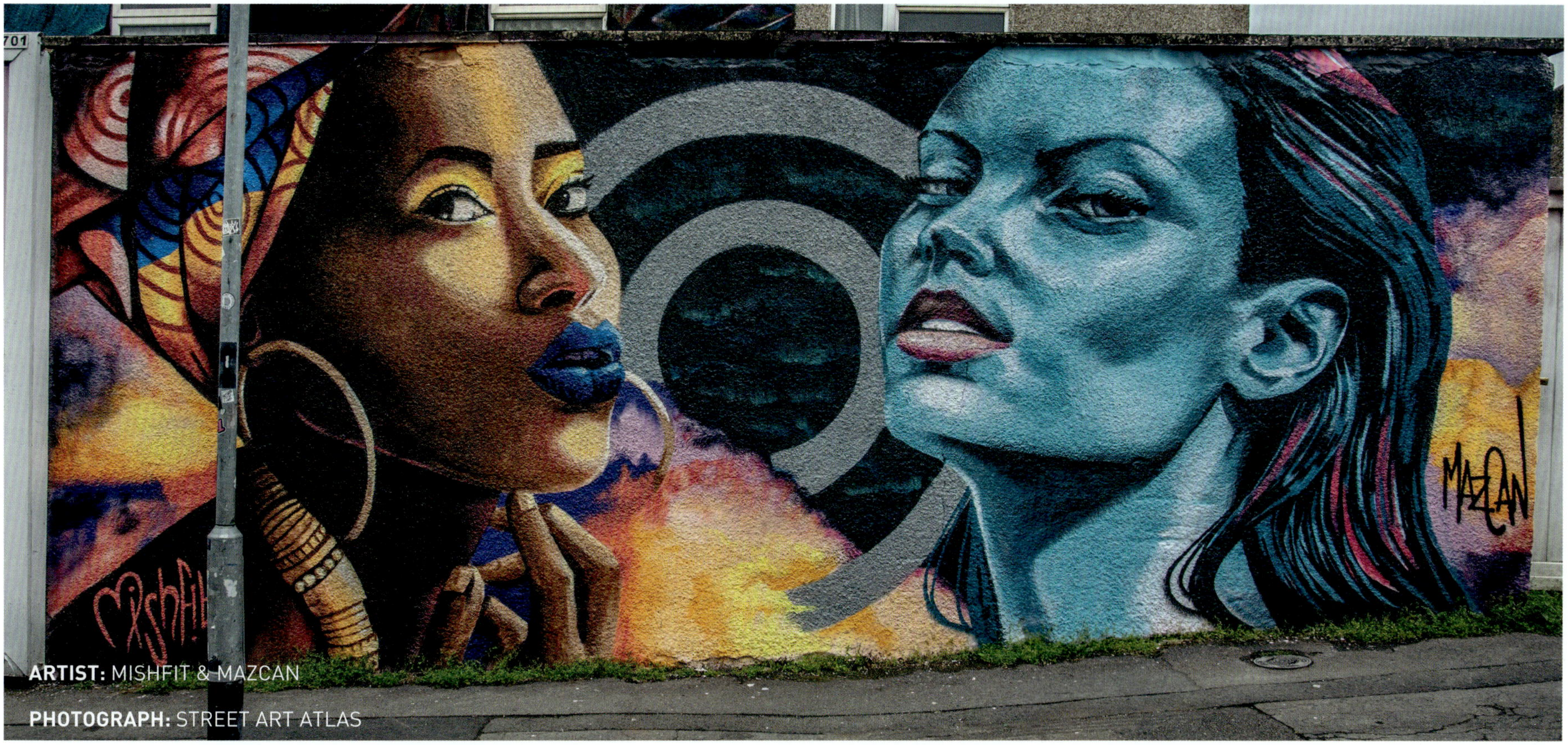

ARTIST: MISHFIT & MAZCAN

PHOTOGRAPH: STREET ART ATLAS

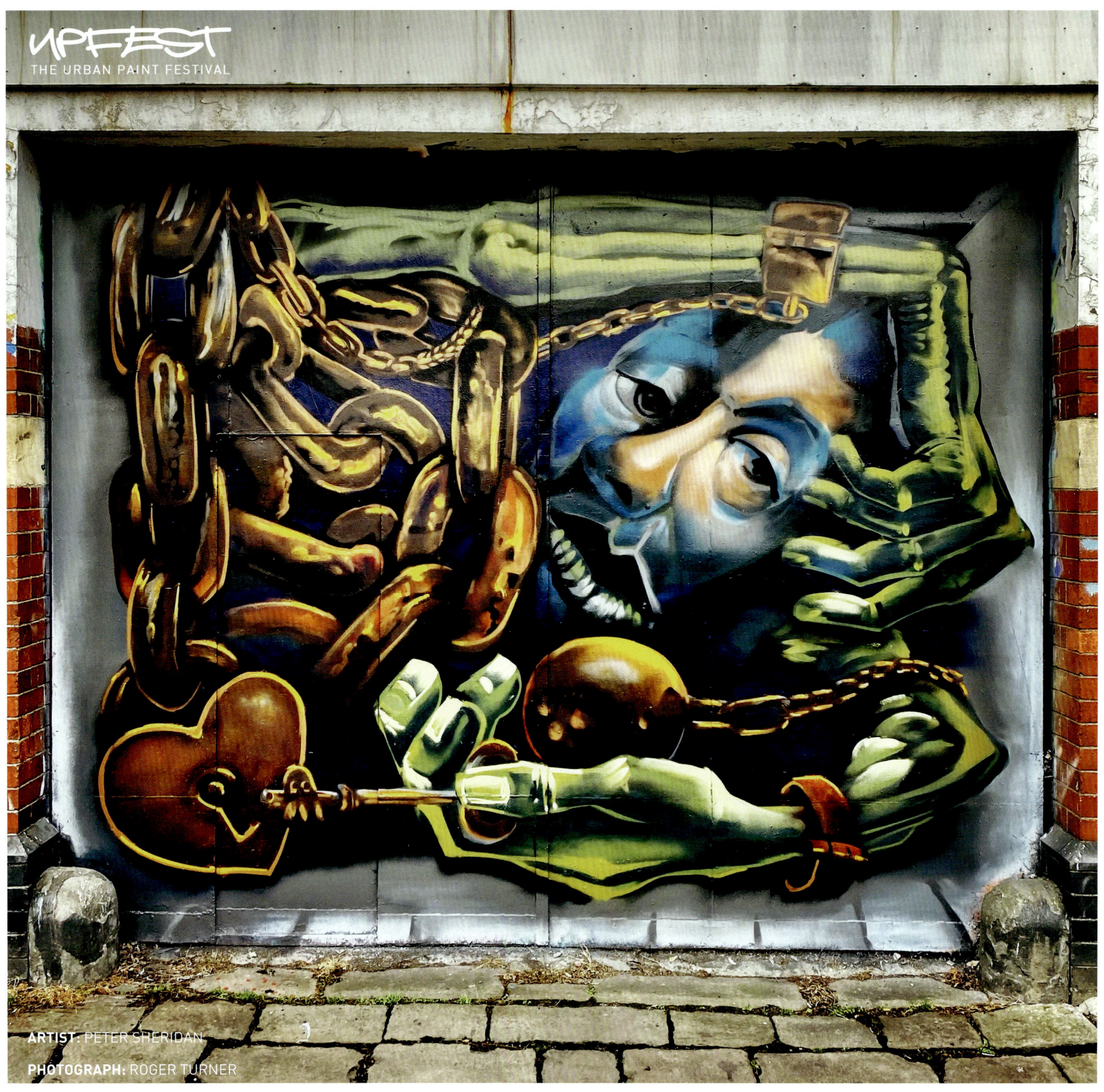

ARTIST: PETER SHERIDAN

PHOTOGRAPH: ROGER TURNER

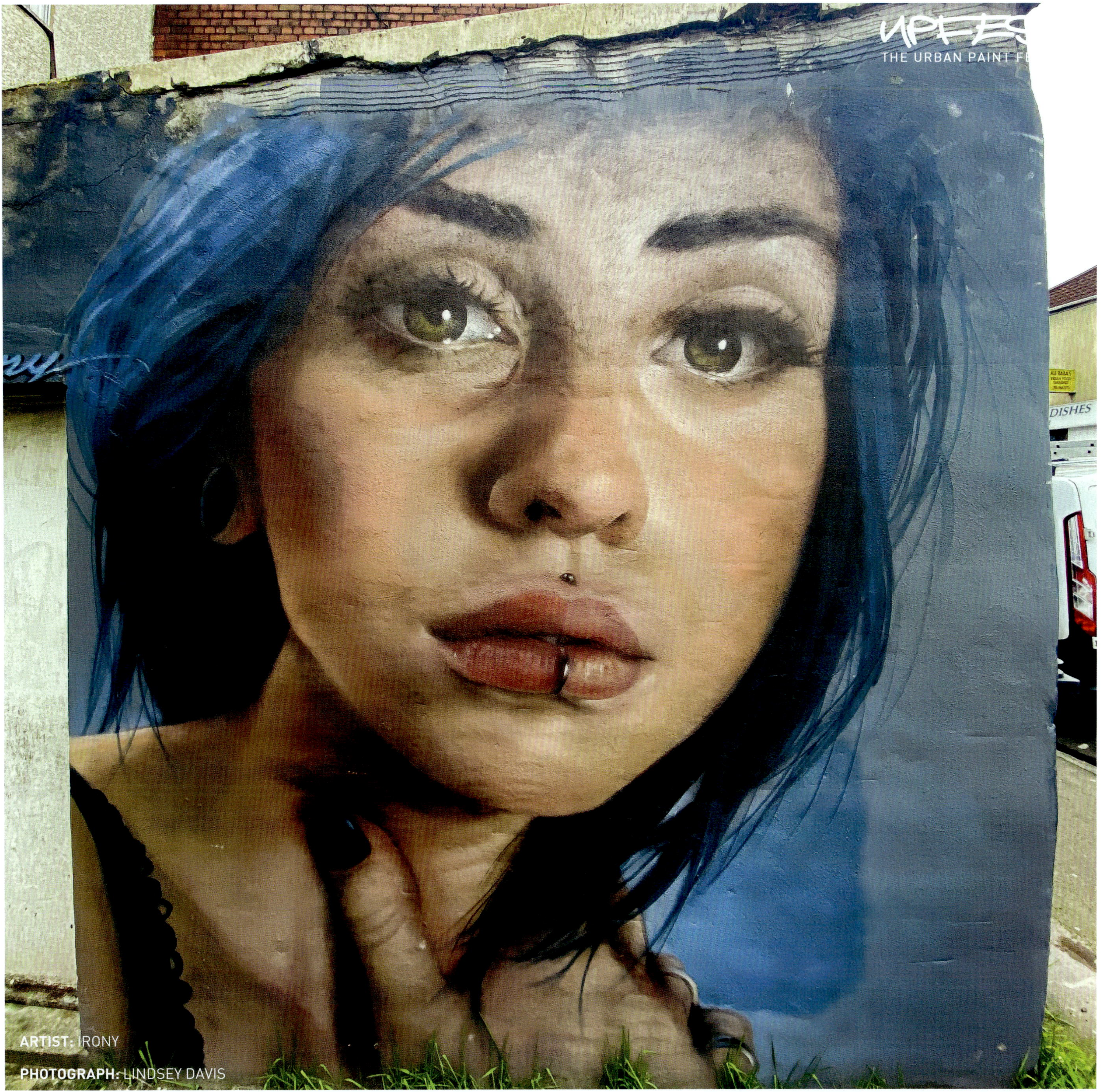
UPFEST
THE URBAN PAINT FE
DISHES

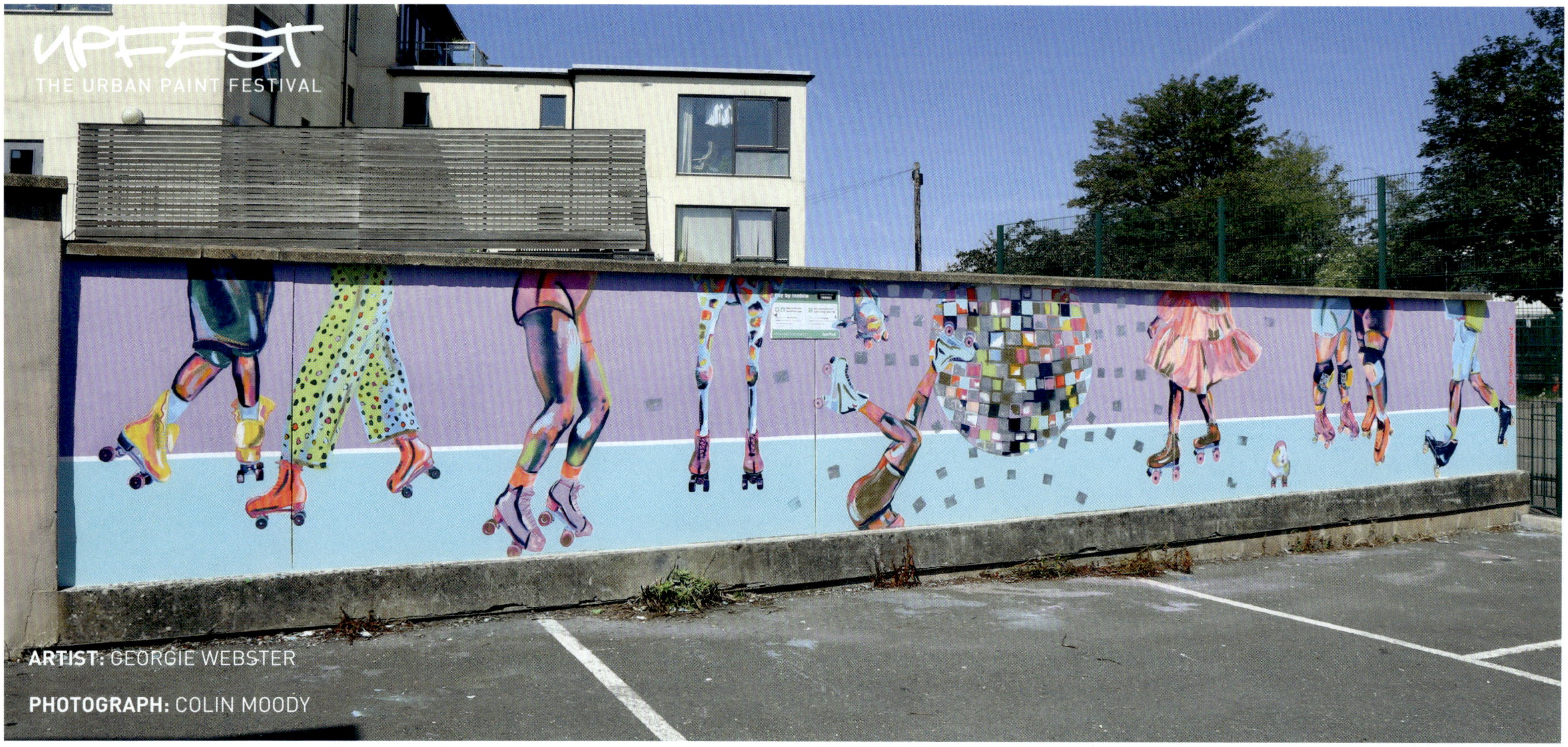

ARTIST: GEORGIE WEBSTER

PHOTOGRAPH: COLIN MOODY

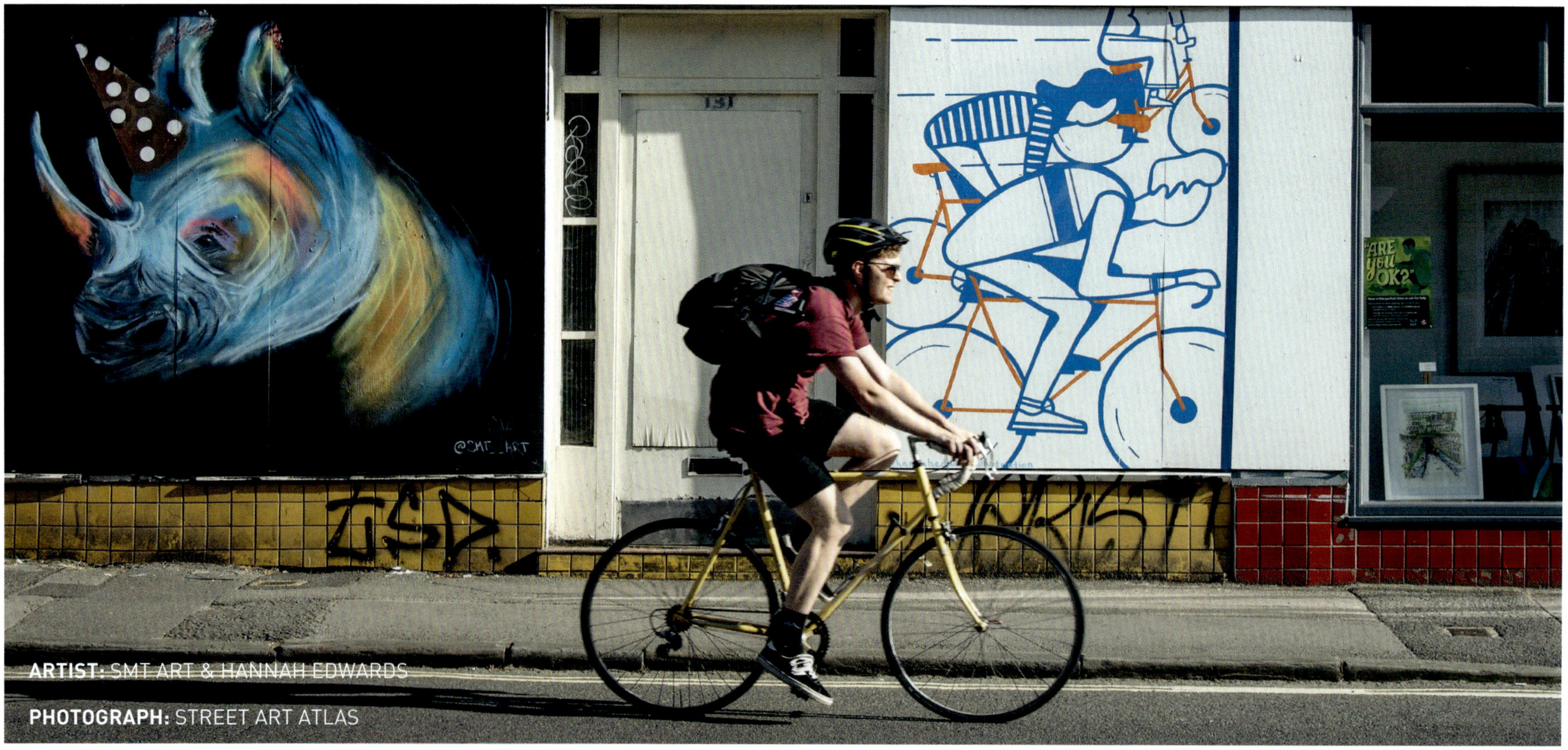

ARTIST: SMT ART & HANNAH EDWARDS

PHOTOGRAPH: STREET ART ATLAS

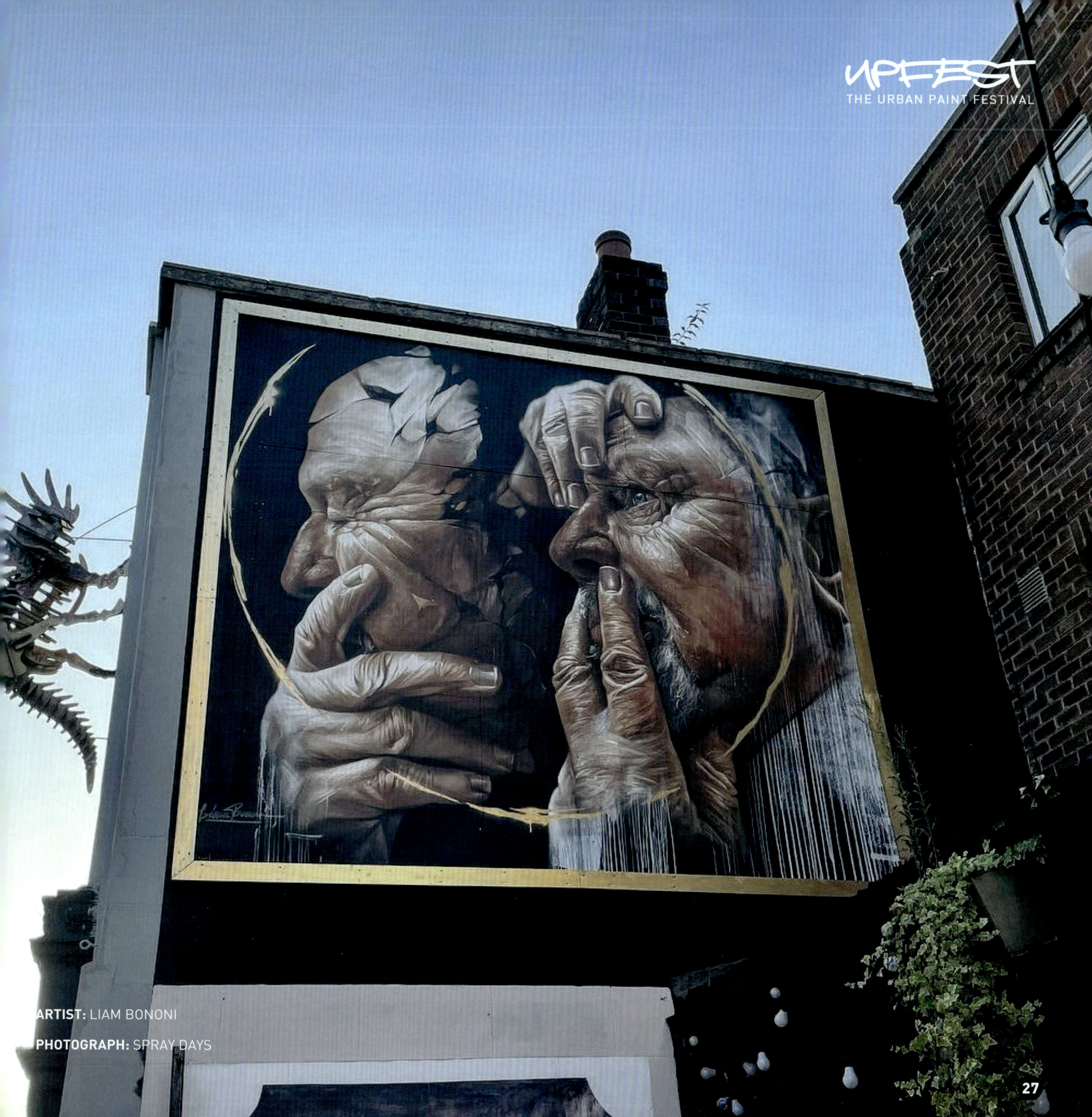

ARTIST: LIAM BONONI

PHOTOGRAPH: SPRAY DAYS

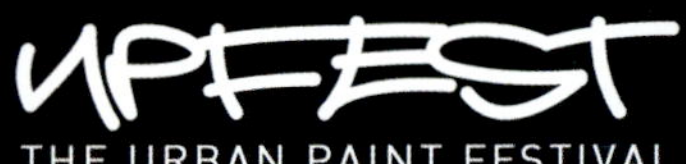

ARTIST: SOKER

PHOTOGRAPH: LINDSEY DAVIS

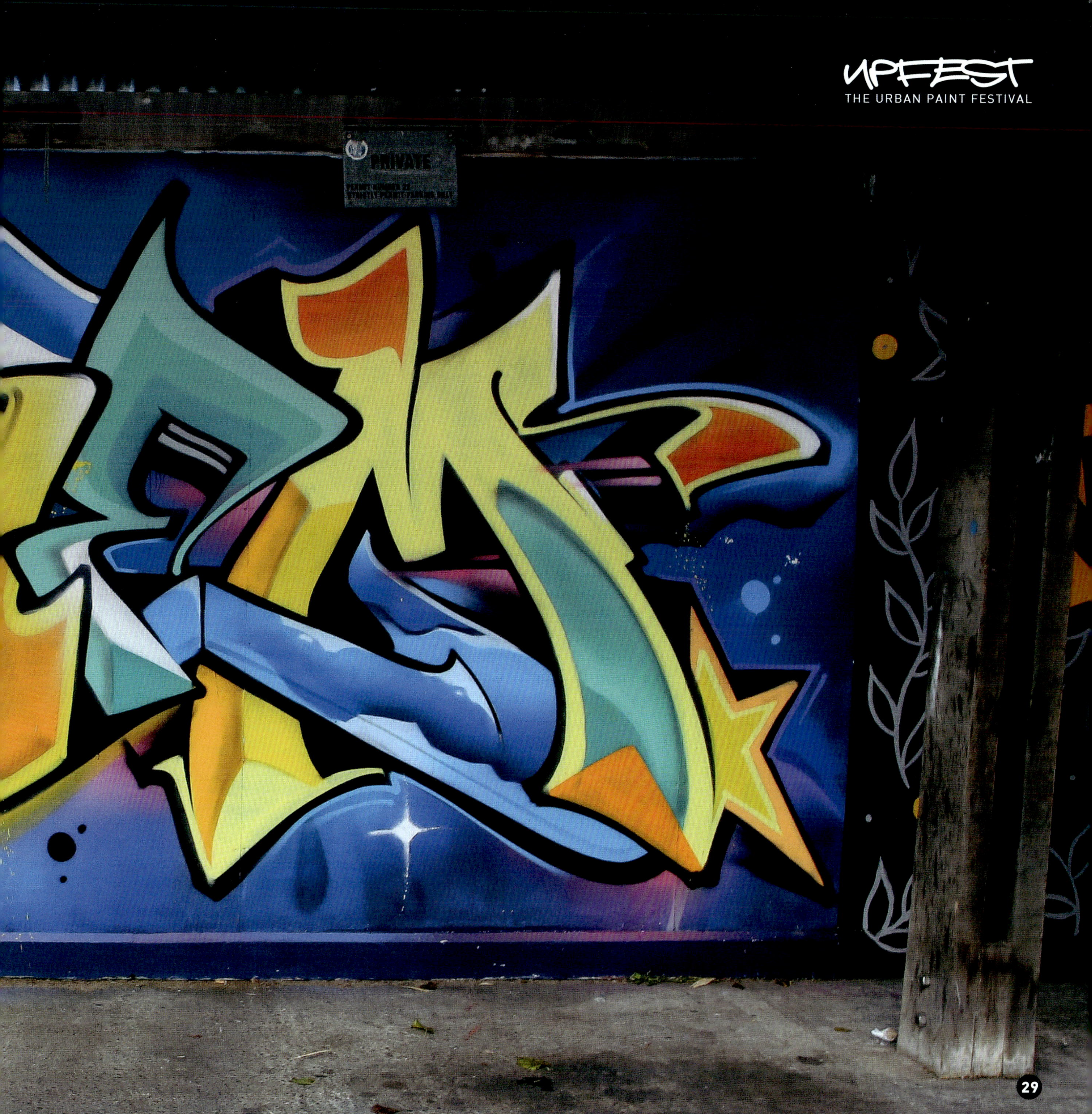

UPFEST
THE URBAN PAINT FESTIVAL
PRIVATE

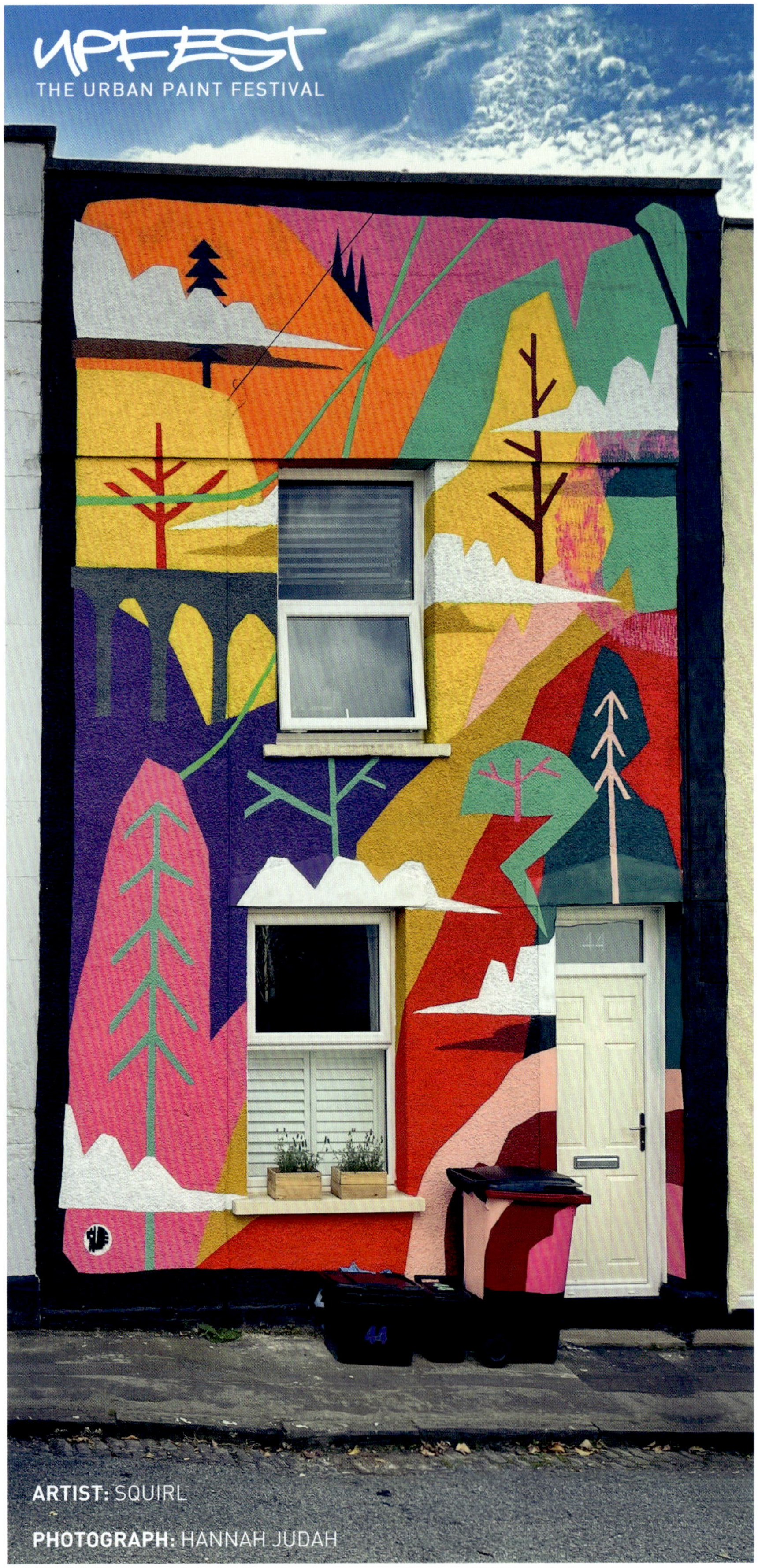

ARTIST: SQUIRL

PHOTOGRAPH: HANNAH JUDAH

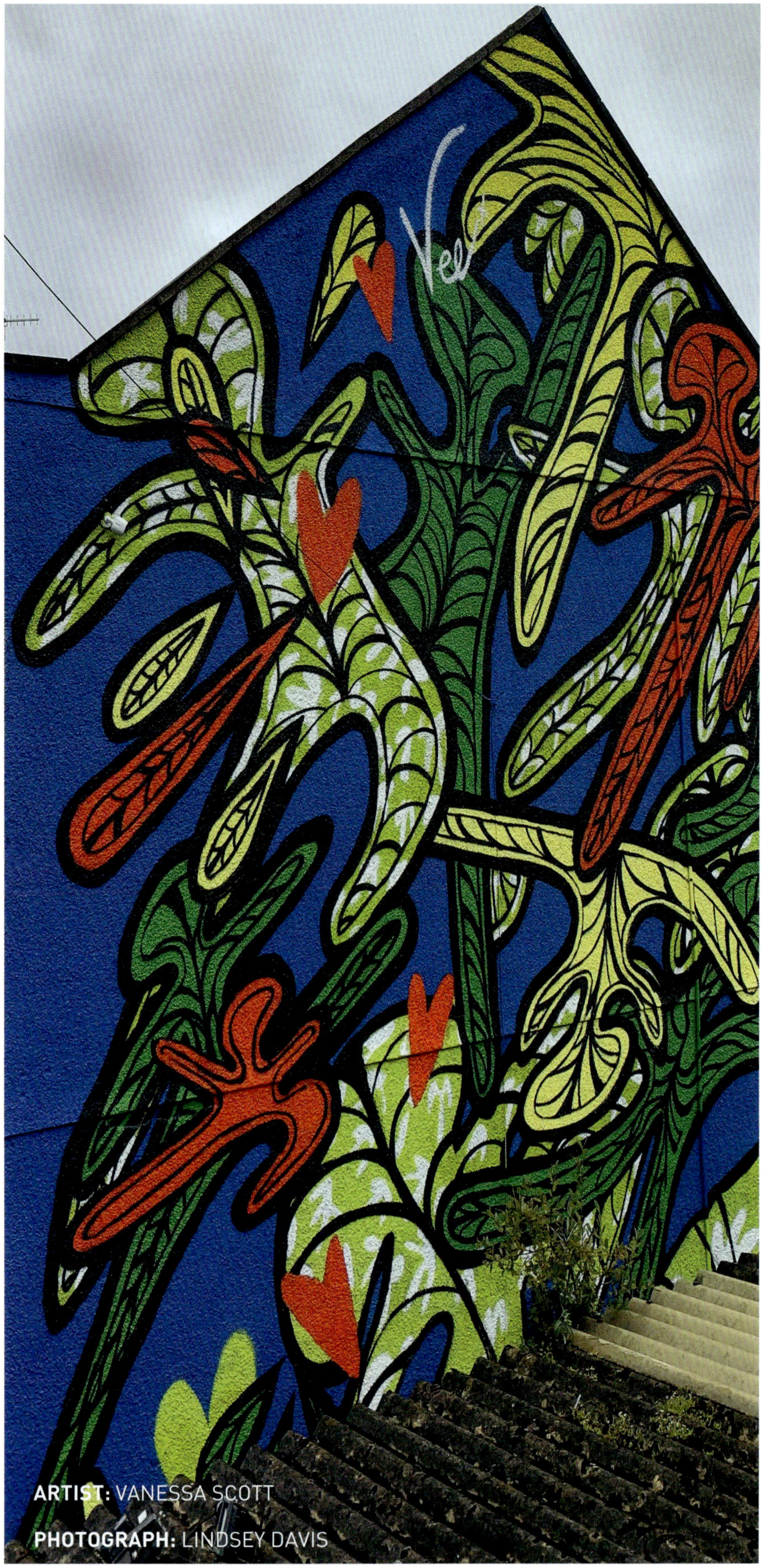

ARTIST: VANESSA SCOTT

PHOTOGRAPH: LINDSEY DAVIS

UPFEST
THE URBAN PAINT FESTIVAL
Except for loading

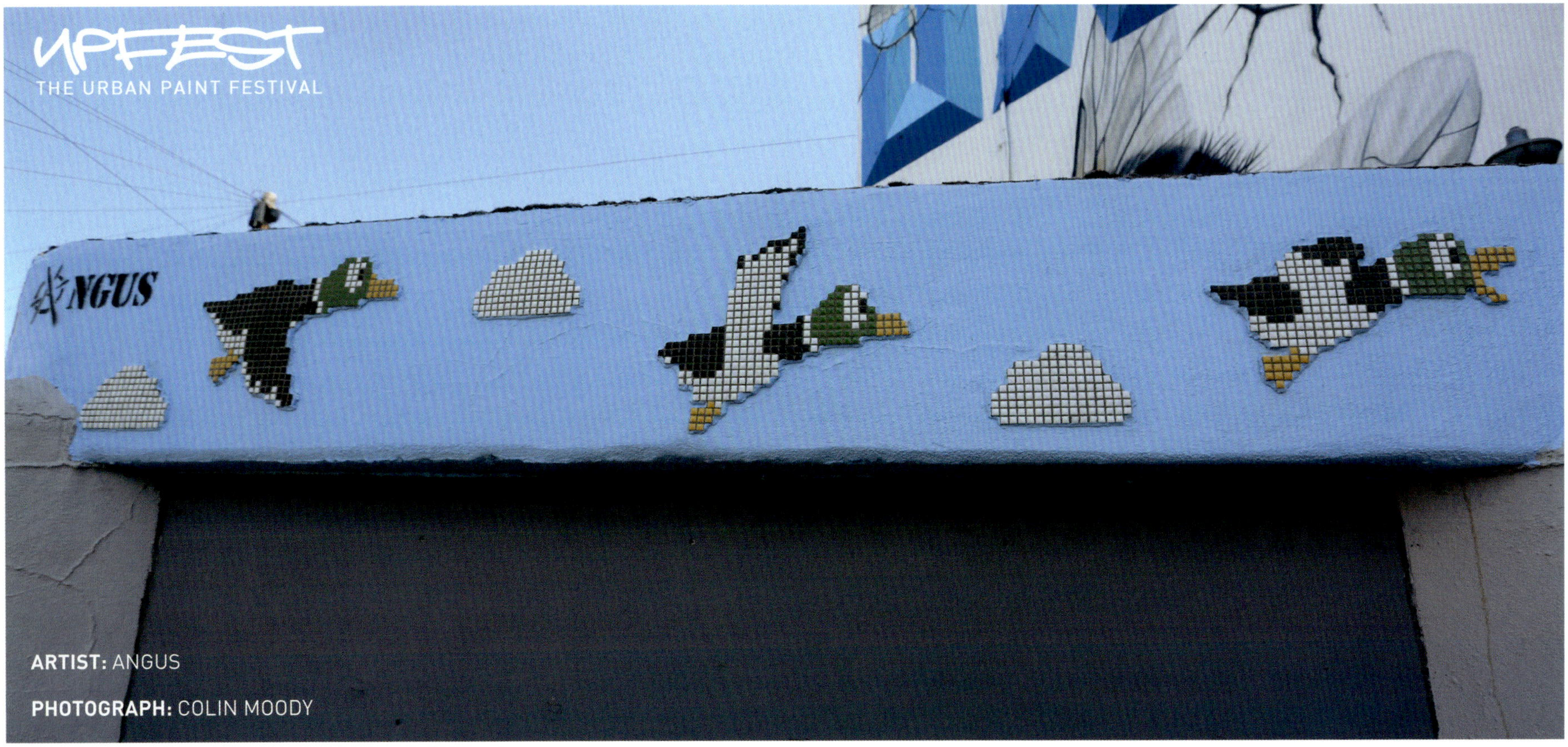

ARTIST: ANGUS

PHOTOGRAPH: COLIN MOODY

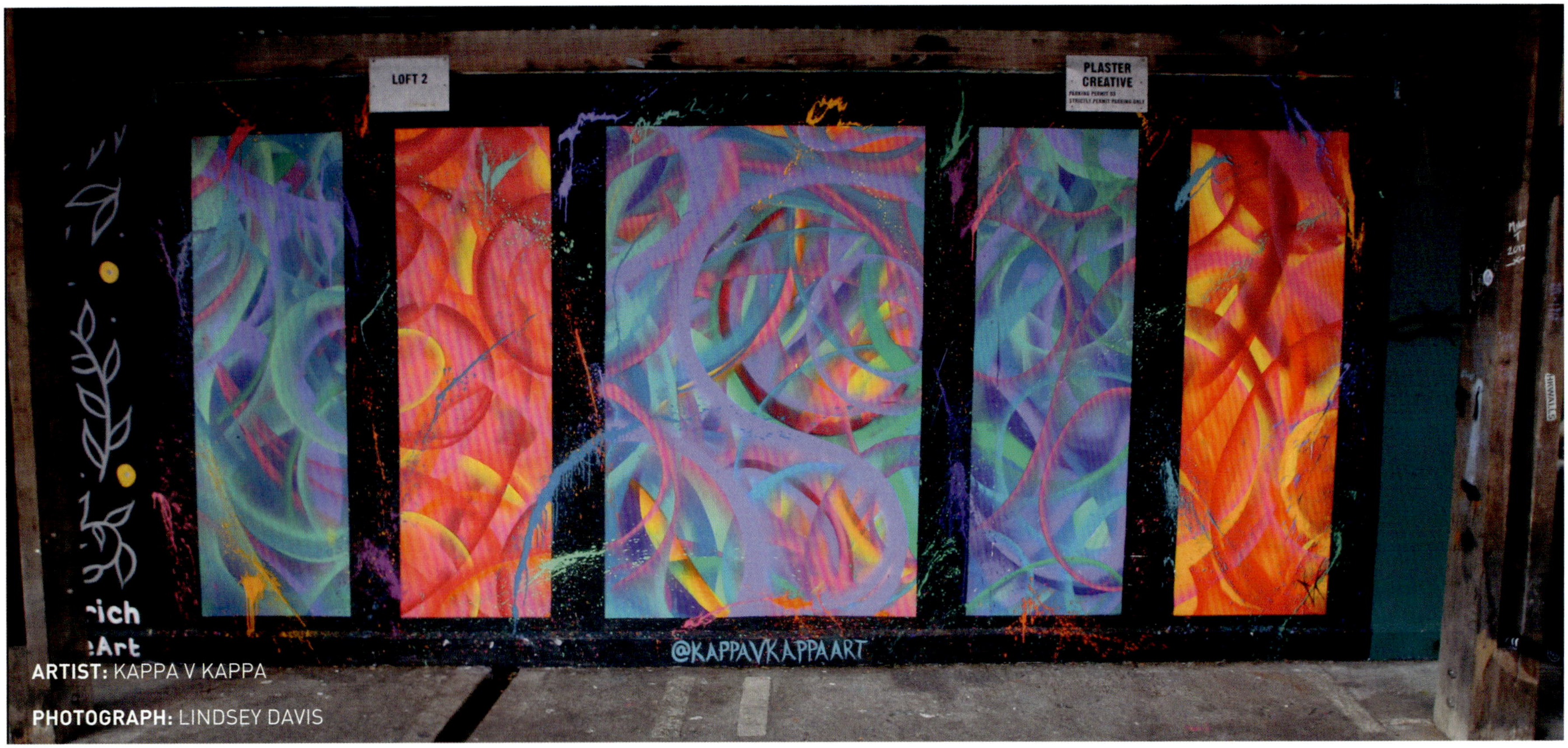

ARTIST: KAPPA V KAPPA

PHOTOGRAPH: LINDSEY DAVIS

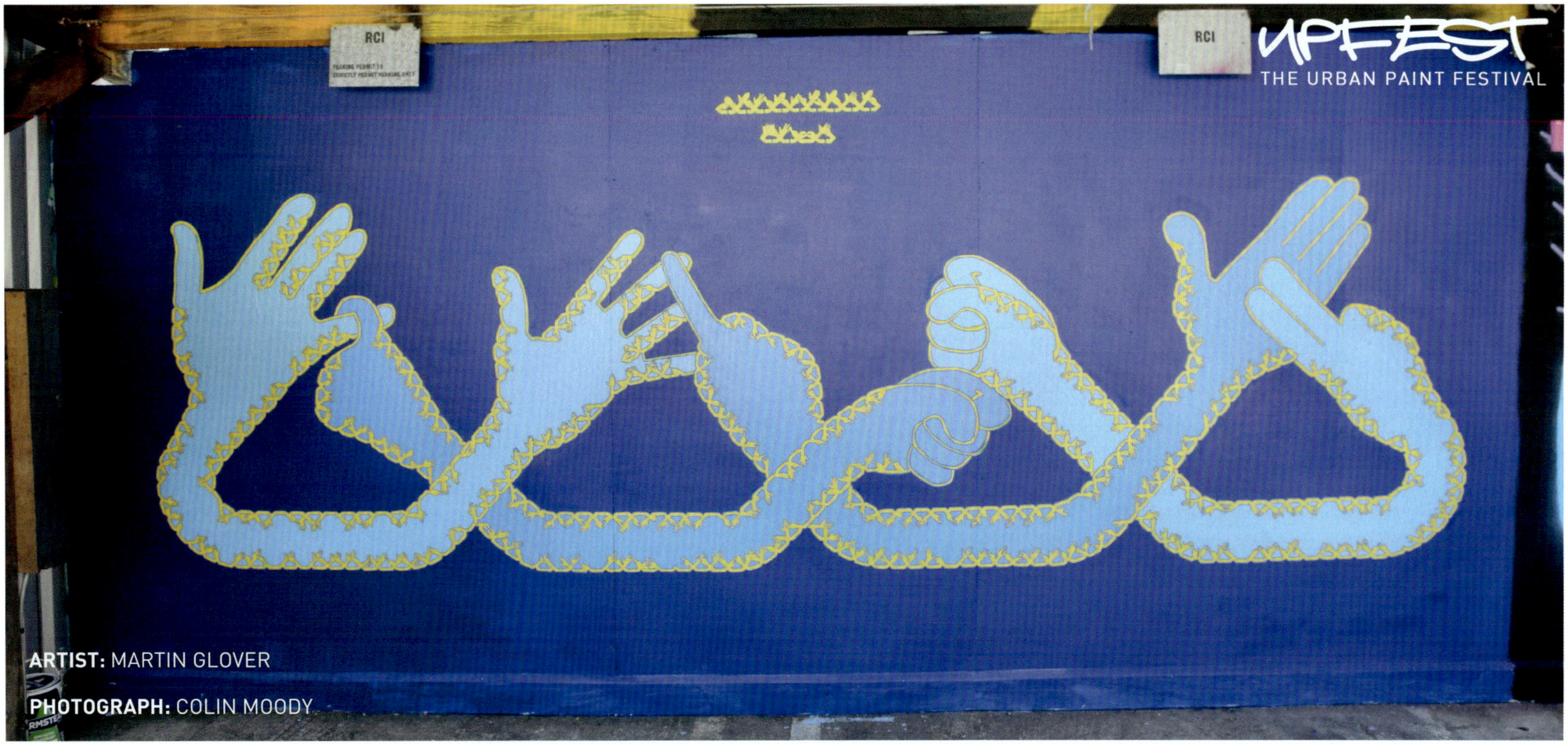

ARTIST: MARTIN GLOVER

PHOTOGRAPH: COLIN MOODY

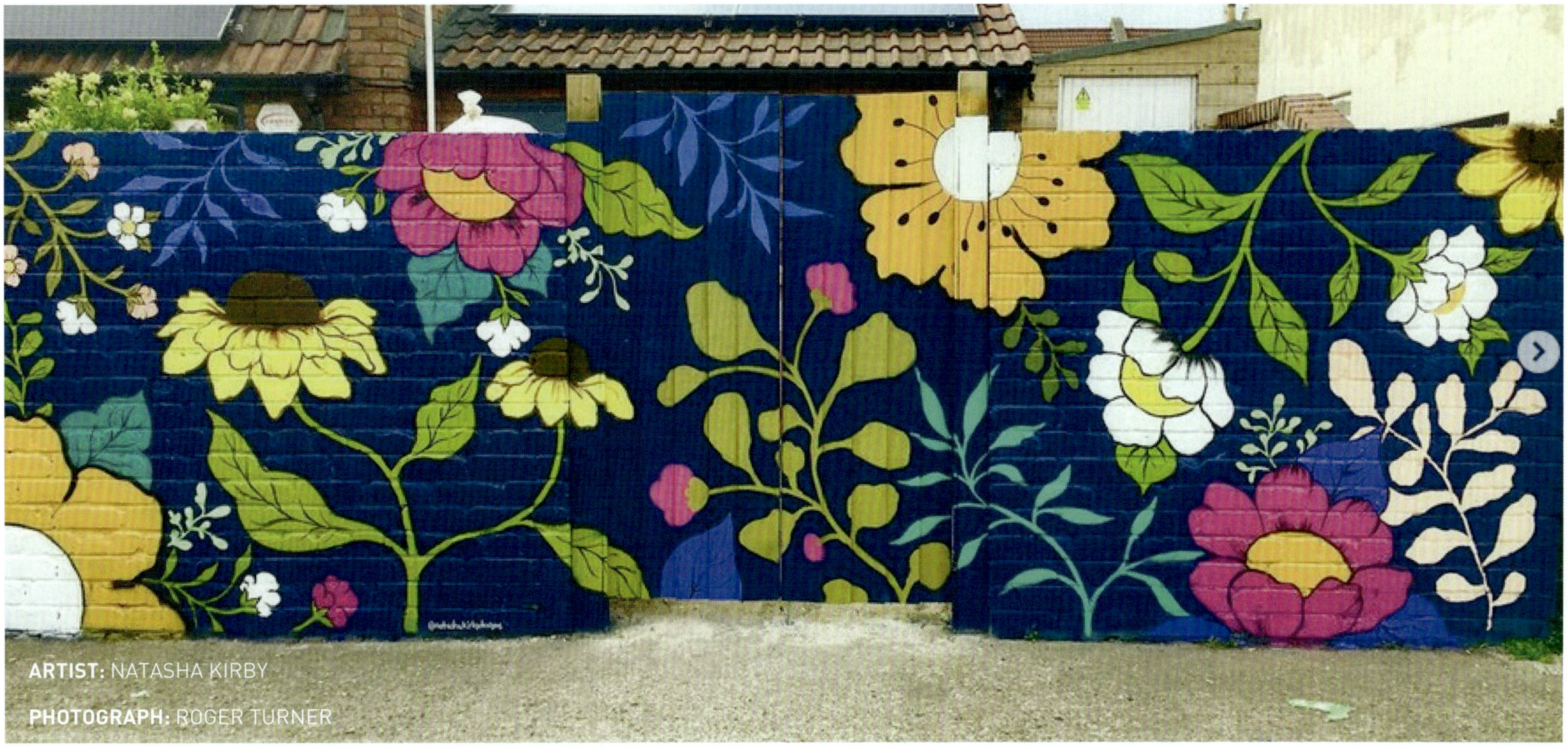

ARTIST: NATASHA KIRBY

PHOTOGRAPH: ROGER TURNER

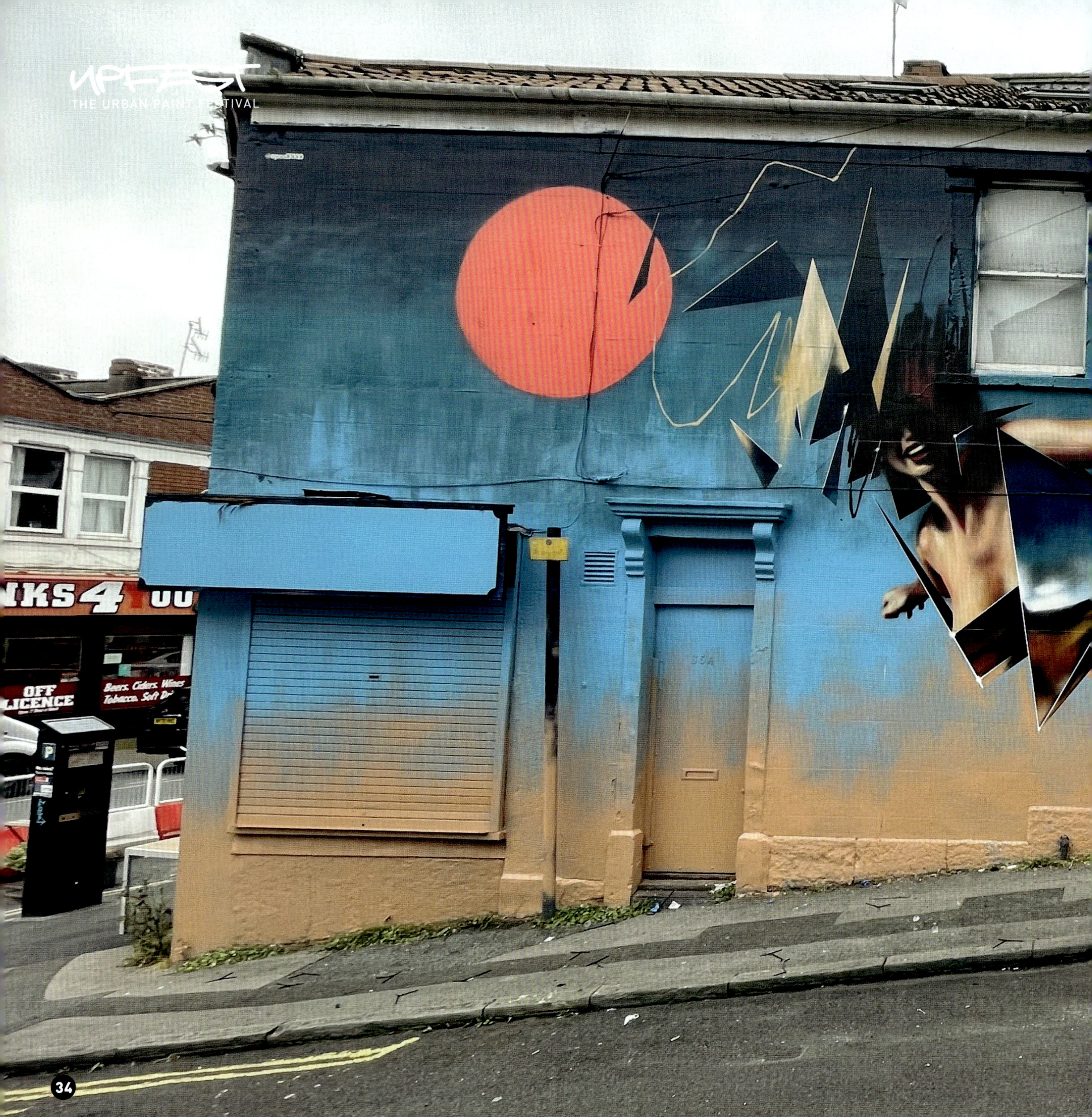
UPFEST
THE URBAN PAINT FESTIVAL

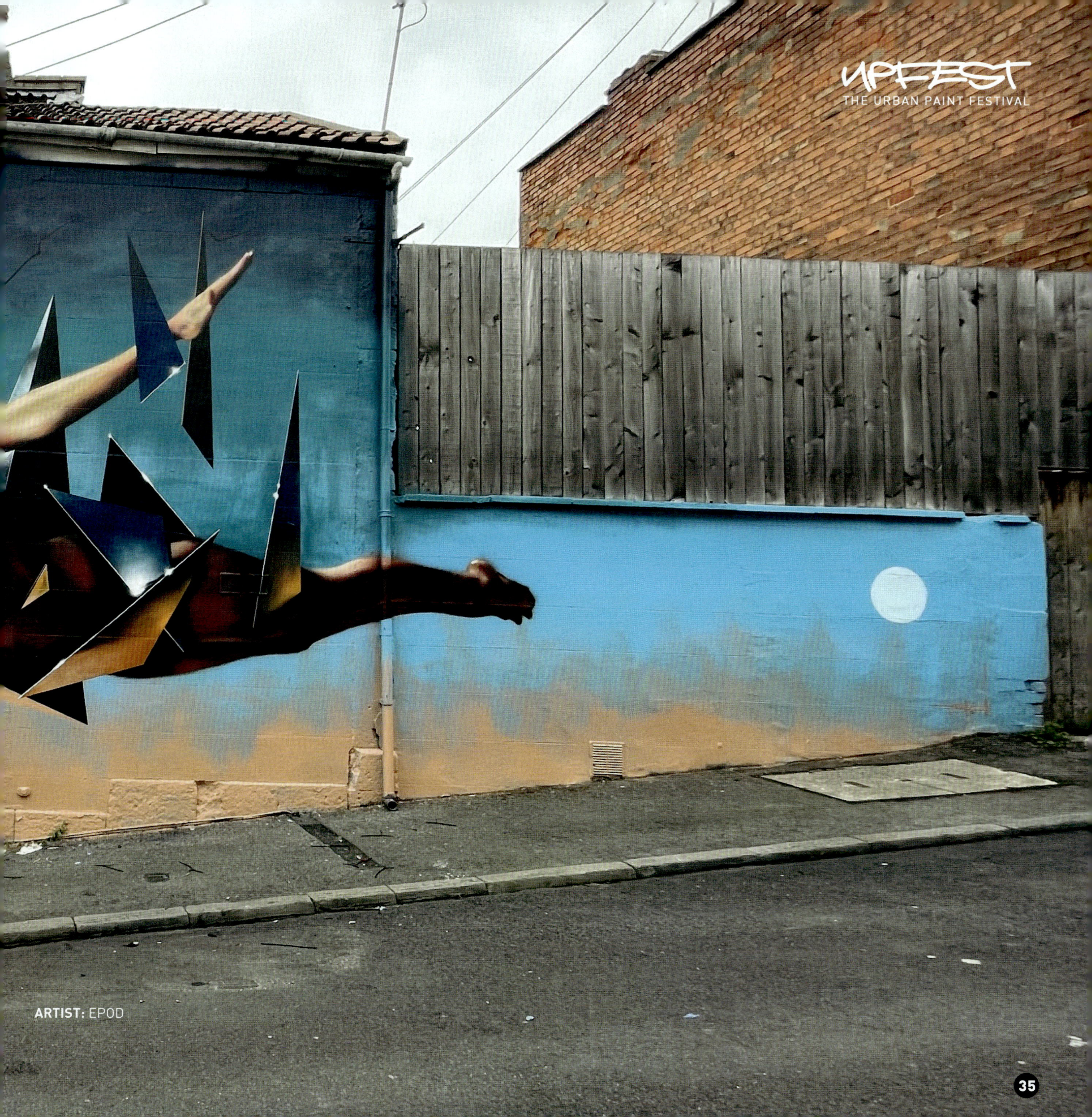
UPFEST
THE URBAN PAINT FESTIVAL
ARTIST: EPOD

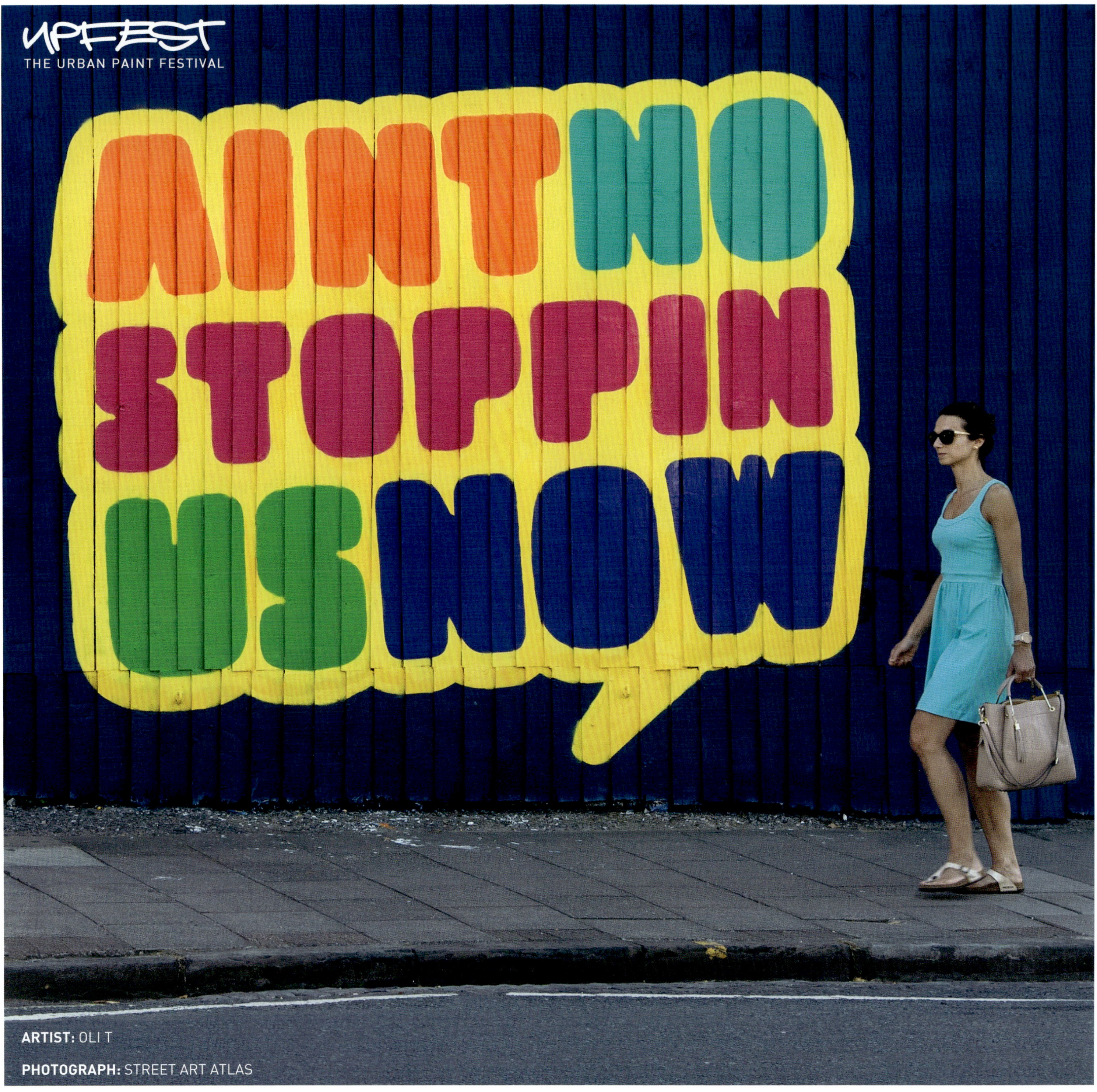

UPFEST
THE URBAN PAINT FESTIVAL
AINT NO STOPPIN US NOW

ARTIST: OLI T
PHOTOGRAPH: STREET ART ATLAS

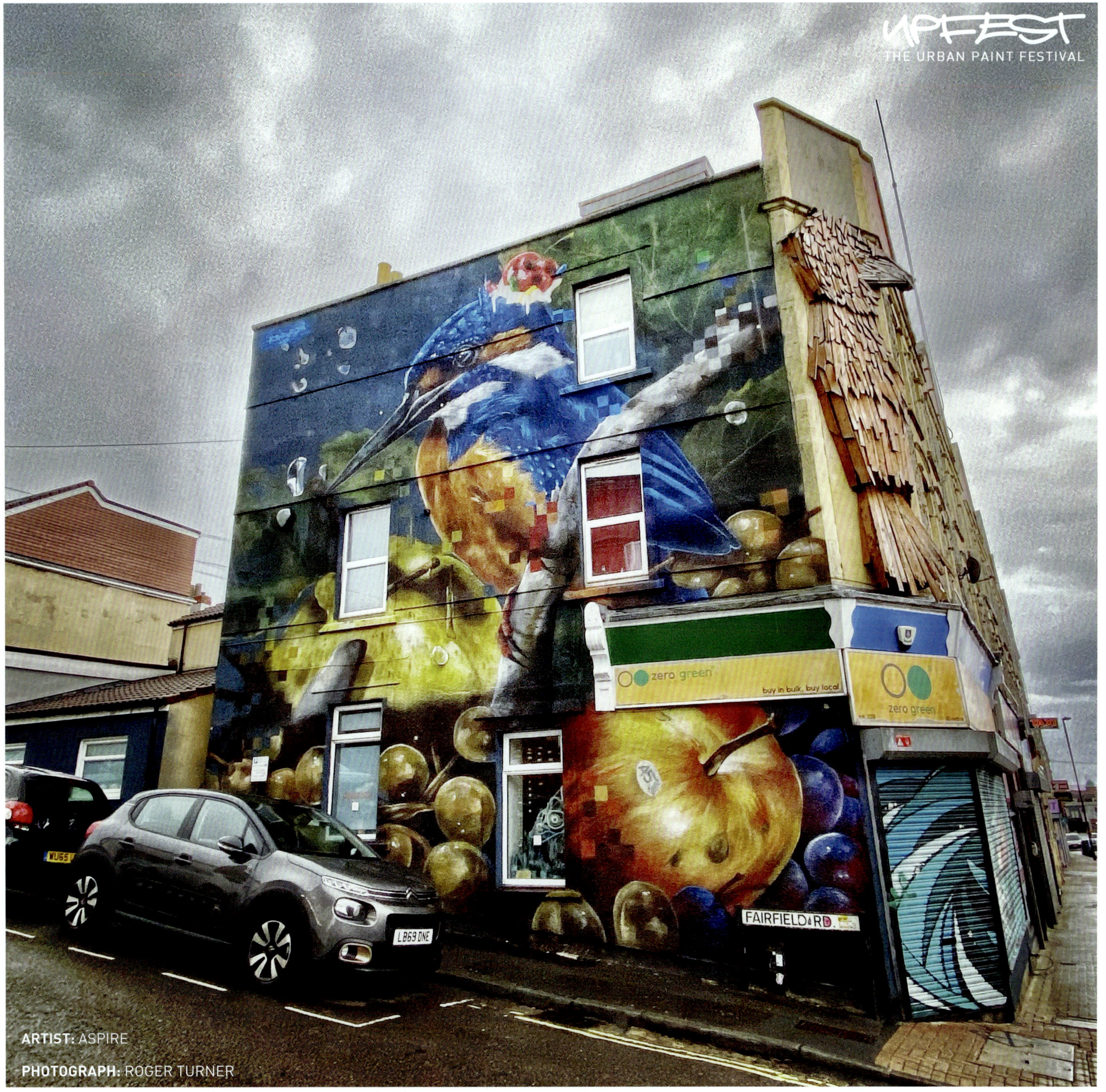

ARTIST: ASPIRE

PHOTOGRAPH: ROGER TURNER

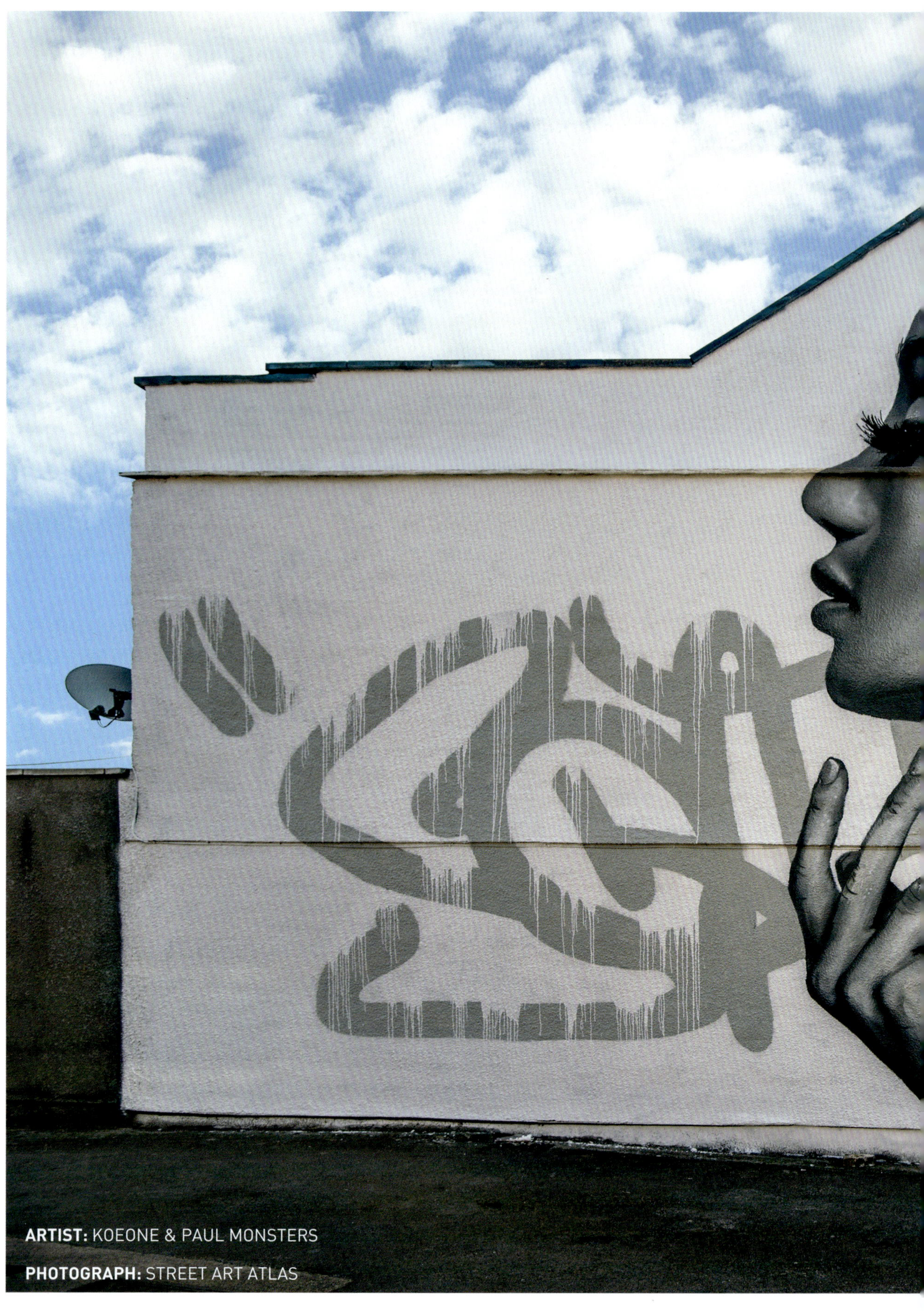

ARTIST: KOEONE & PAUL MONSTERS

PHOTOGRAPH: STREET ART ATLAS

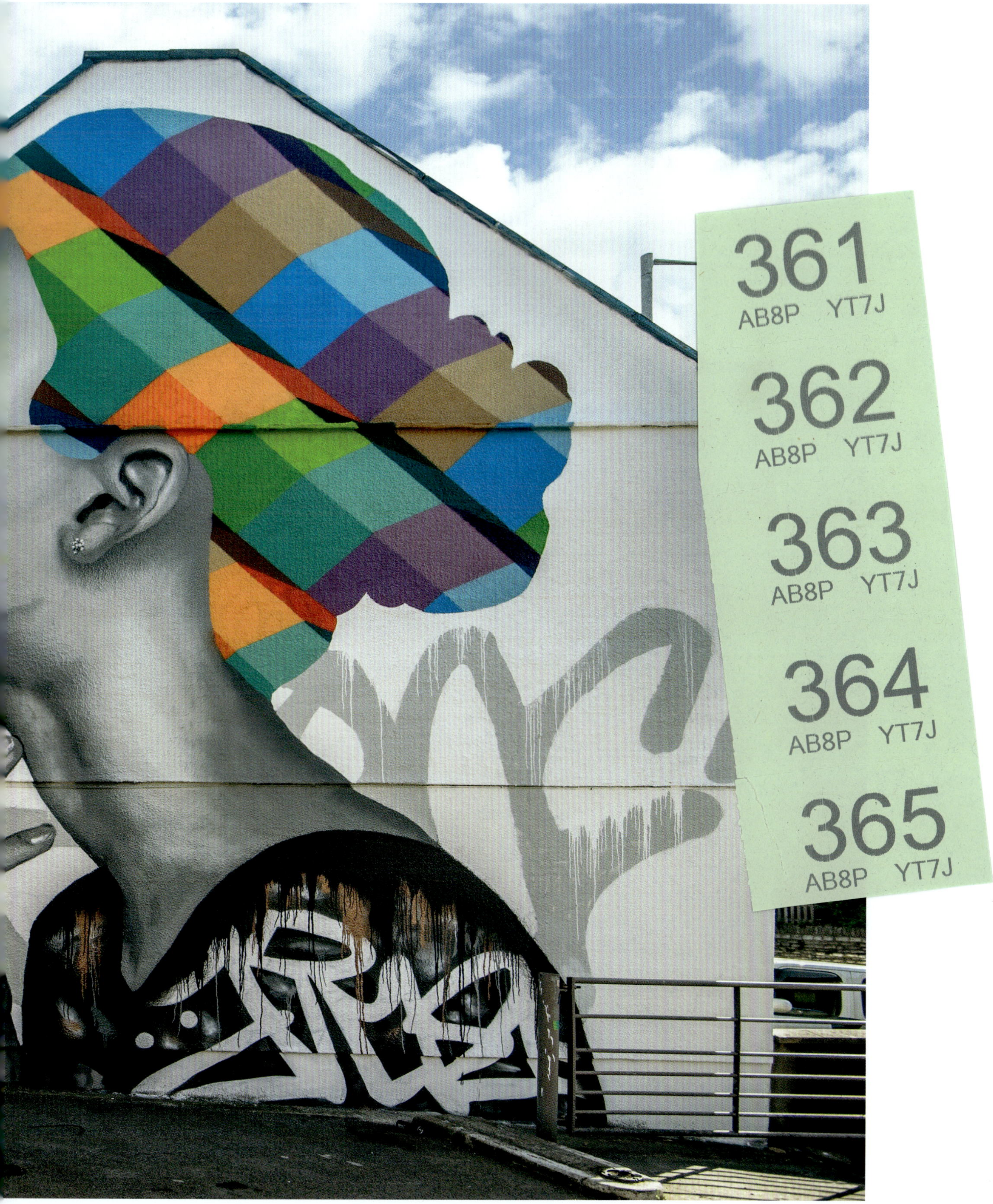

361
AB8P   YT7J
362
AB8P   YT7J
363
AB8P   YT7J
364
AB8P   YT7J
365
AB8P   YT7J

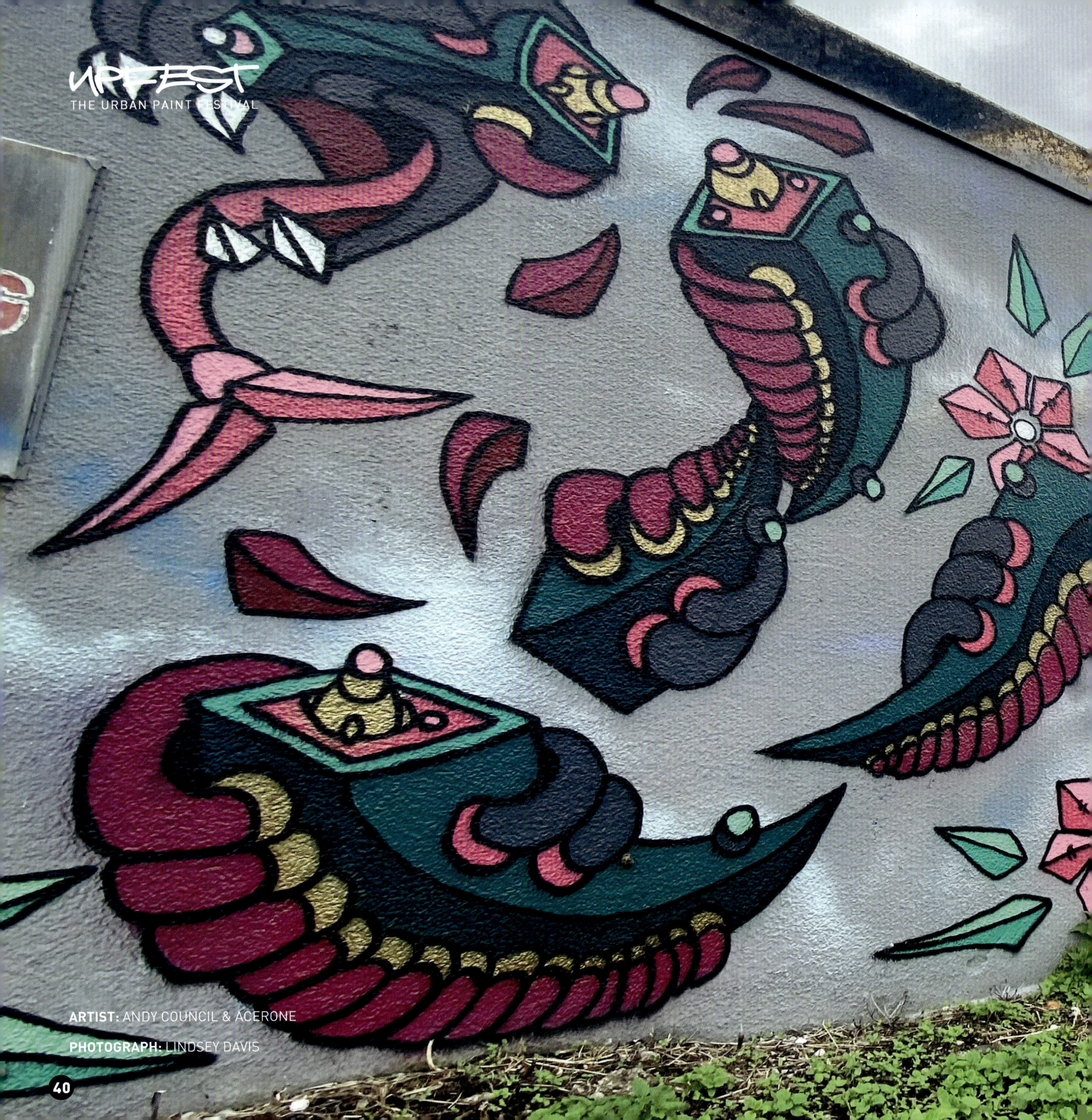
UPFEST
THE URBAN PAINT FESTIVAL

ARTIST: ANDY COUNCIL & ACERONE
PHOTOGRAPH: LINDSEY DAVIS

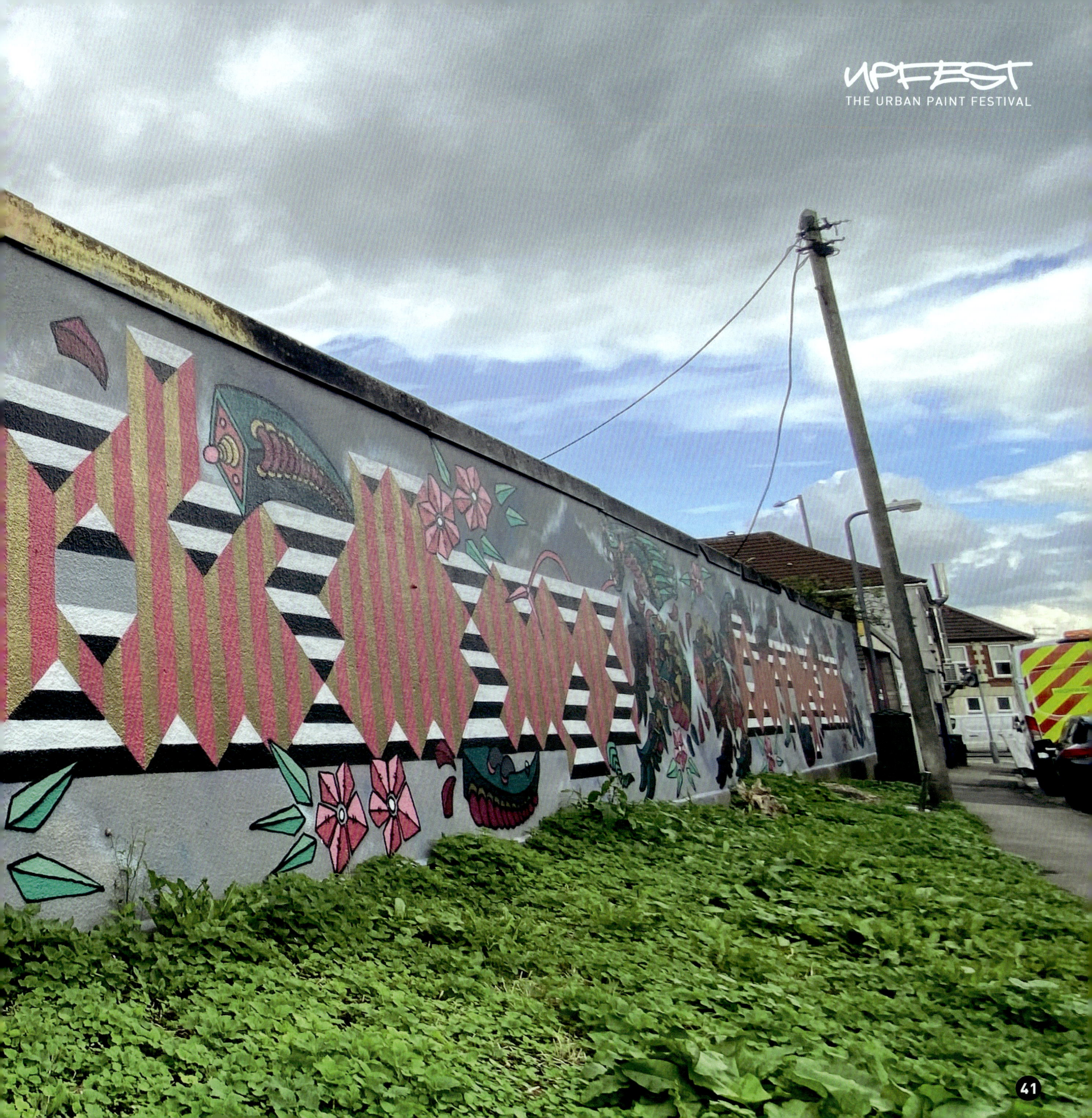
UPFEST
THE URBAN PAINT FESTIVAL

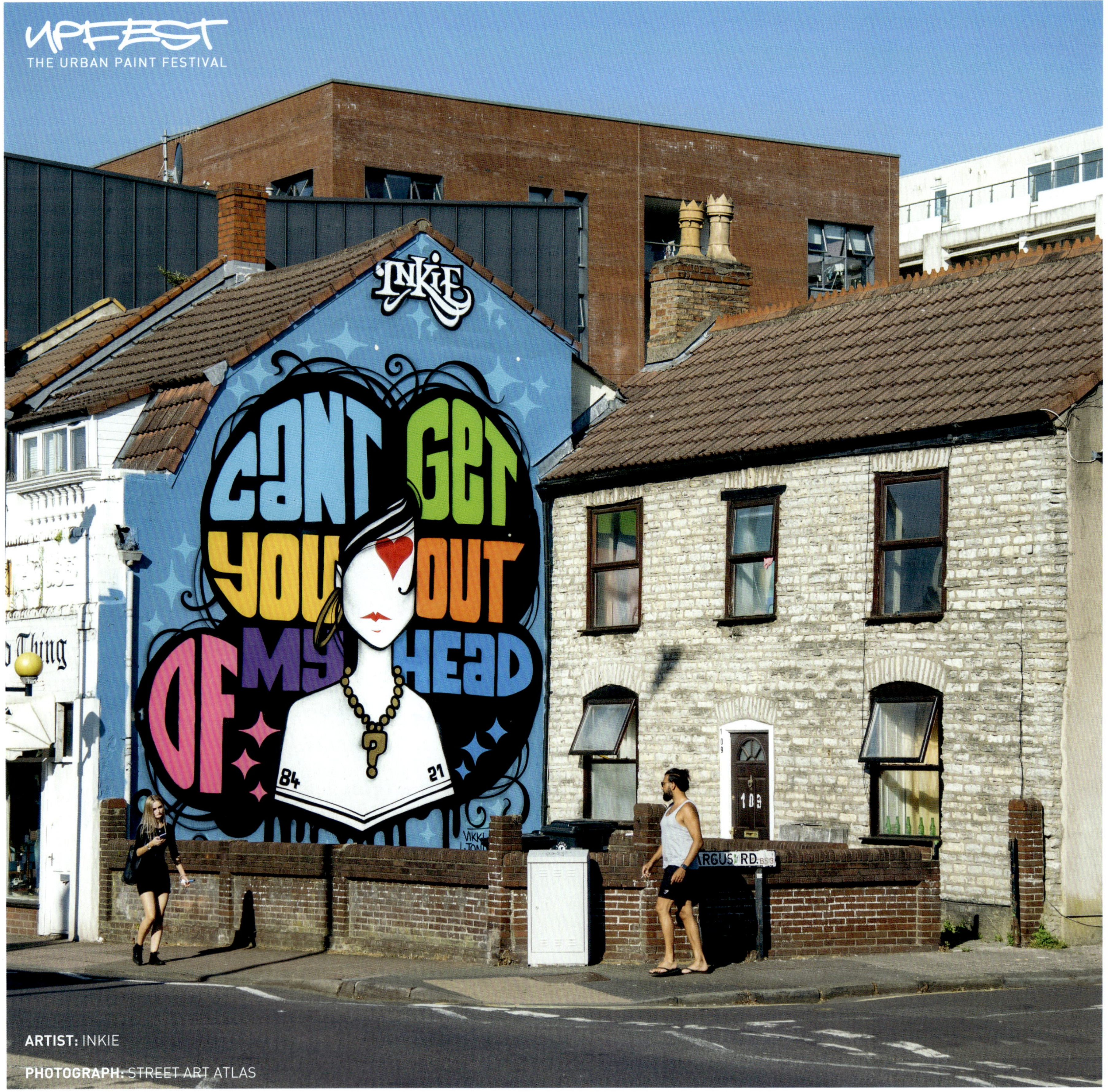
UPFEST
THE URBAN PAINT FESTIVAL
INKiE
CANT GET
YOU OUT
OF MY HEAD
84
21
VIKKI
I-TONI
109
103
ARGUS RD. BS3
o Thing

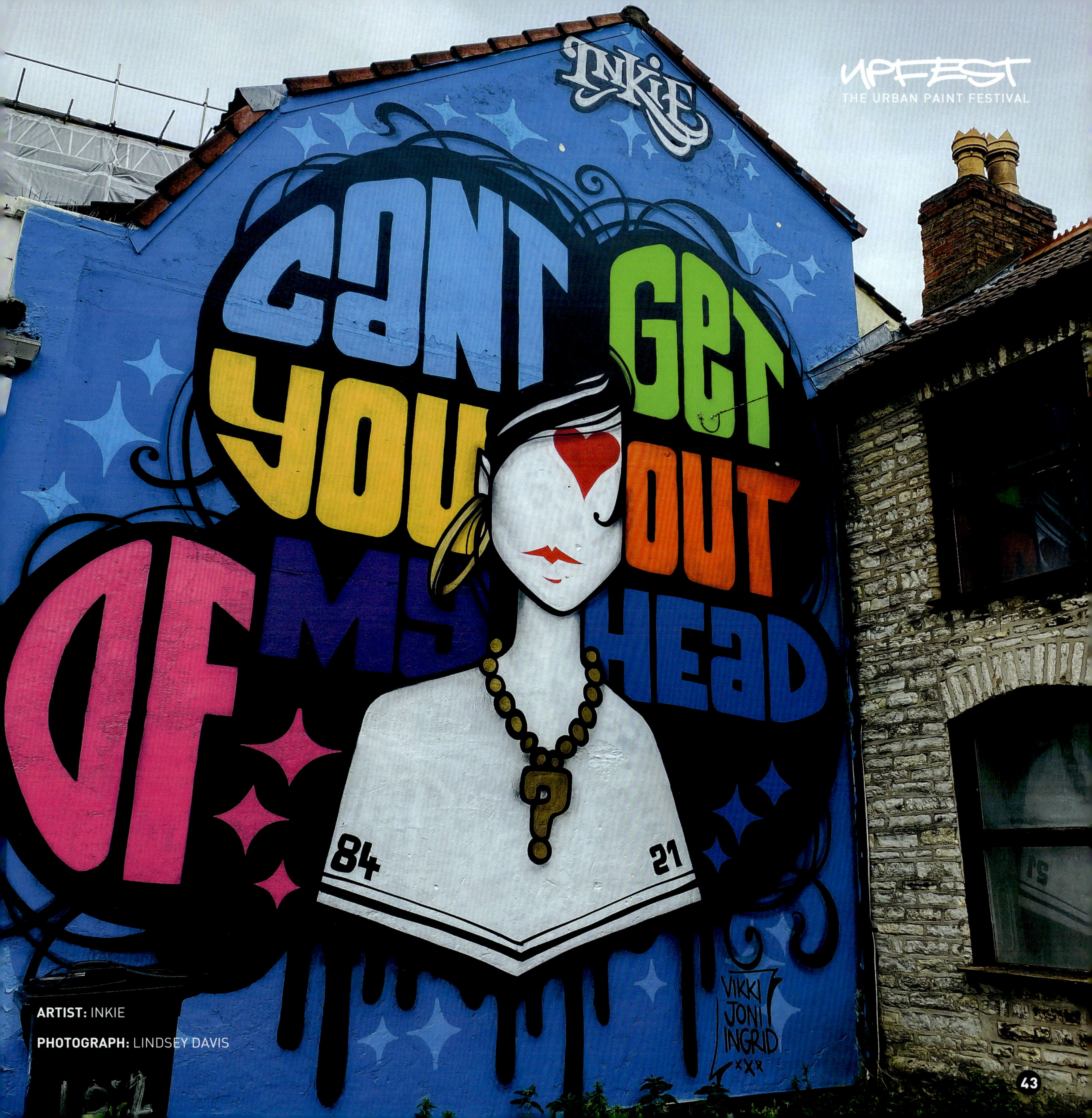

ARTIST: INKIE

PHOTOGRAPH: LINDSEY DAVIS

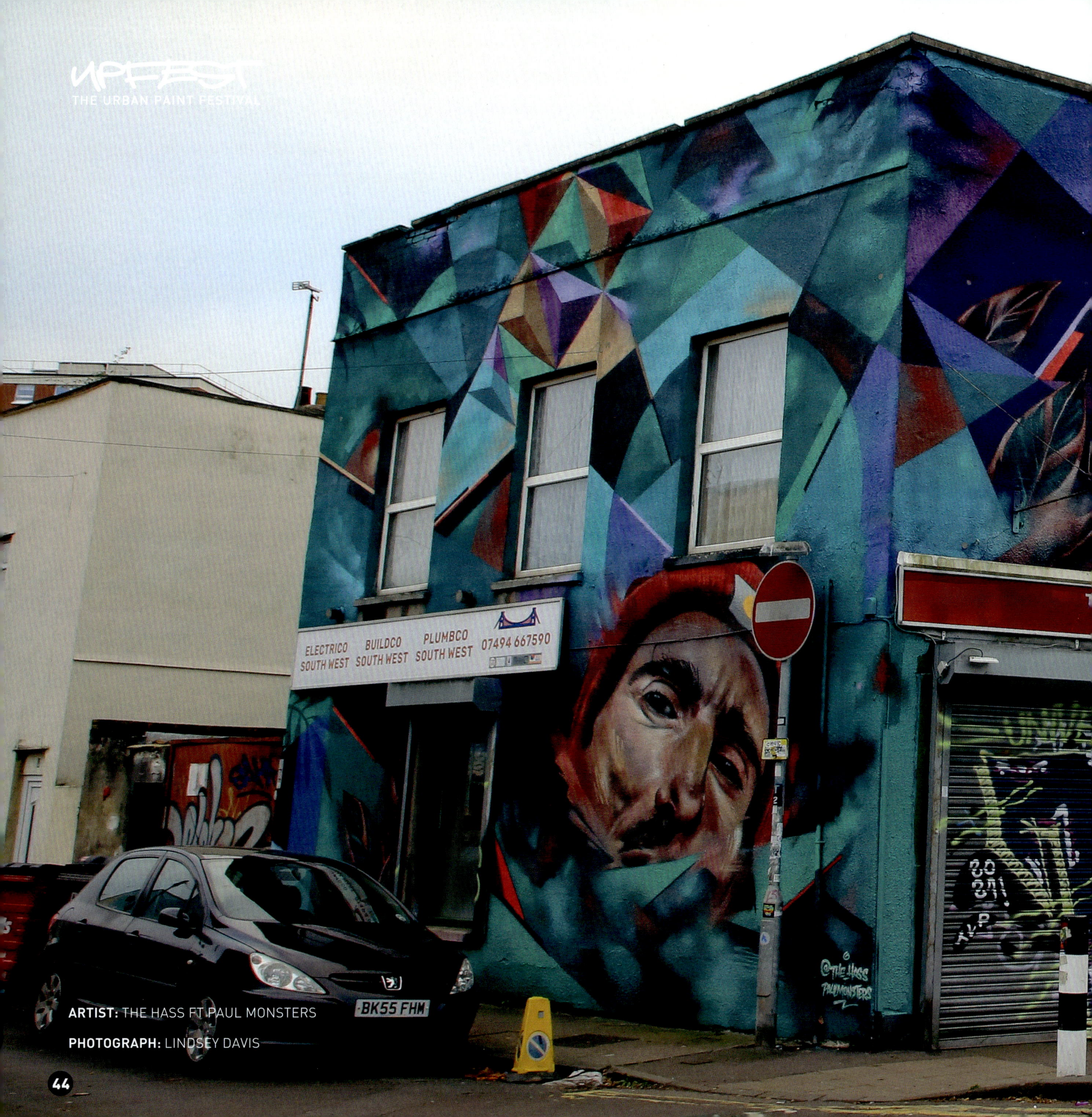

ARTIST: THE HASS FT PAUL MONSTERS

PHOTOGRAPH: LINDSEY DAVIS

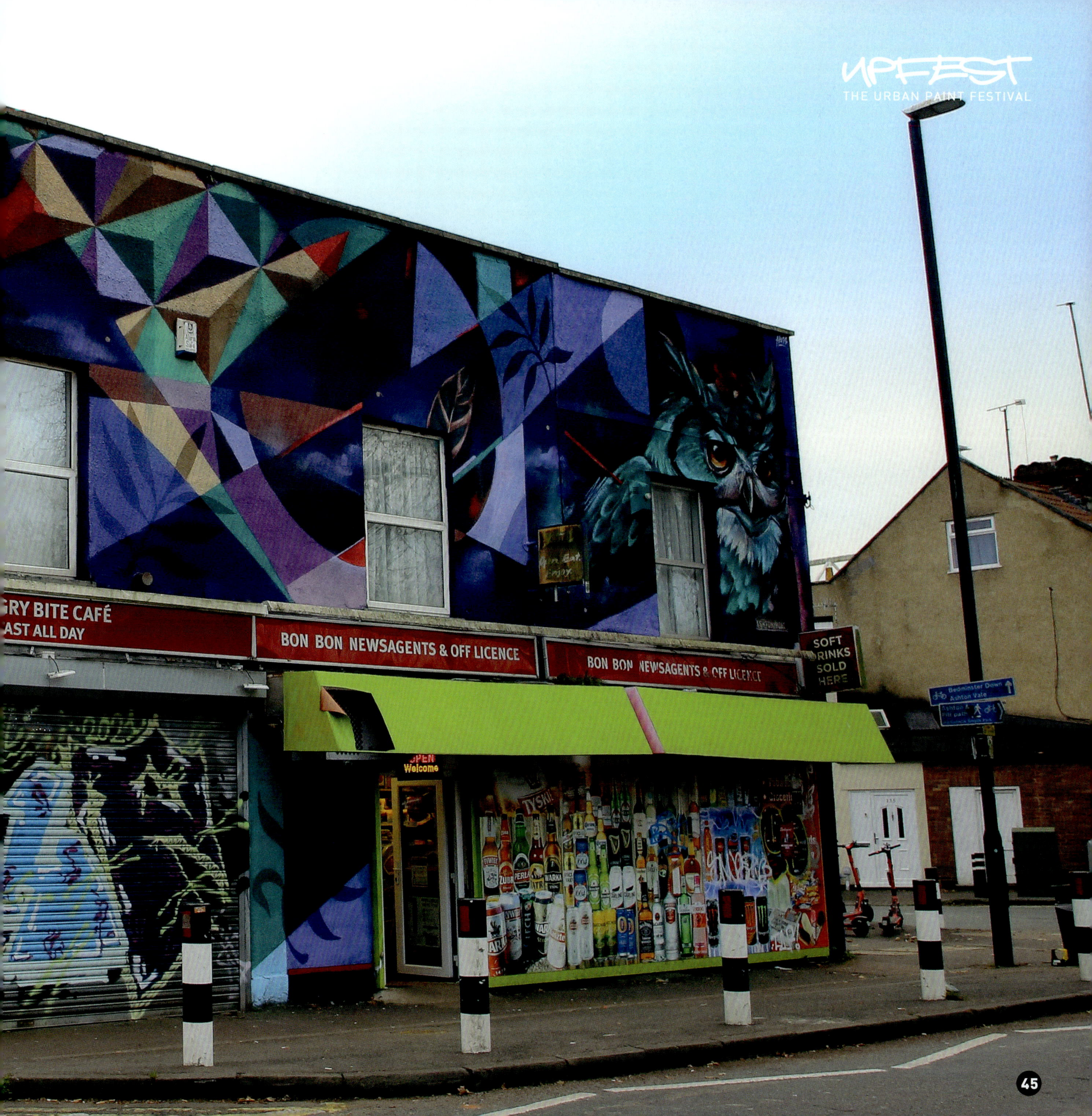
UPFEST
THE URBAN PAINT FESTIVAL
GRY BITE CAFÉ
AST ALL DAY
BON BON NEWSAGENTS & OFF LICENCE
BON BON NEWSAGENTS & OFF LICENCE
SOFT DRINKS SOLD HERE
OPEN
Welcome
Bedminster Down
Ashton Vale
TYSKIE

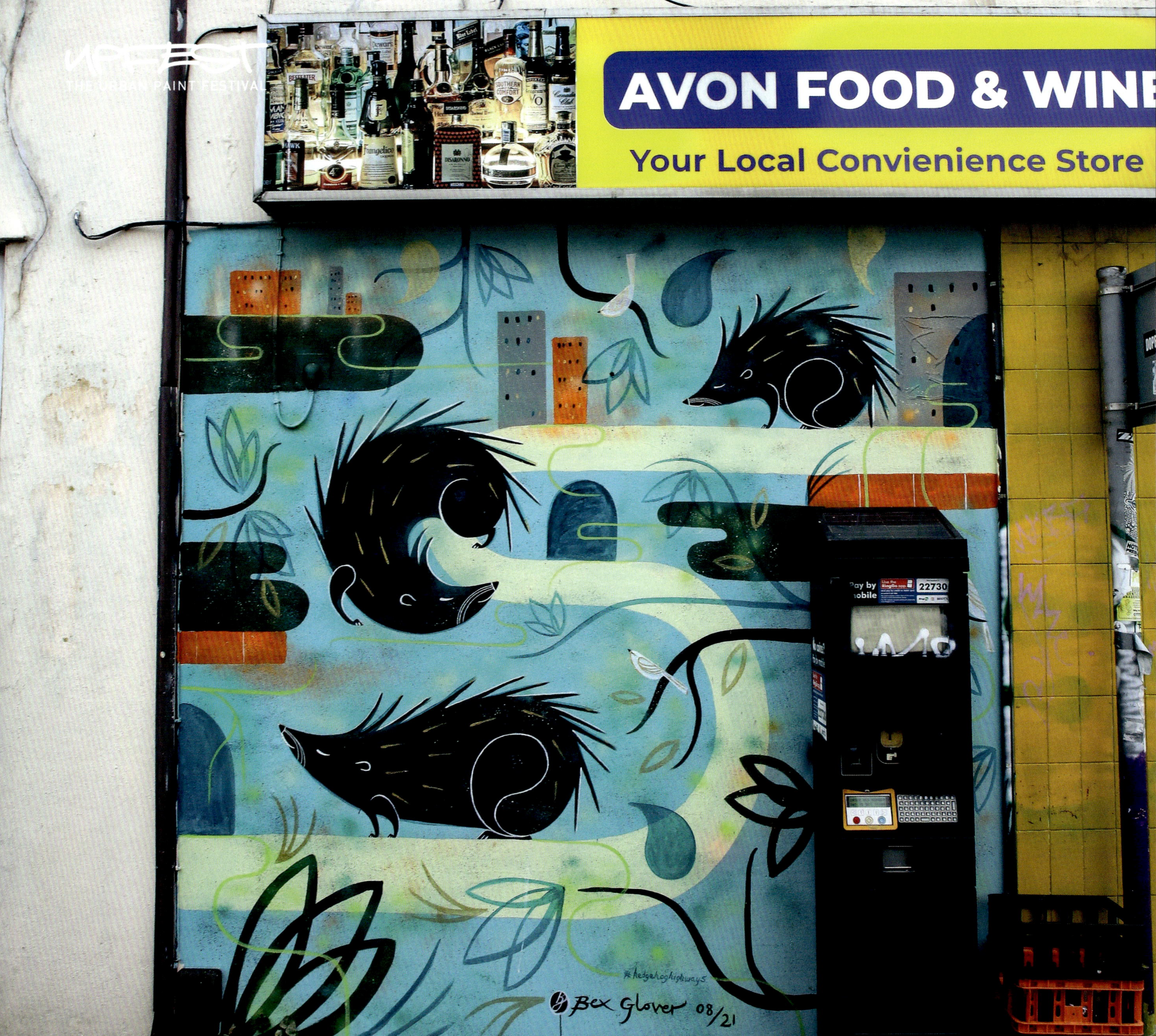

ARTIST: BEX GLOVER

PHOTOGRAPH: LINDSEY DAVIS

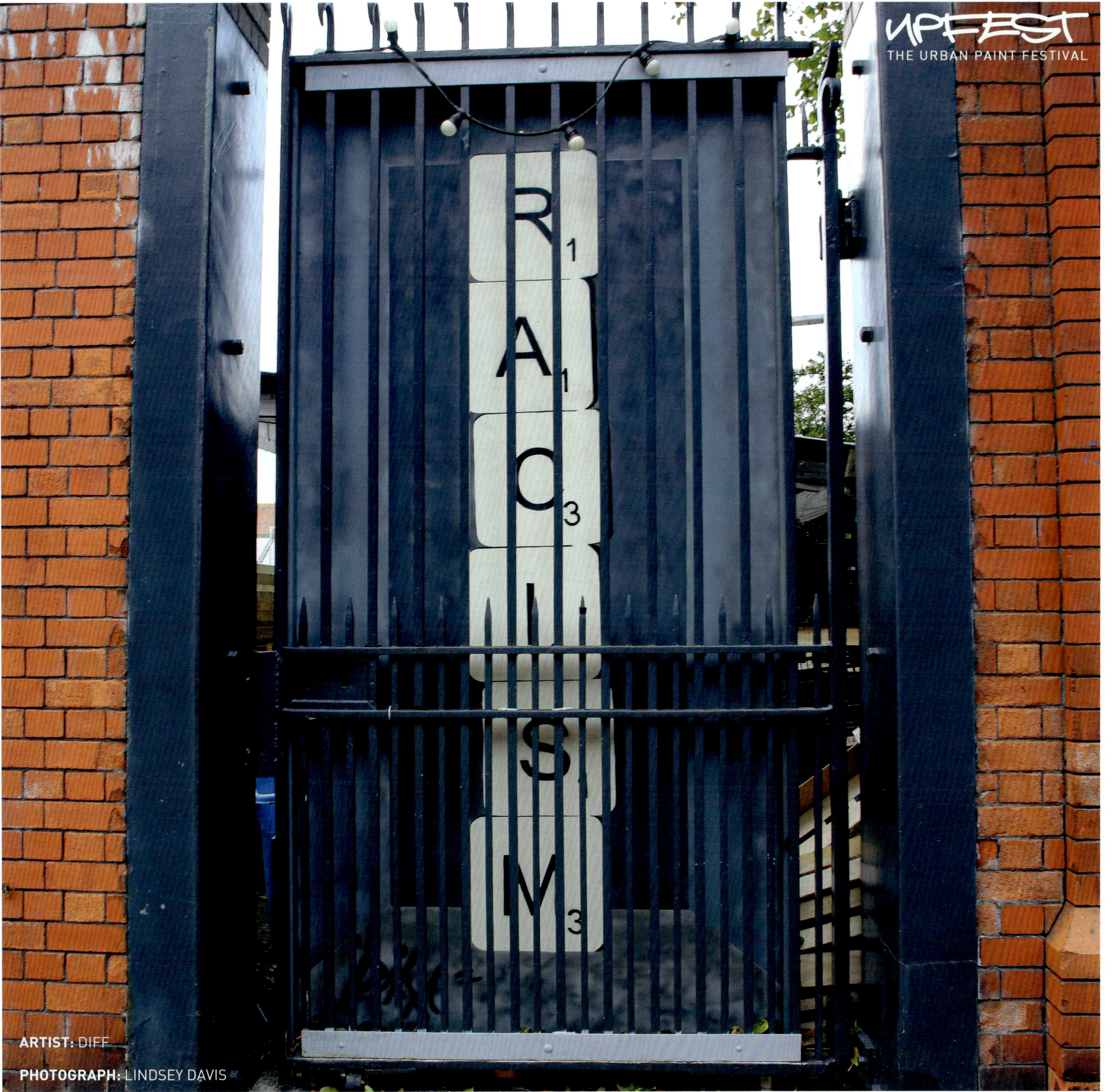

ARTIST: DIFF

PHOTOGRAPH: LINDSEY DAVIS

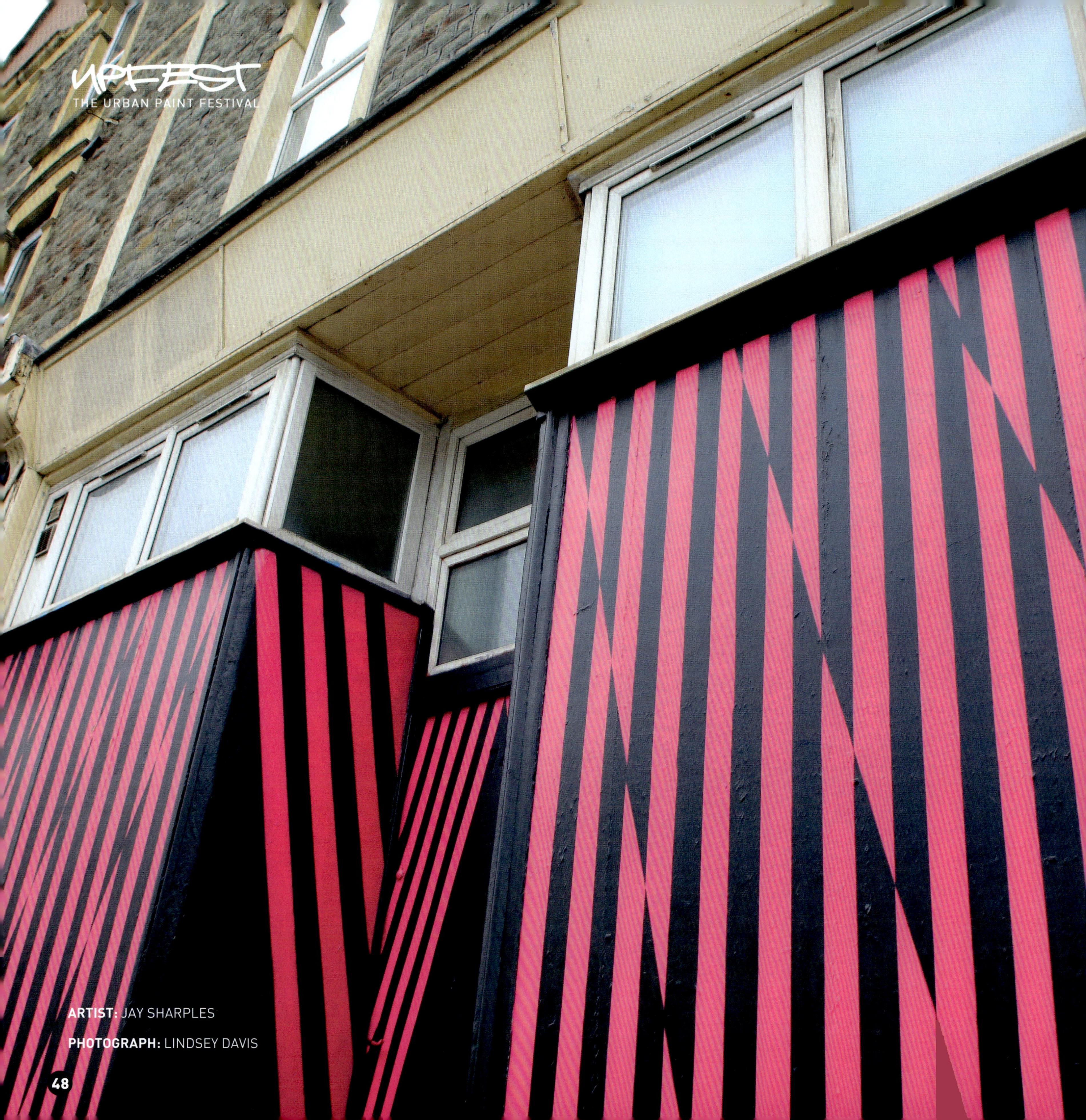

ARTIST: JAY SHARPLES

PHOTOGRAPH: LINDSEY DAVIS

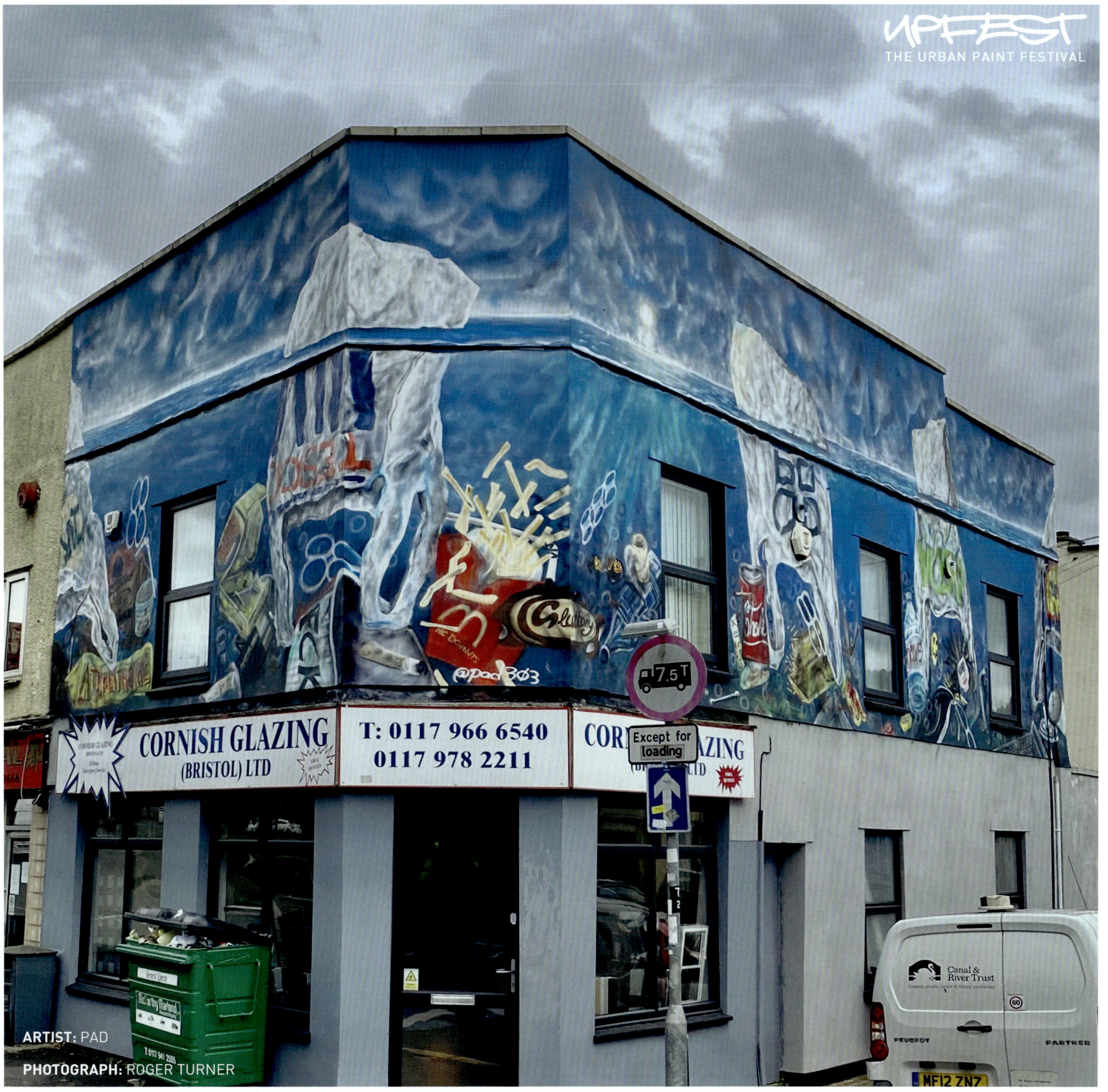

ARTIST: PAD

PHOTOGRAPH: ROGER TURNER

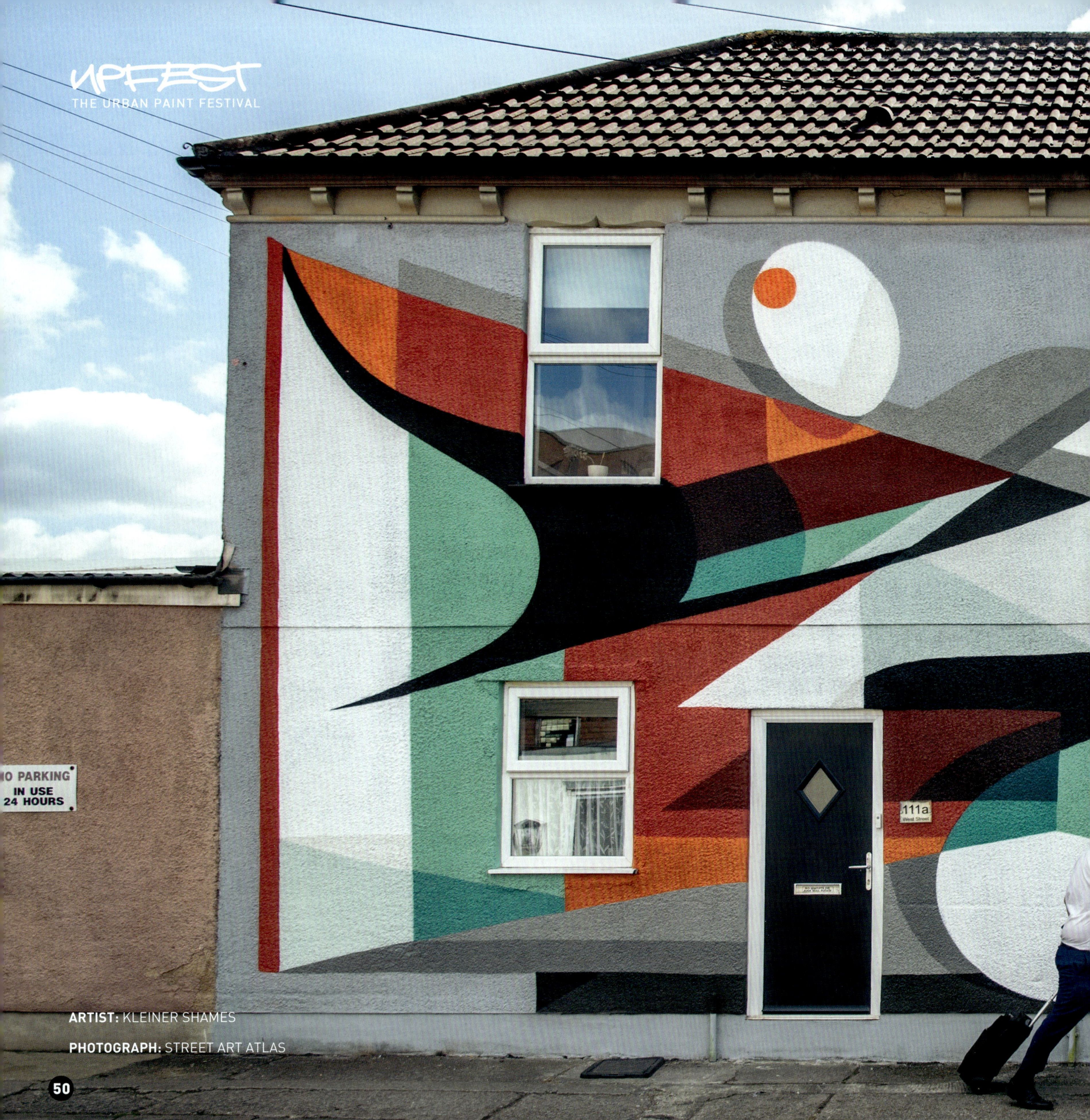

ARTIST: KLEINER SHAMES

PHOTOGRAPH: STREET ART ATLAS

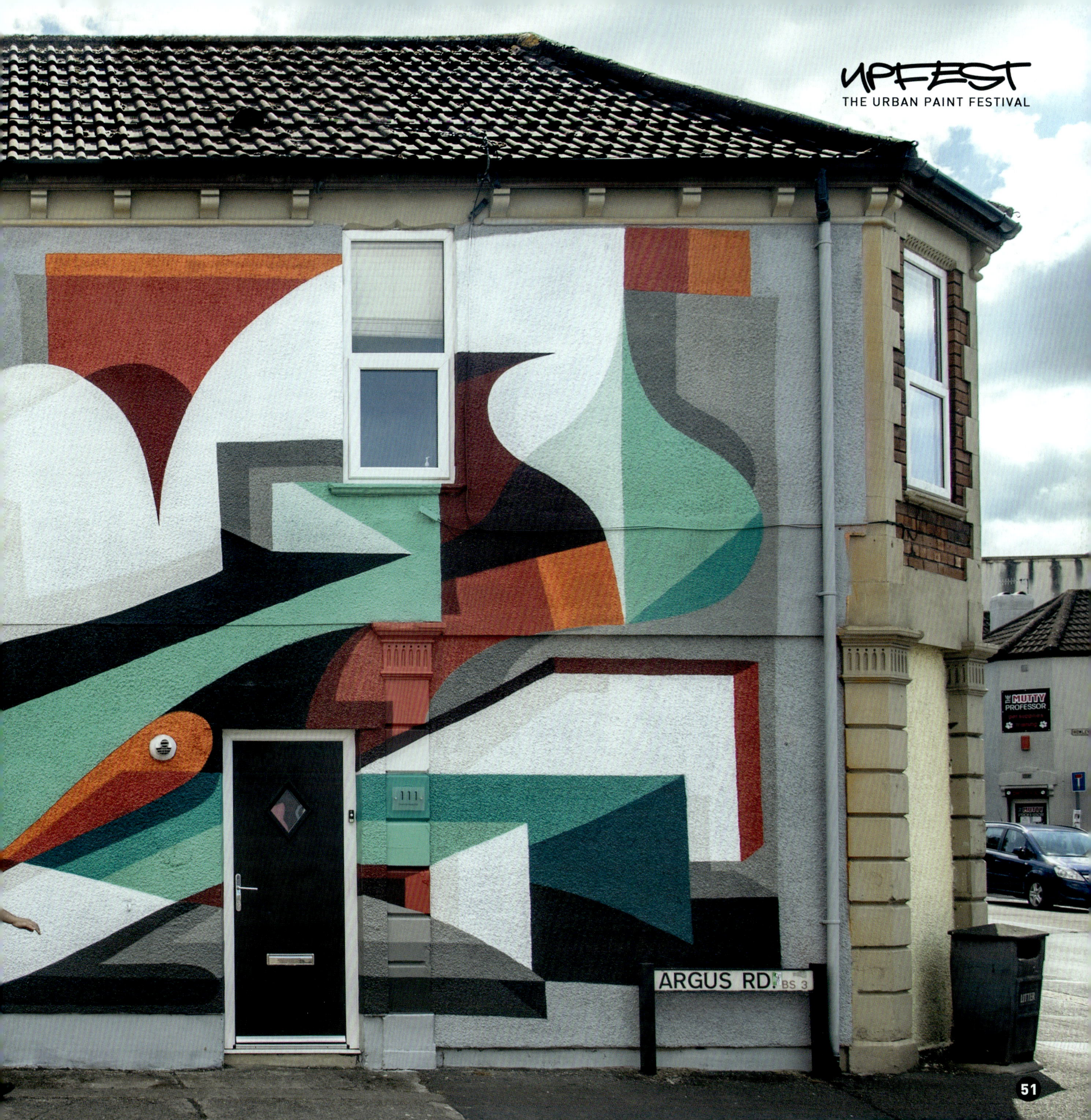

UPFEST
THE URBAN PAINT FESTIVAL
111
ARGUS RD. BS 3
THE MUTTY PROFESSOR
LITTER

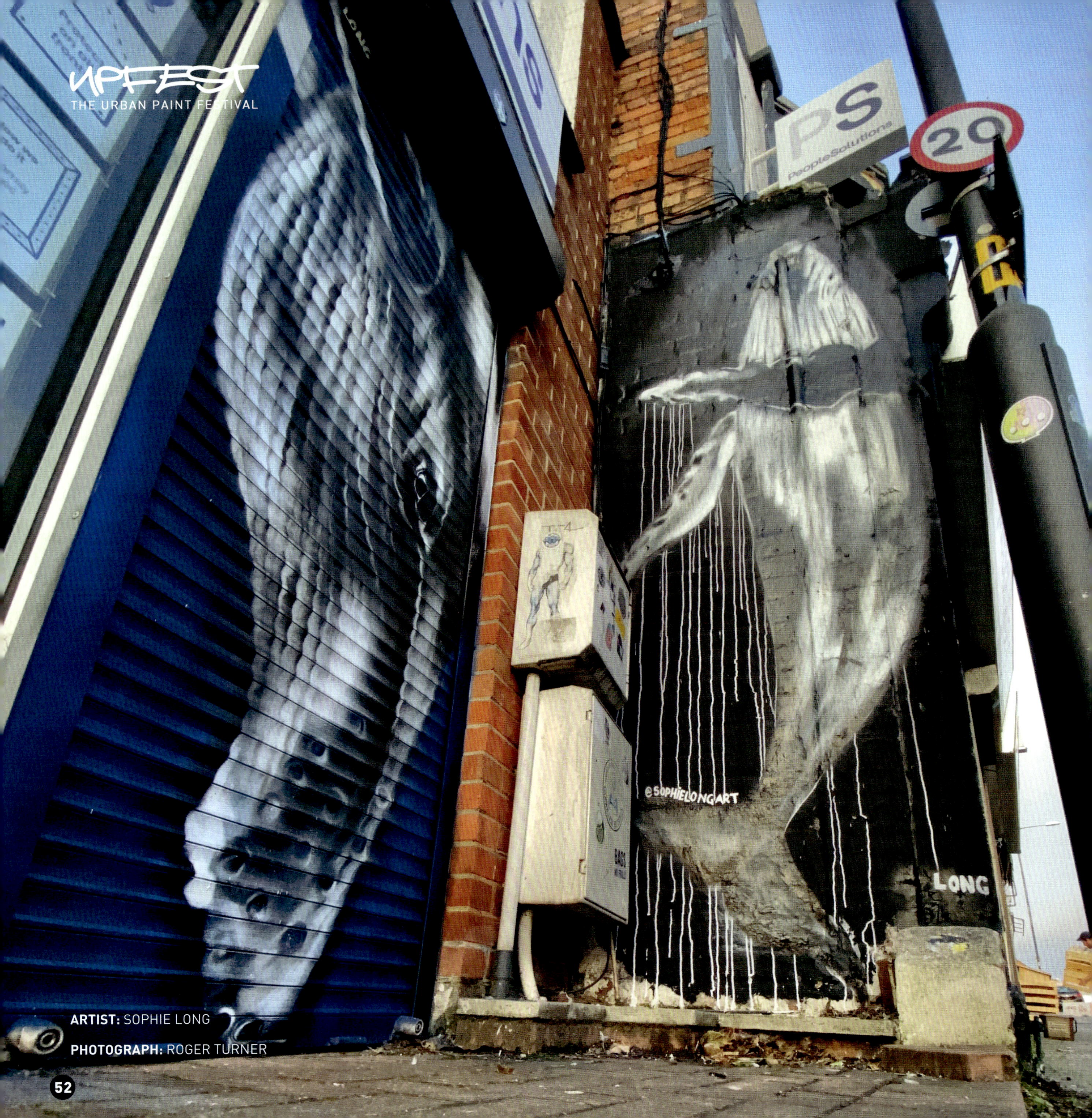

ARTIST: SOPHIE LONG

PHOTOGRAPH: ROGER TURNER

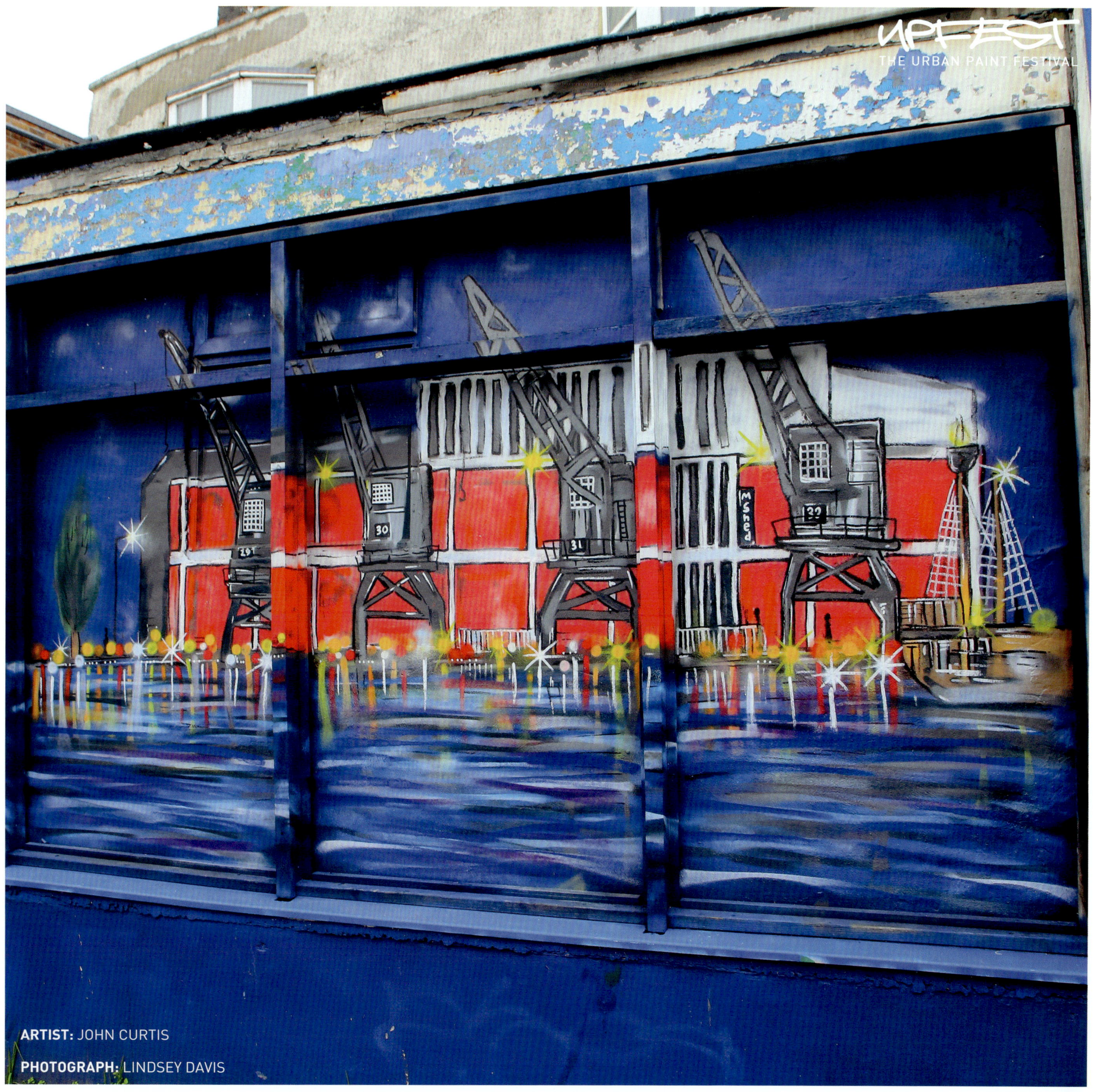

ARTIST: JOHN CURTIS

PHOTOGRAPH: LINDSEY DAVIS

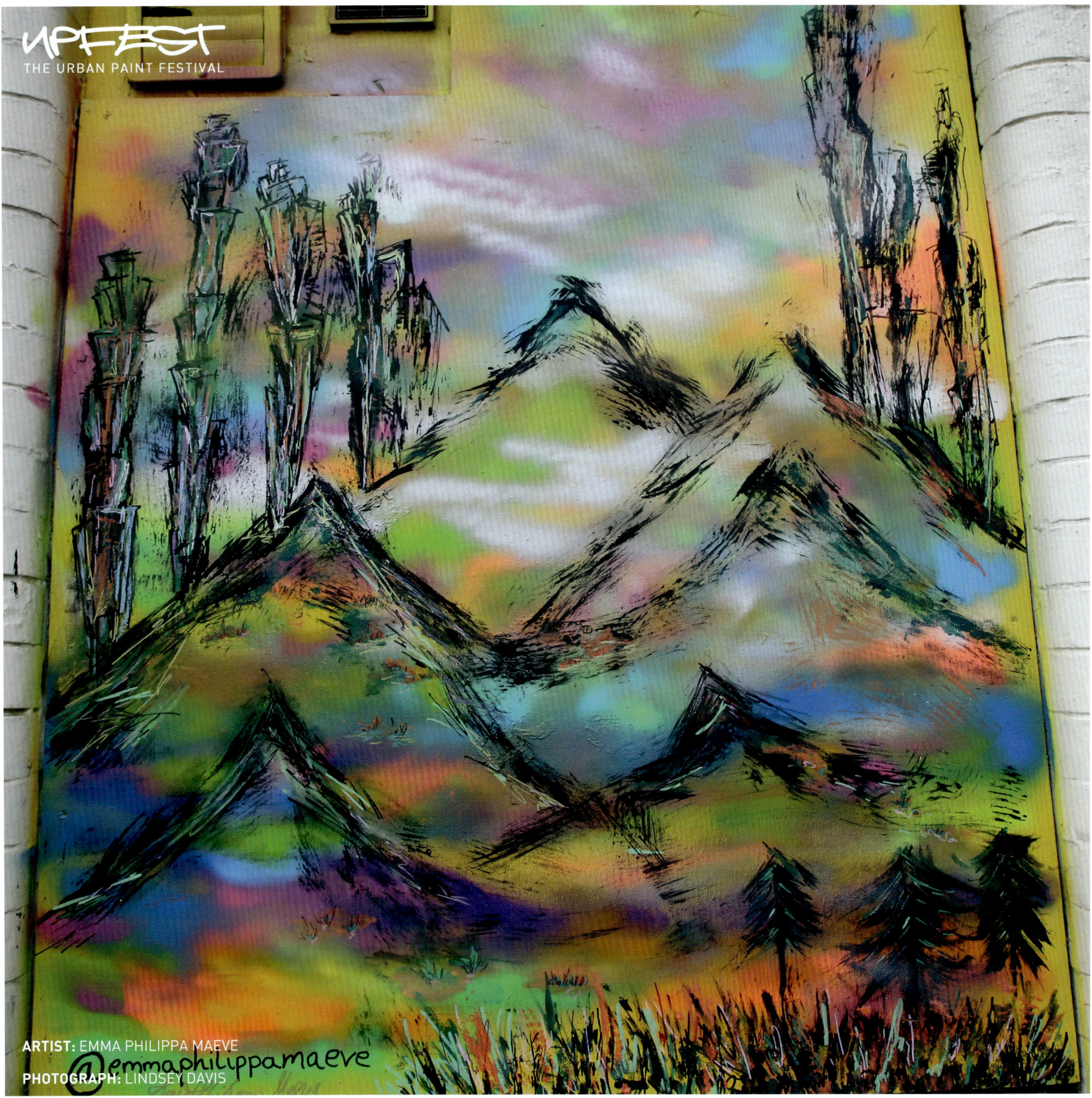

ARTIST: EMMA PHILIPPA MAEVE
PHOTOGRAPH: LINDSEY DAVIS

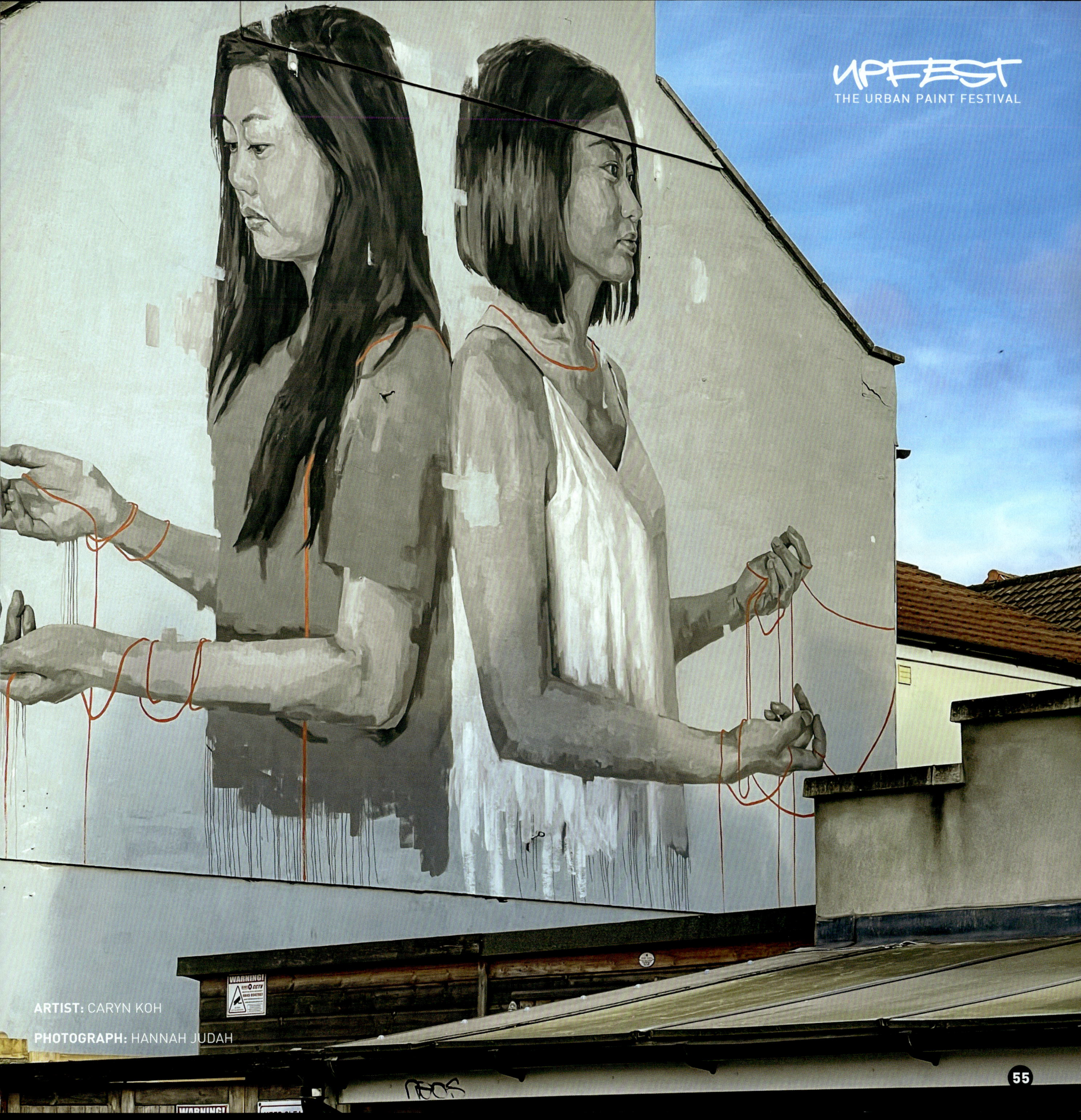
UPFEST
THE URBAN PAINT FESTIVAL

ARTIST: CARYN KOH
PHOTOGRAPH: HANNAH JUDAH

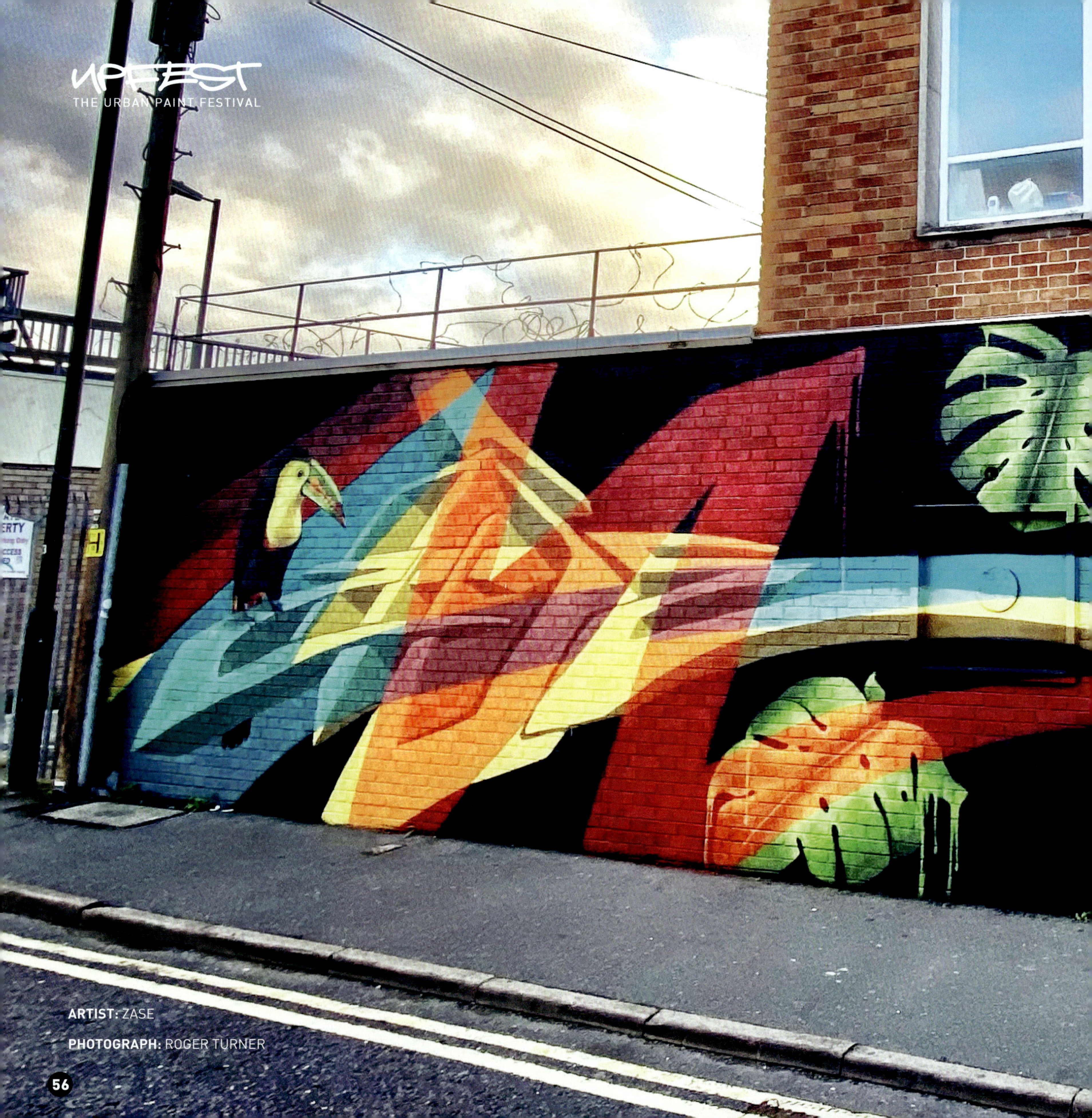

ARTIST: ZASE

PHOTOGRAPH: ROGER TURNER

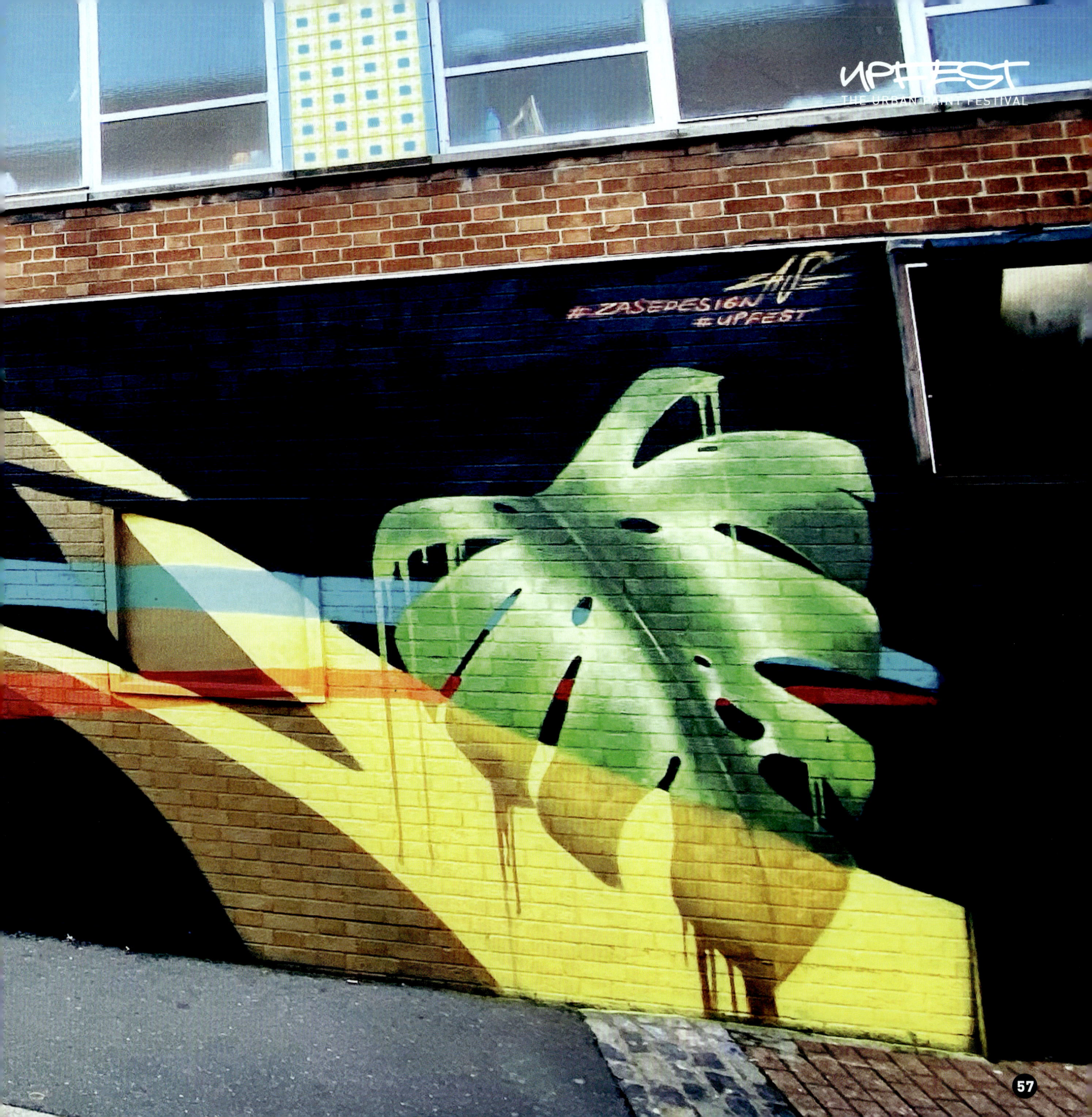
#ZASEDESIGN
#UPFEST

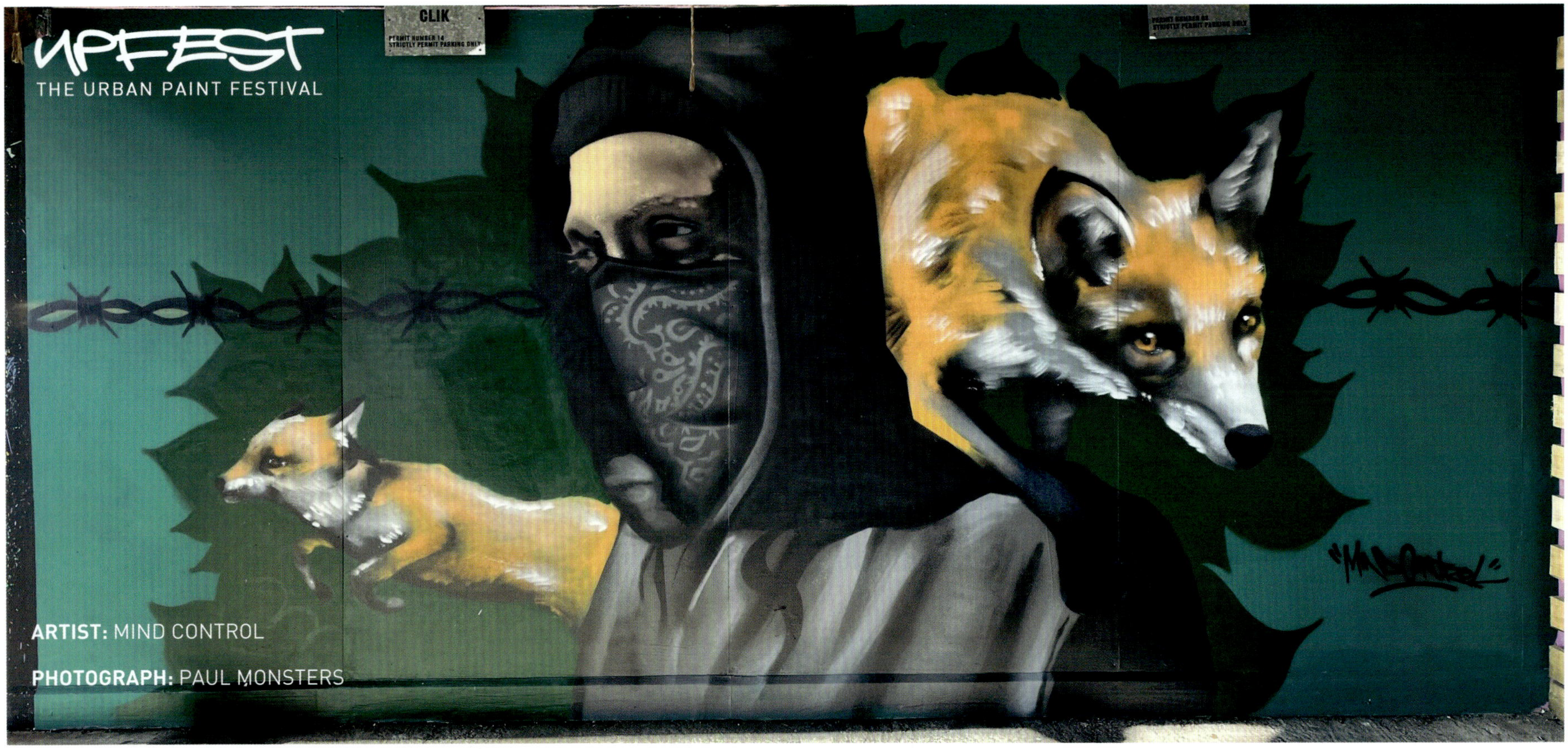

ARTIST: MIND CONTROL

PHOTOGRAPH: PAUL MONSTERS

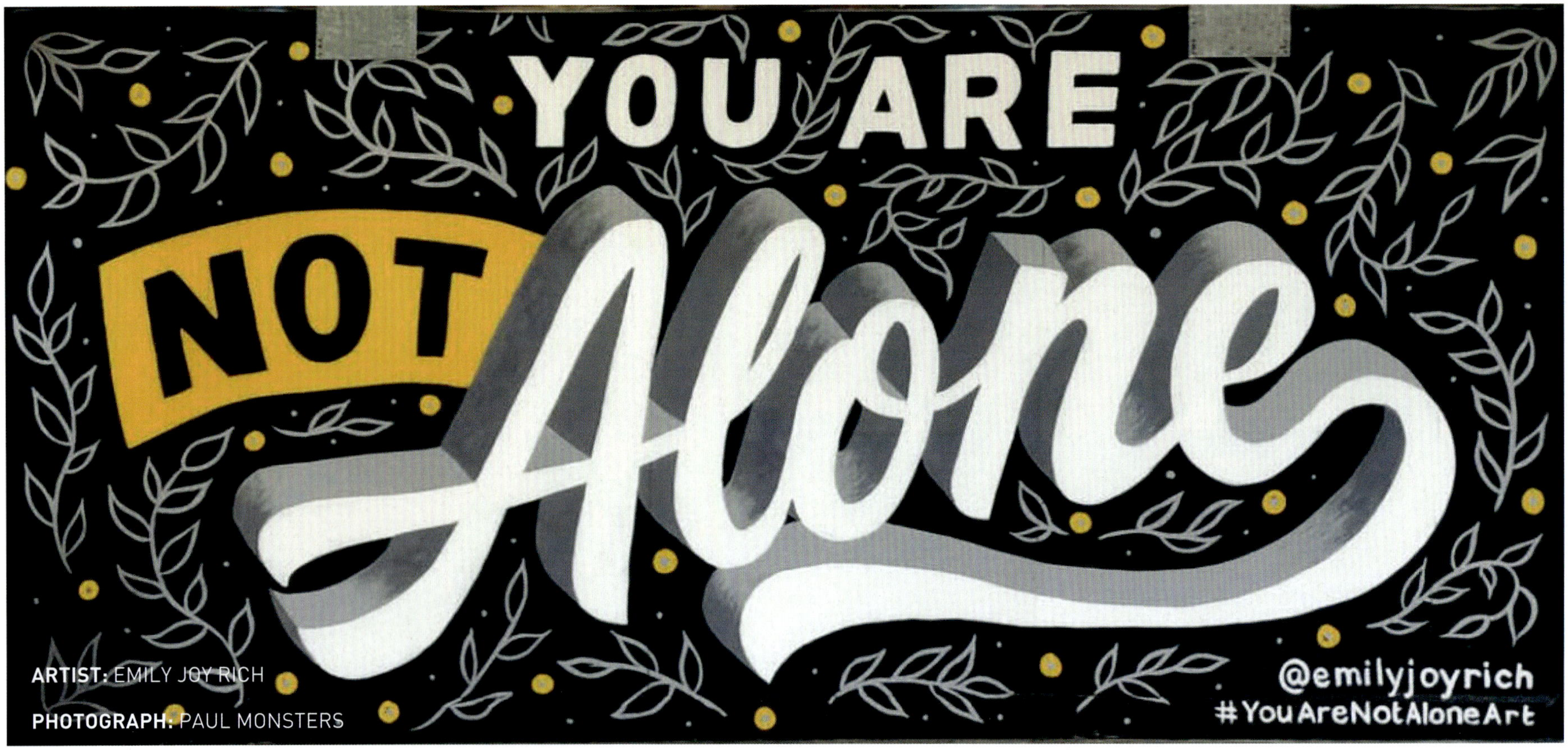

ARTIST: EMILY JOY RICH

PHOTOGRAPH: PAUL MONSTERS

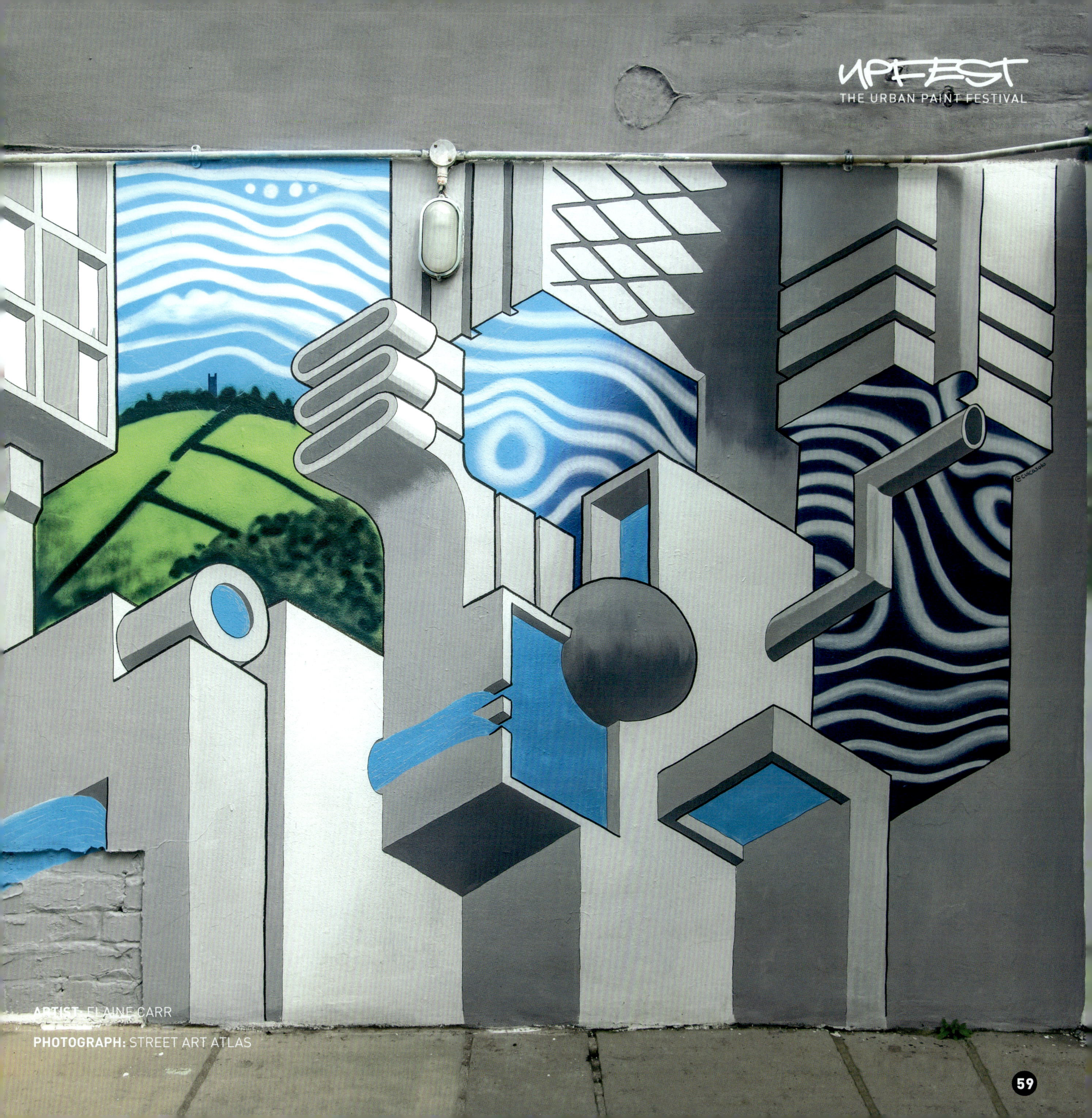

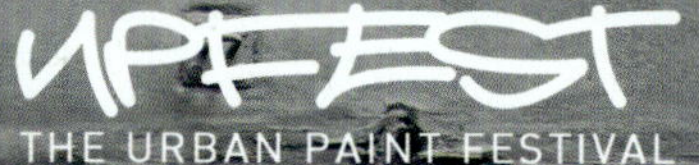

ARTIST: ELAINE CARR

PHOTOGRAPH: STREET ART ATLAS

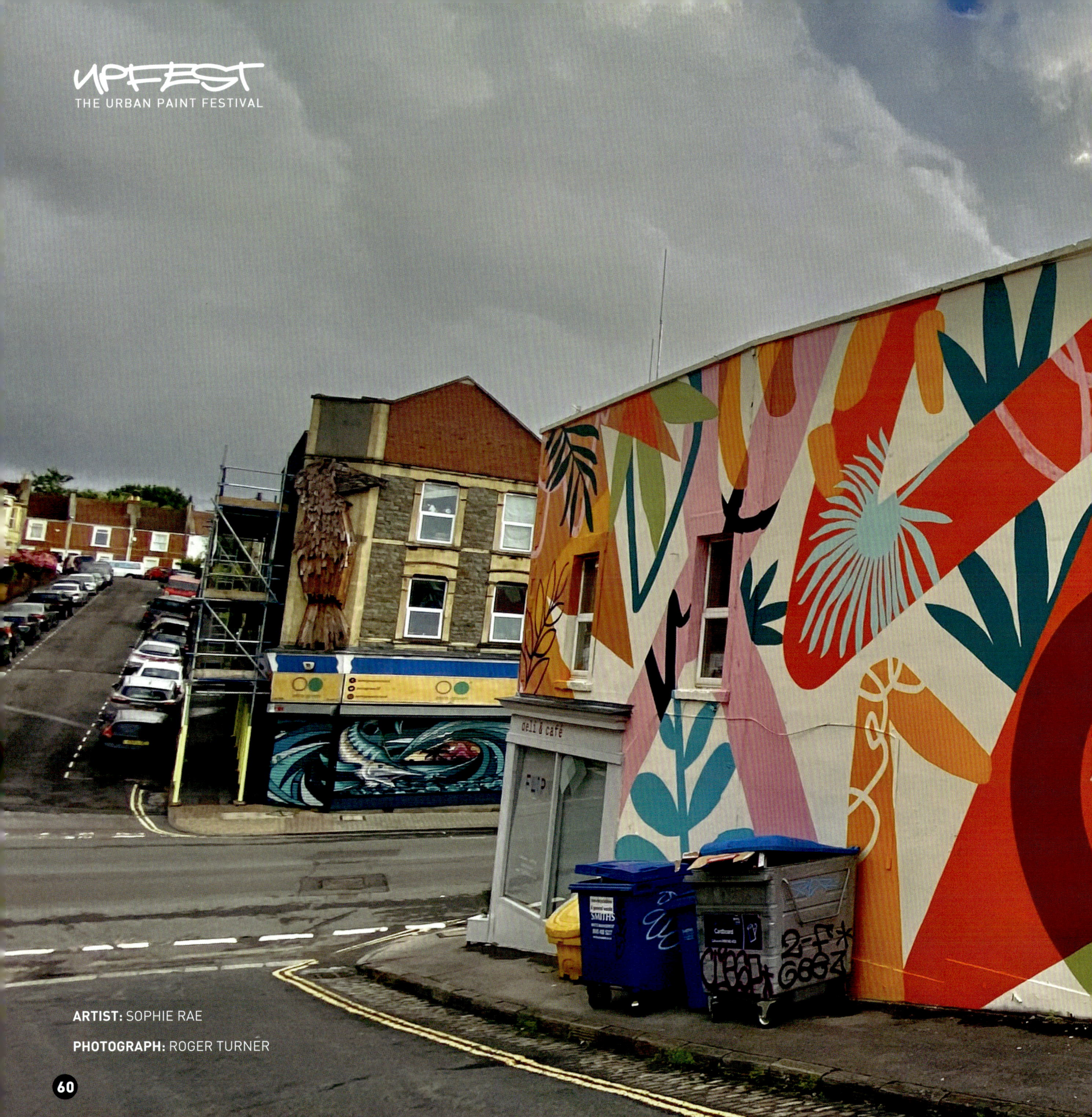

UPFEST
THE URBAN PAINT FESTIVAL

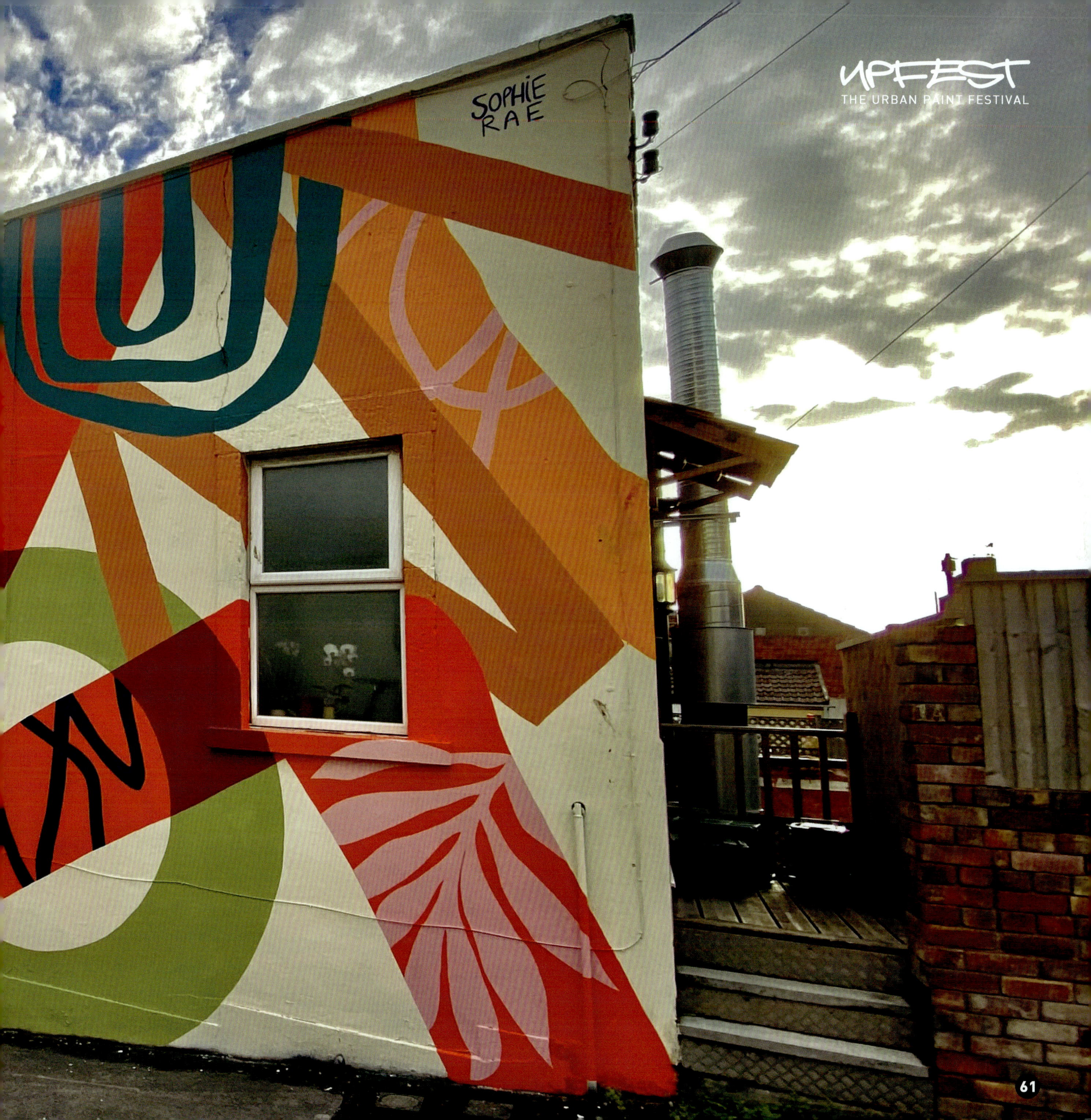
SOPHIE
RAE
UPFEST
THE URBAN PAINT FESTIVAL

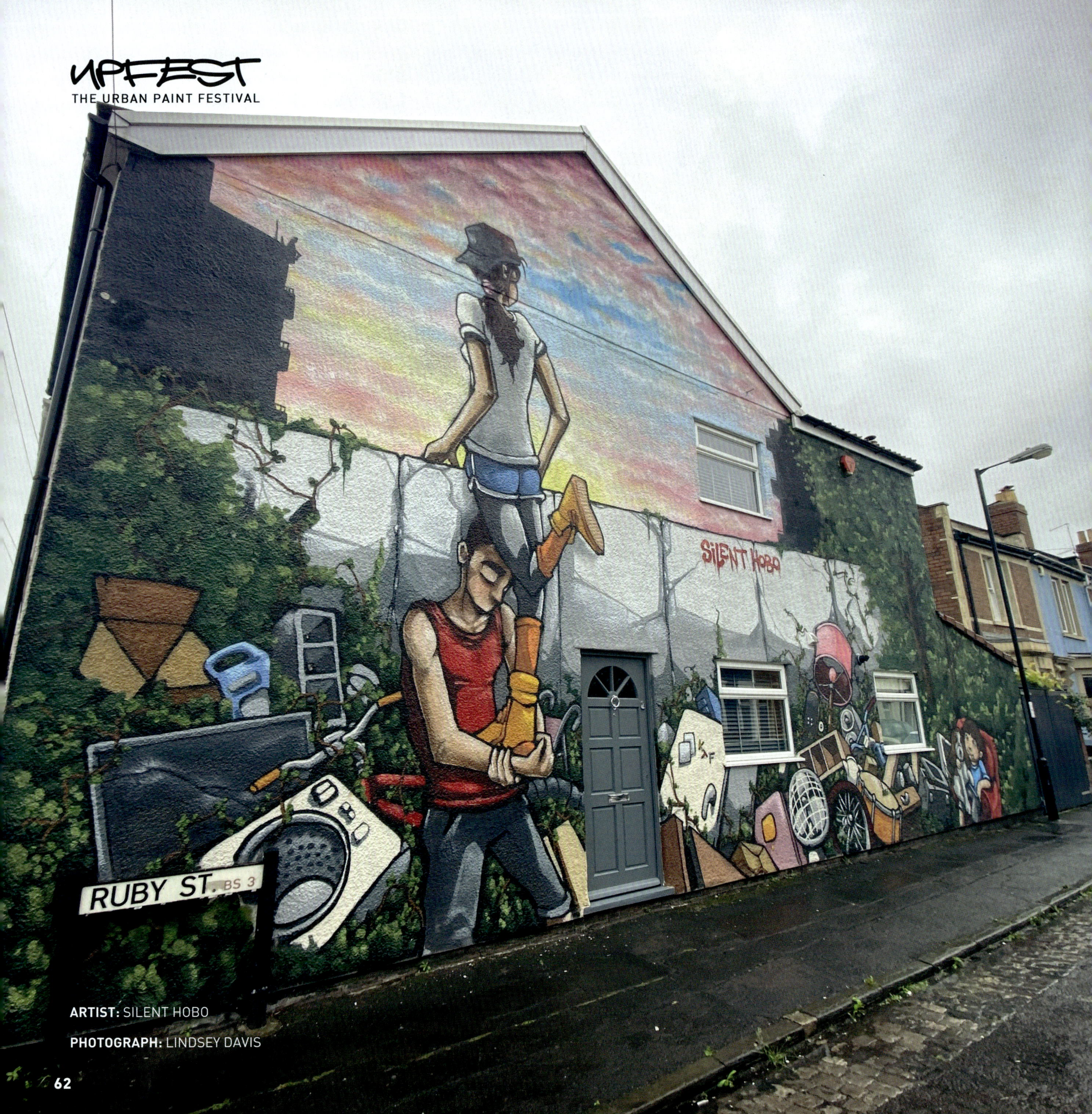

ARTIST: SILENT HOBO

PHOTOGRAPH: LINDSEY DAVIS

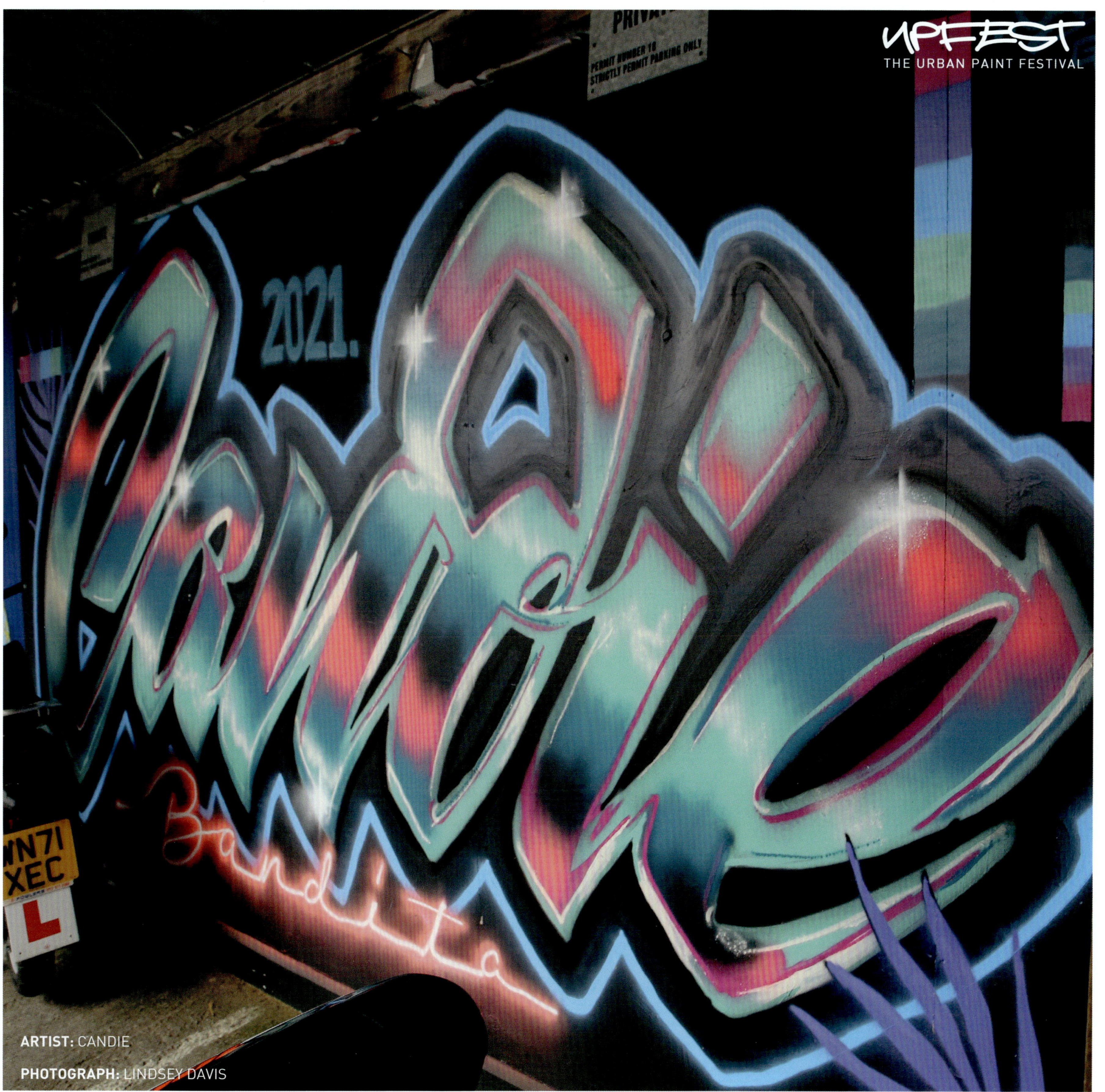

ARTIST: CANDIE

PHOTOGRAPH: LINDSEY DAVIS

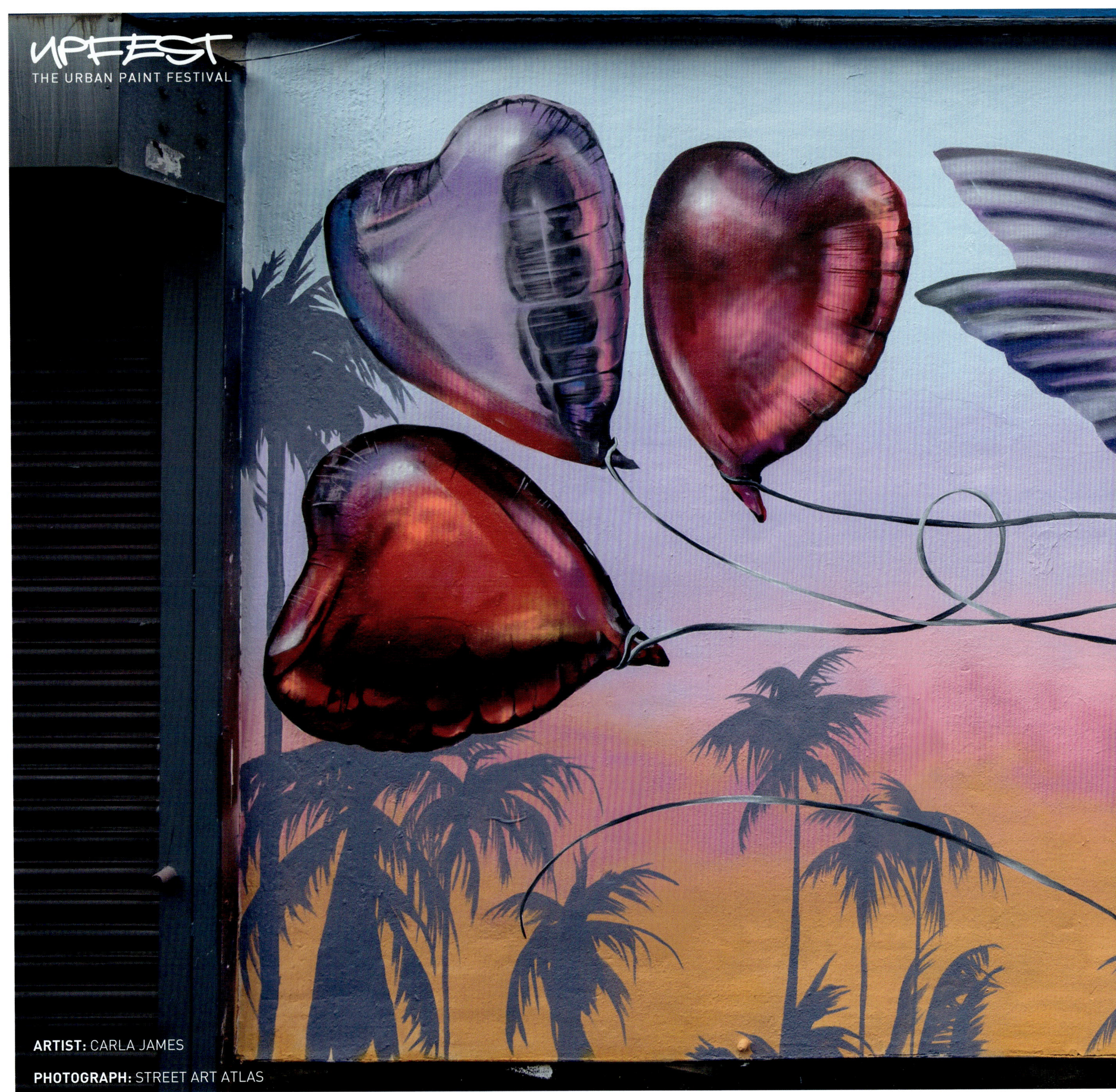
UPFEST
THE URBAN PAINT FESTIVAL

ARTIST: CARLA JAMES
PHOTOGRAPH: STREET ART ATLAS

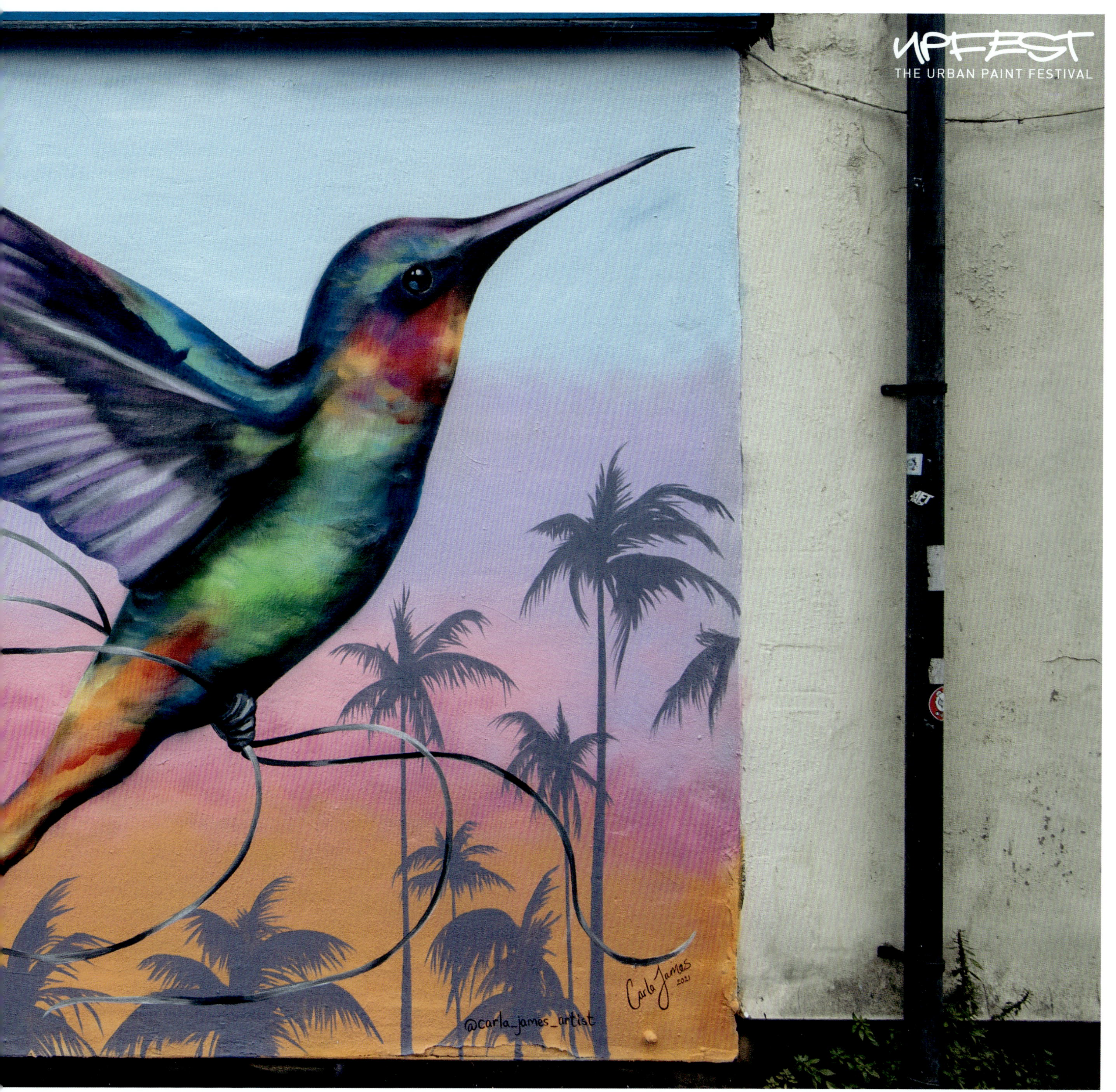

UPFEST
THE URBAN PAINT FESTIVAL
Carla James 2021
@carla_james_artist

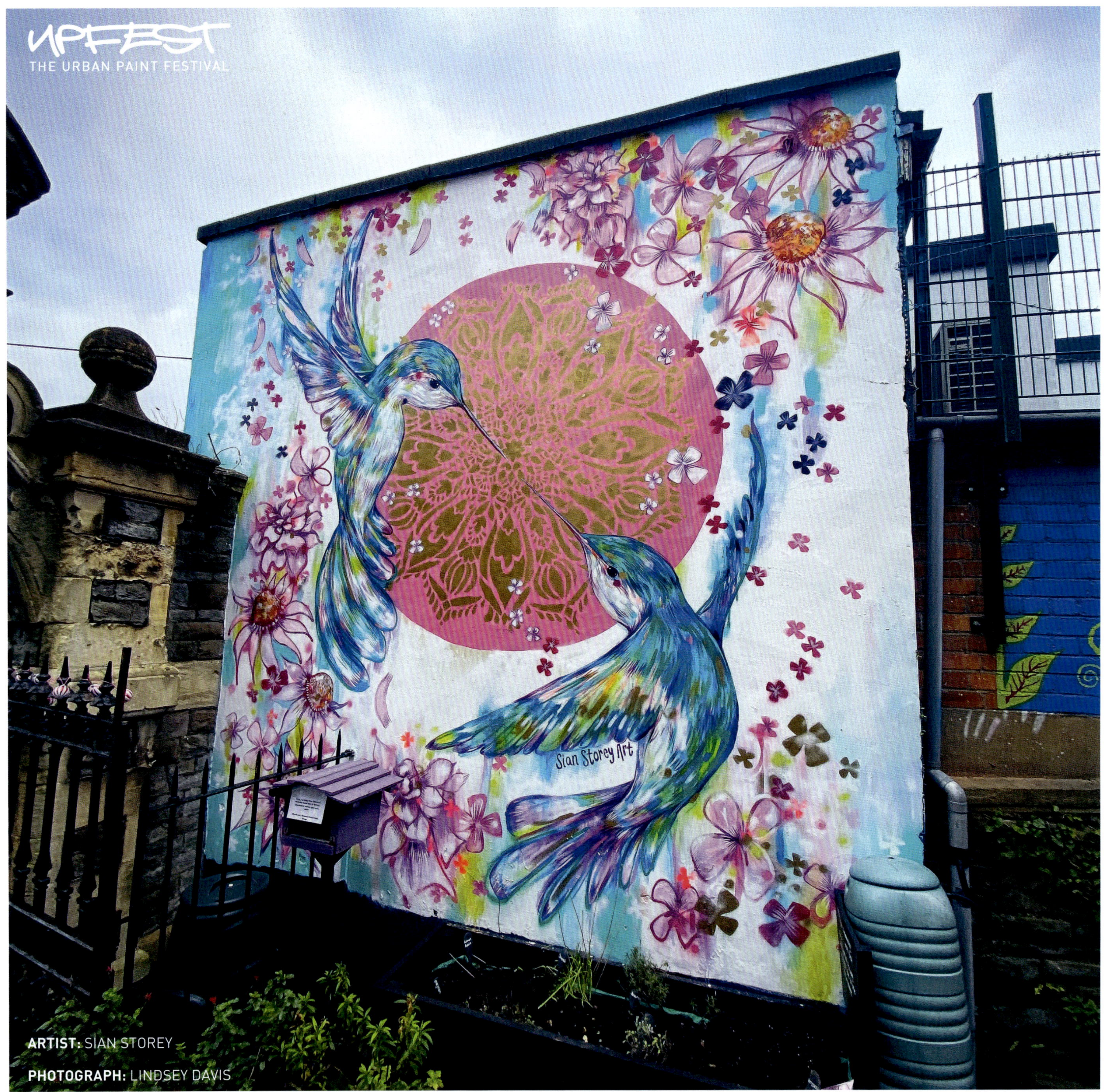
UPFEST
THE URBAN PAINT FESTIVAL
Sian Storey Art

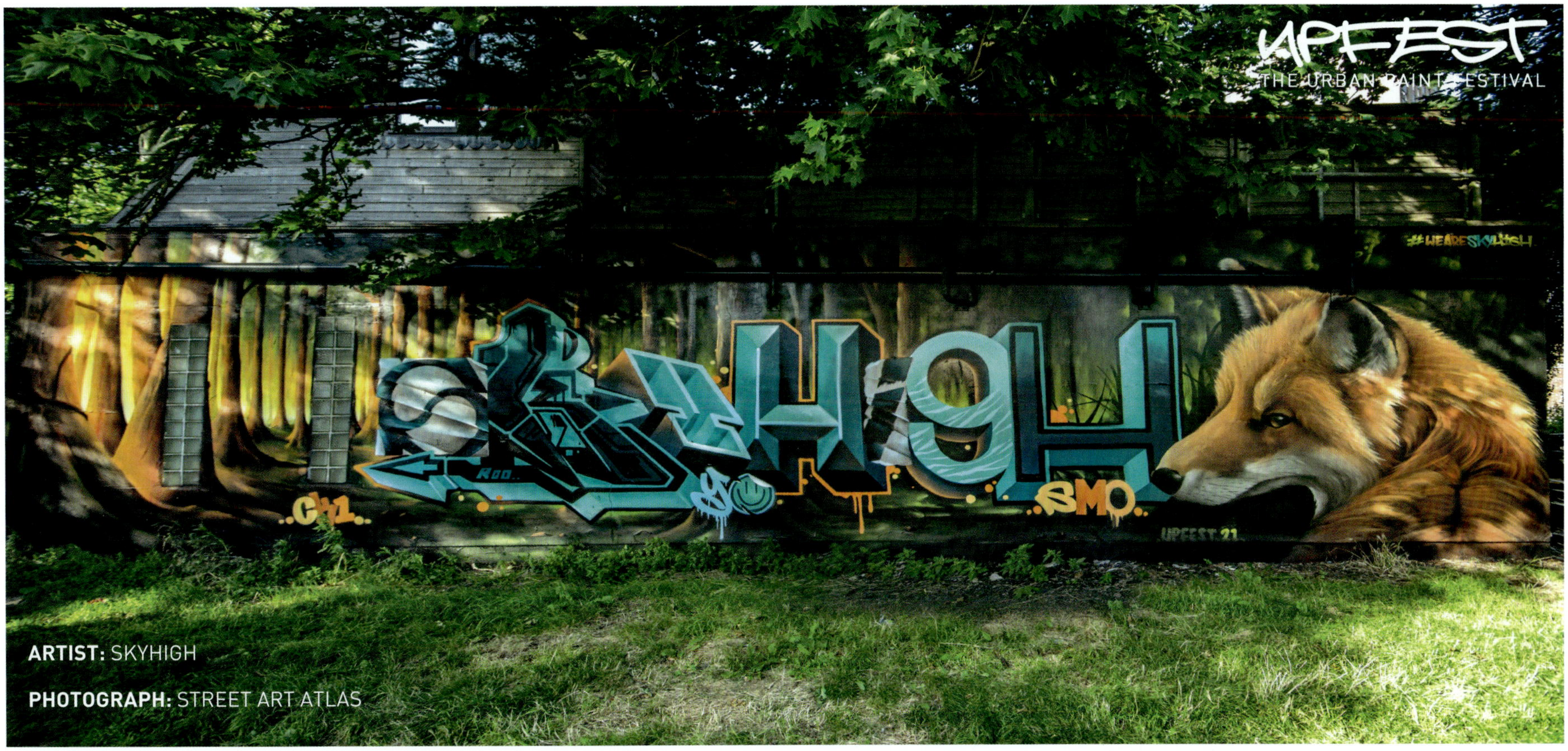

ARTIST: SKYHIGH

PHOTOGRAPH: STREET ART ATLAS

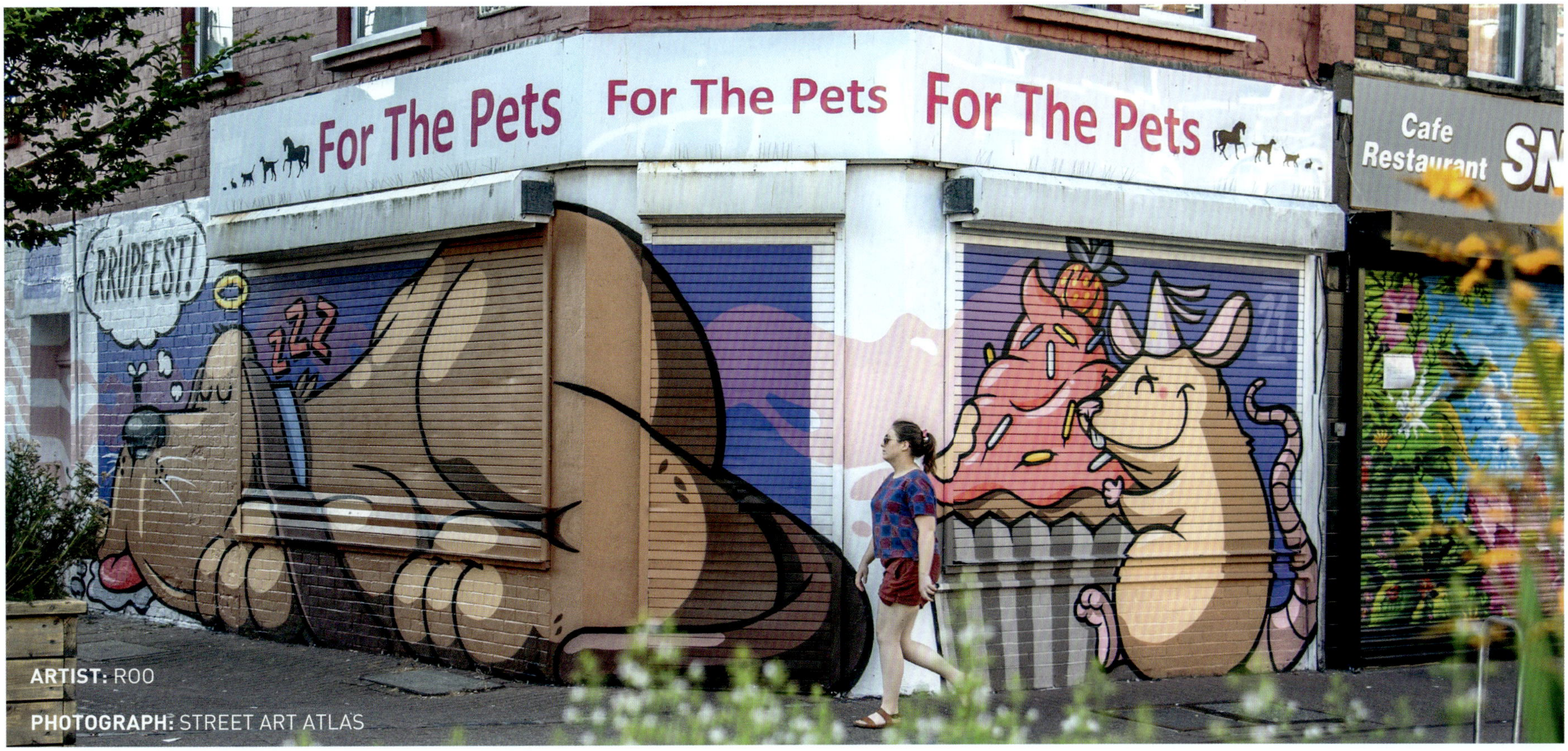

ARTIST: ROO

PHOTOGRAPH: STREET ART ATLAS

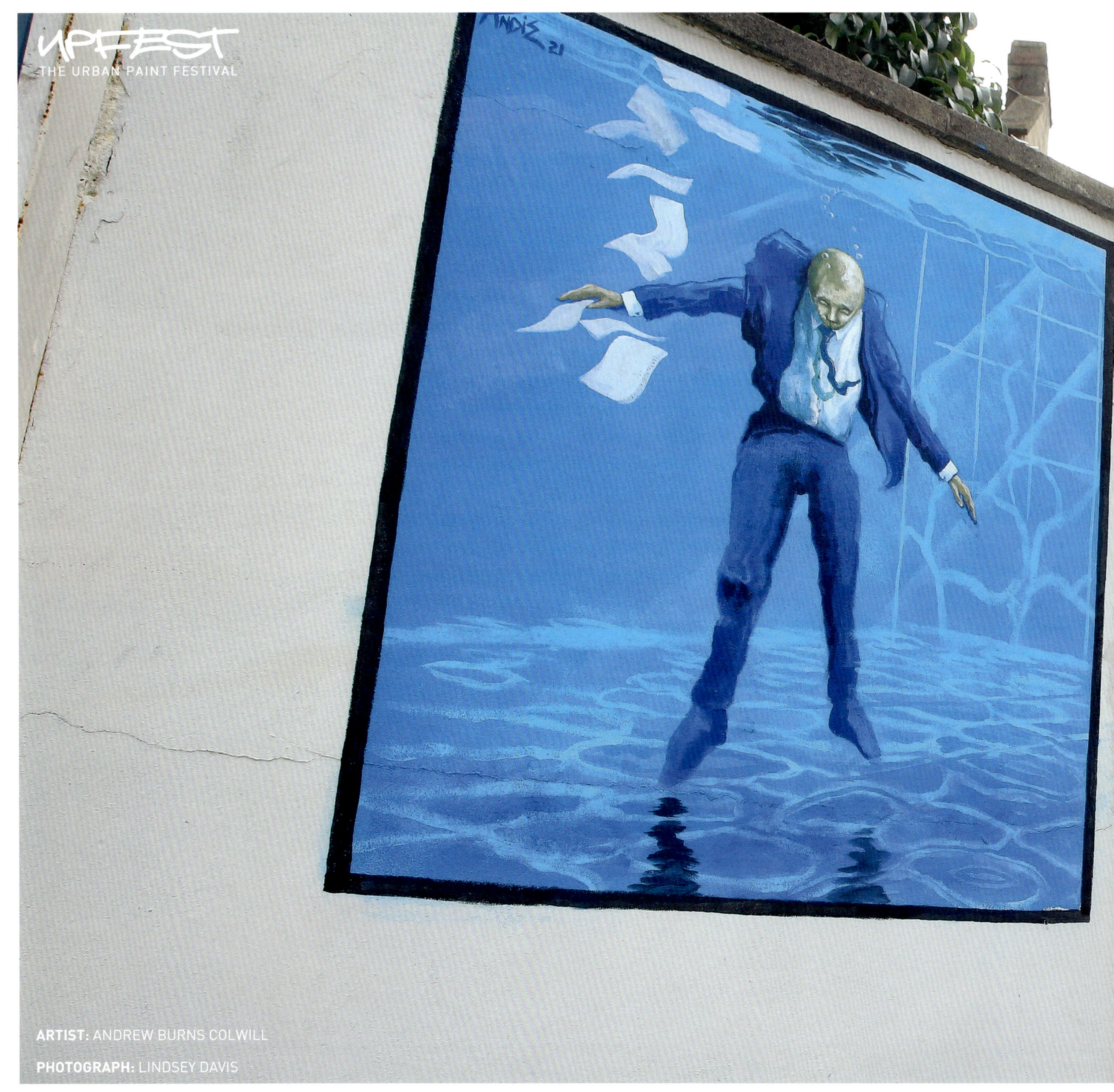

ARTIST: ANDREW BURNS COLWILL

PHOTOGRAPH: LINDSEY DAVIS

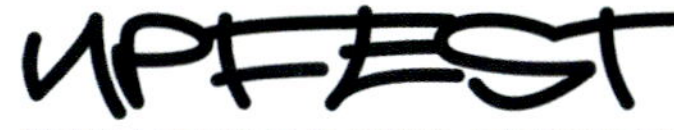
UPFEST
THE URBAN PAINT FESTIVAL

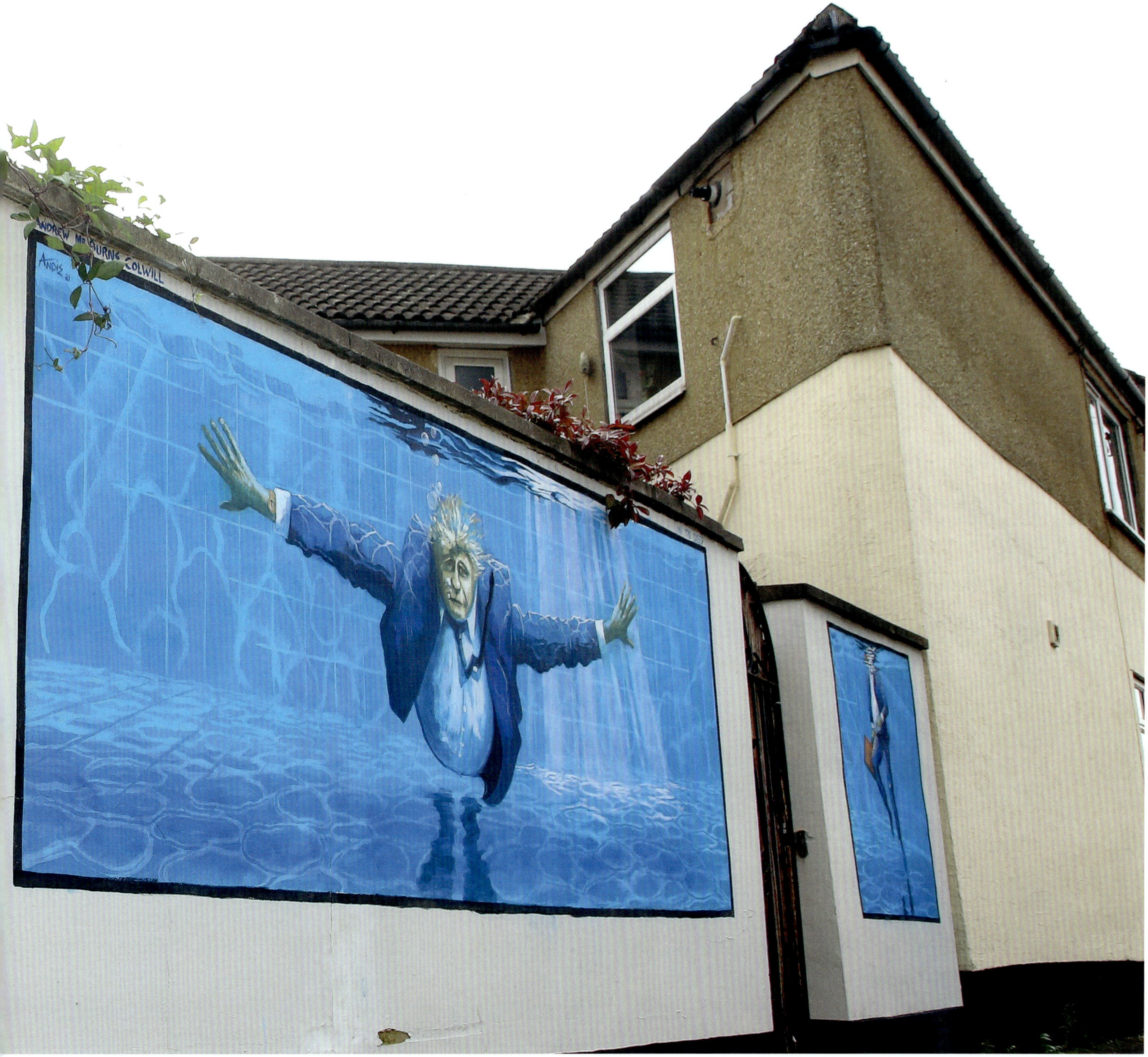

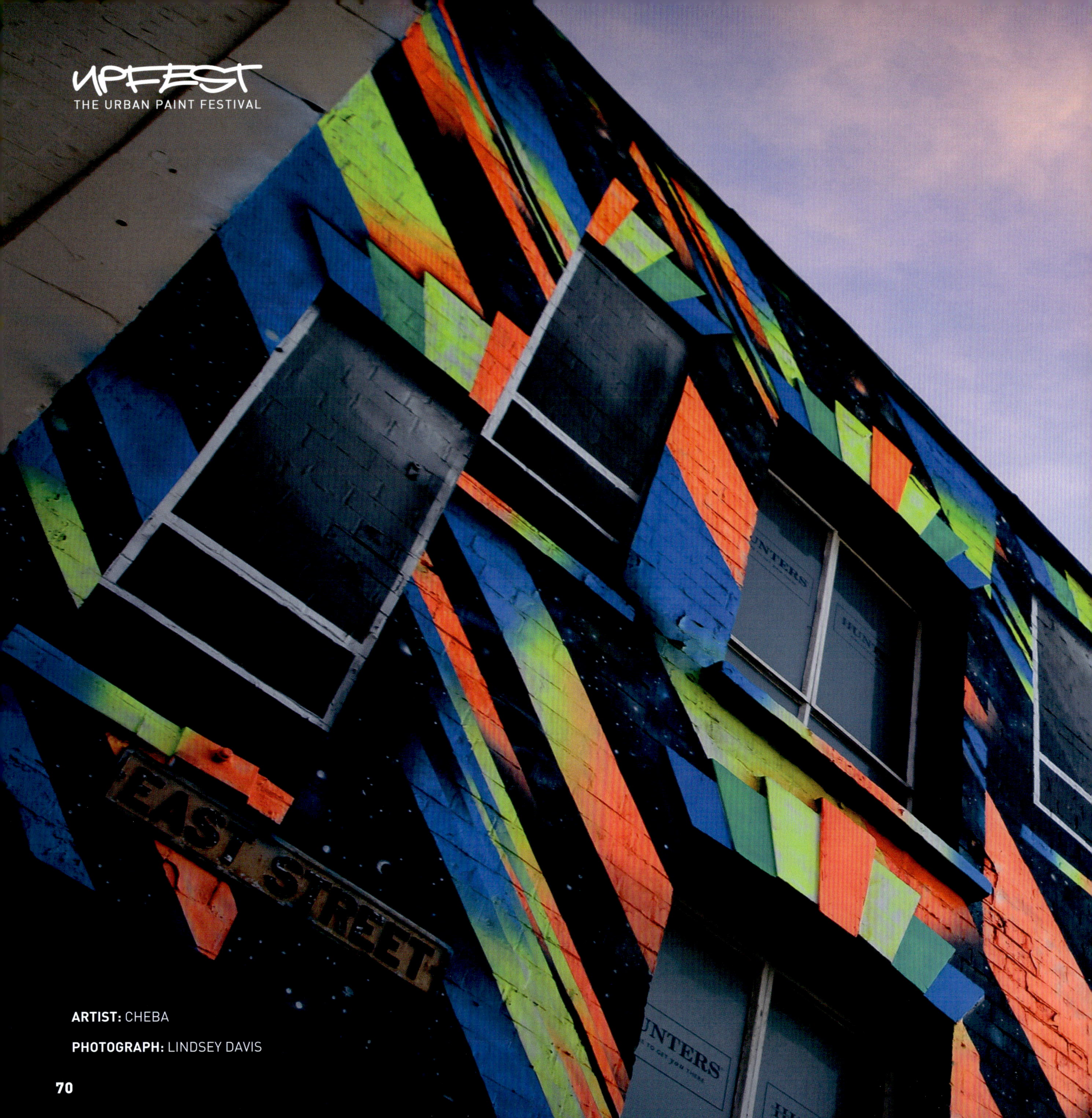

ARTIST: CHEBA

PHOTOGRAPH: LINDSEY DAVIS

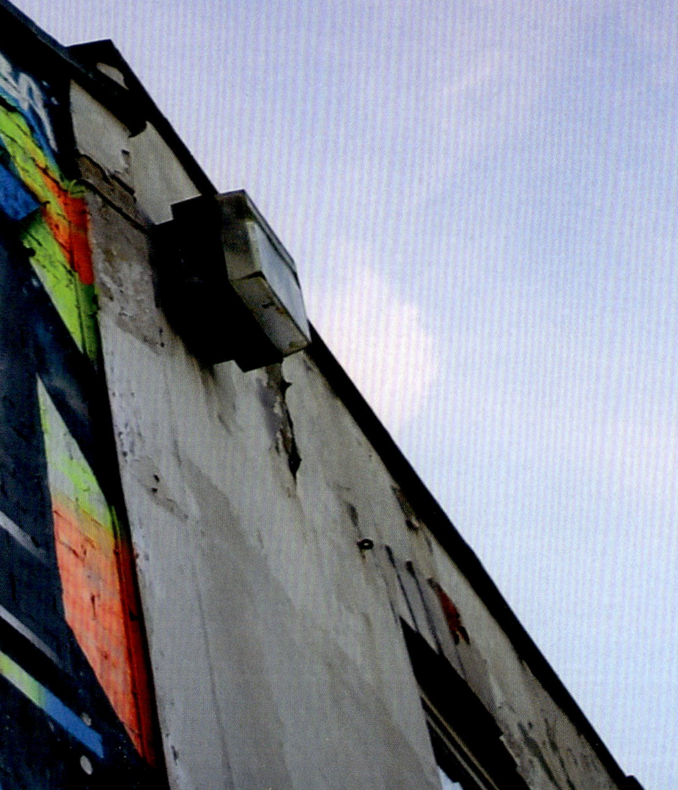

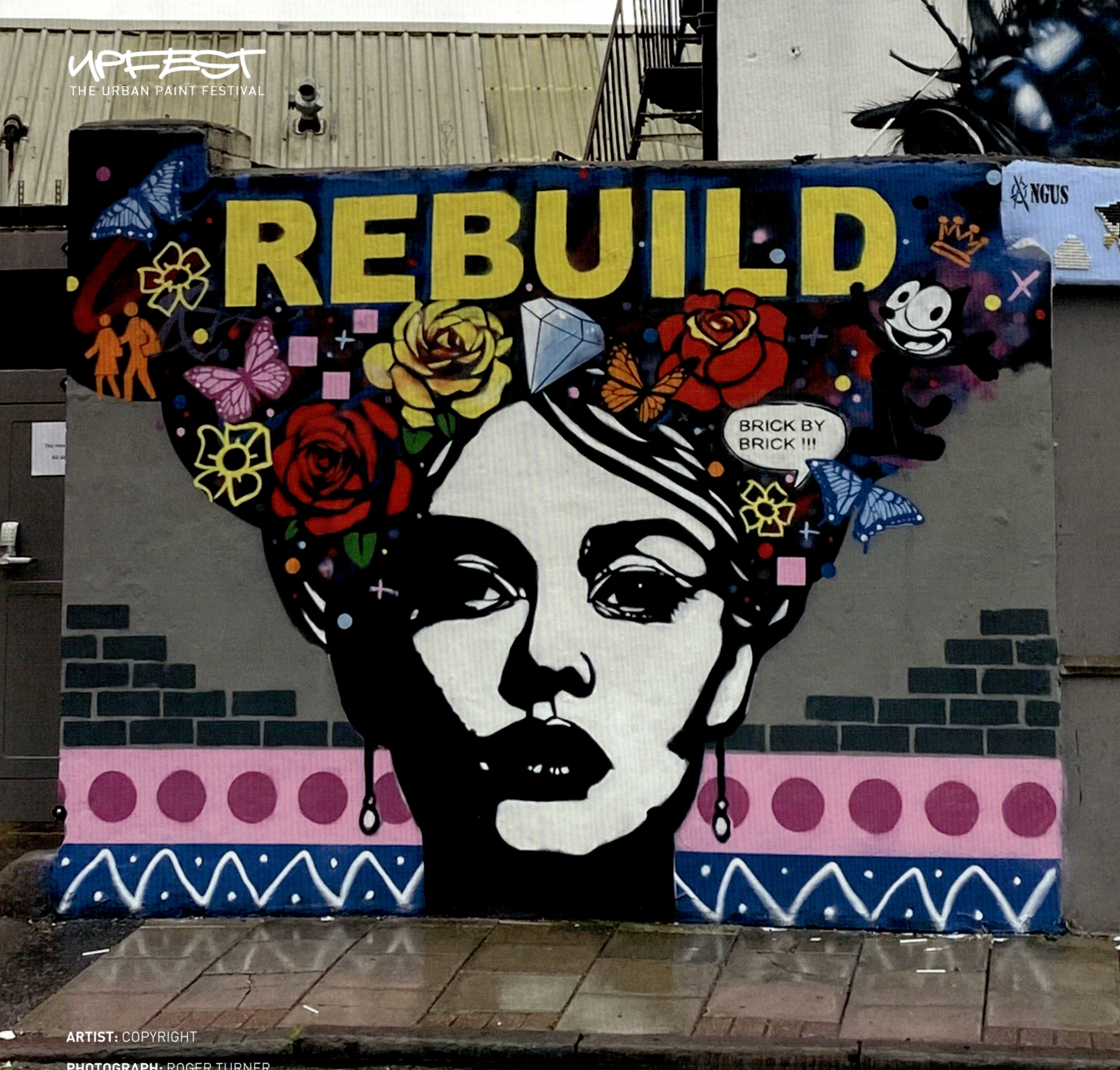

ARTIST: COPYRIGHT

PHOTOGRAPH: ROGER TURNER

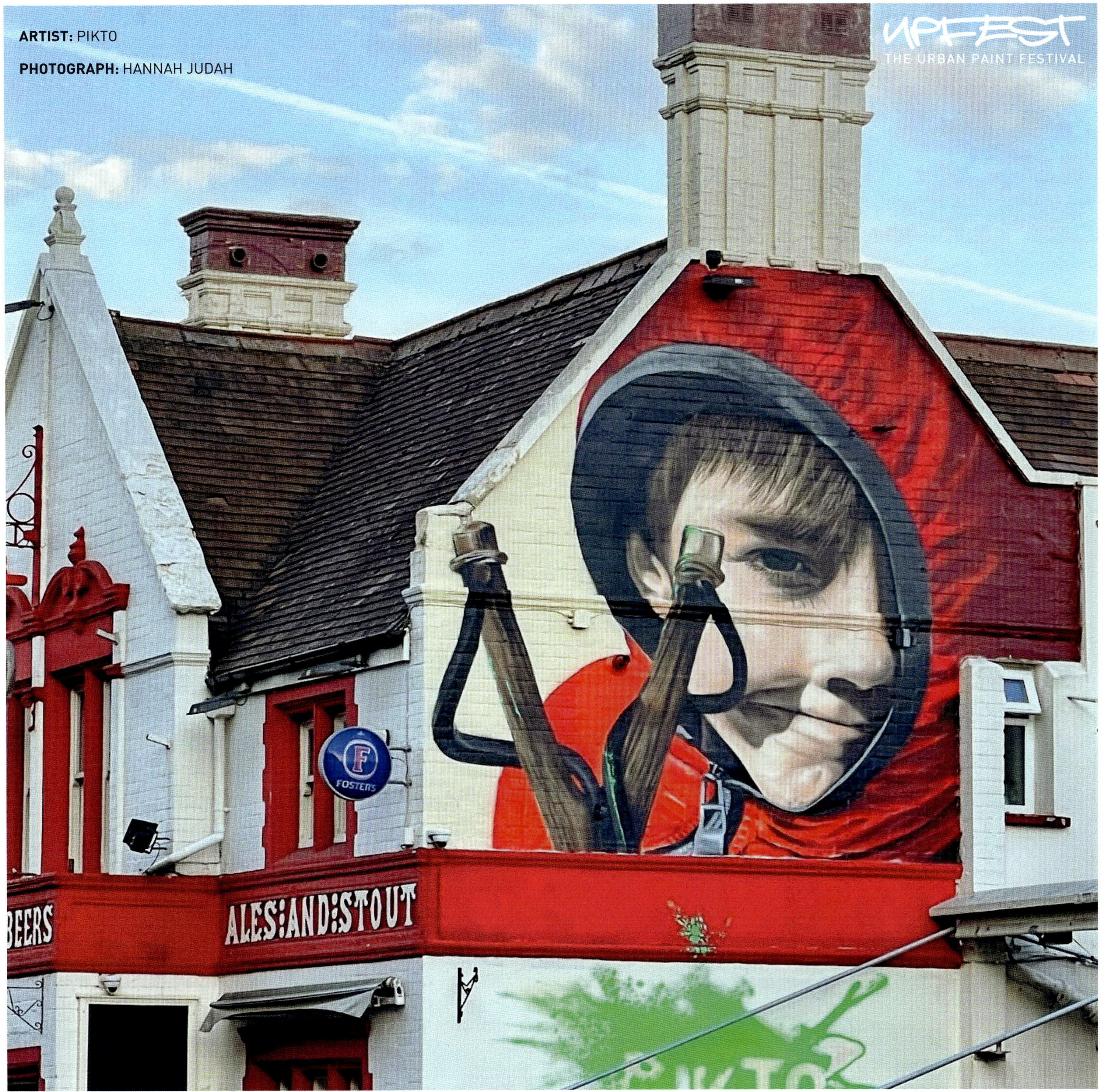

ARTIST: PIKTO

PHOTOGRAPH: HANNAH JUDAH

UPFEST
THE URBAN PAINT FESTIVAL

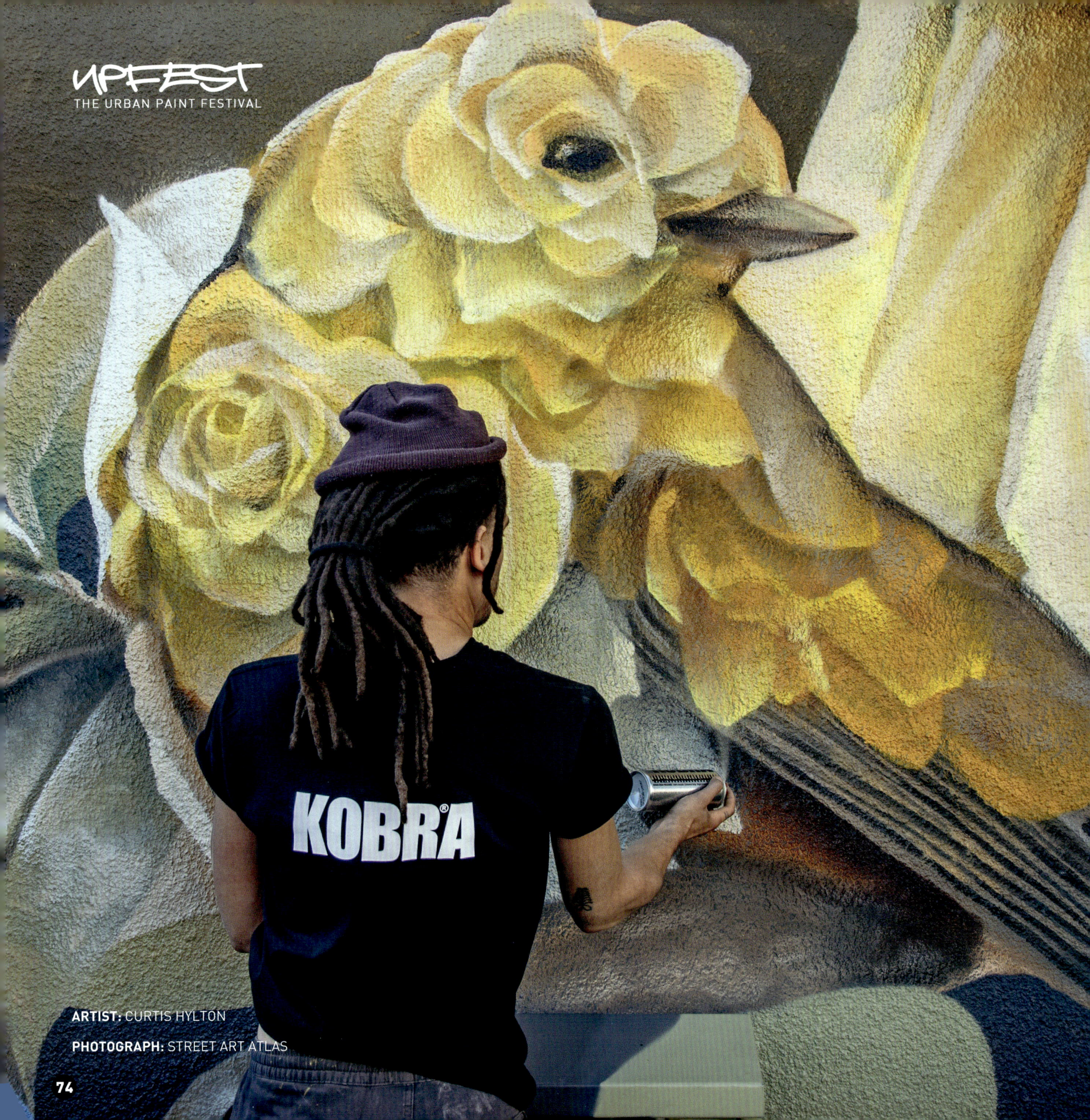

ARTIST: CURTIS HYLTON

PHOTOGRAPH: STREET ART ATLAS

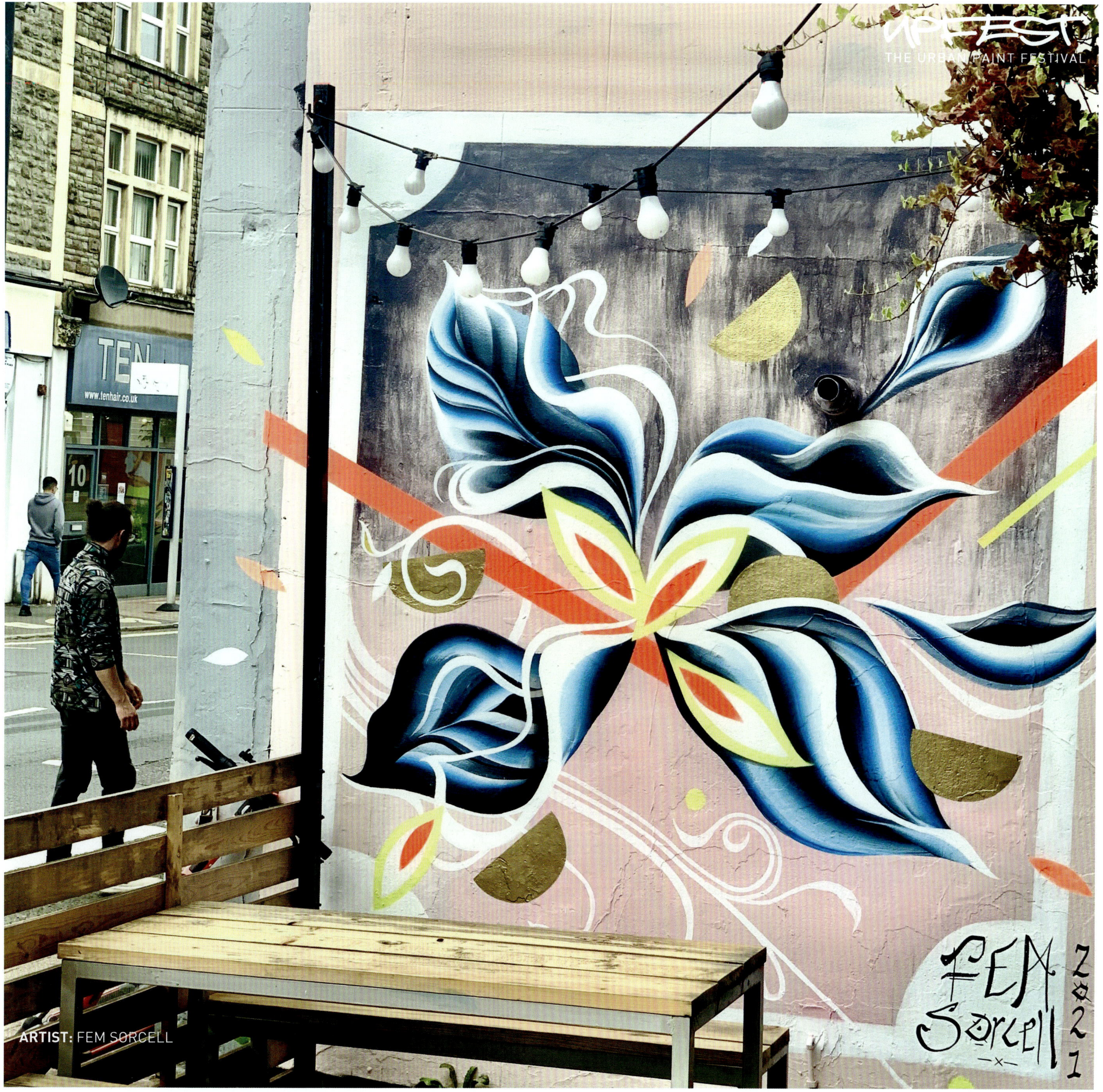
UPFEST
THE URBAN PAINT FESTIVAL
TEN
www.tenhair.co.uk
10
FEM
Sorcell
2021

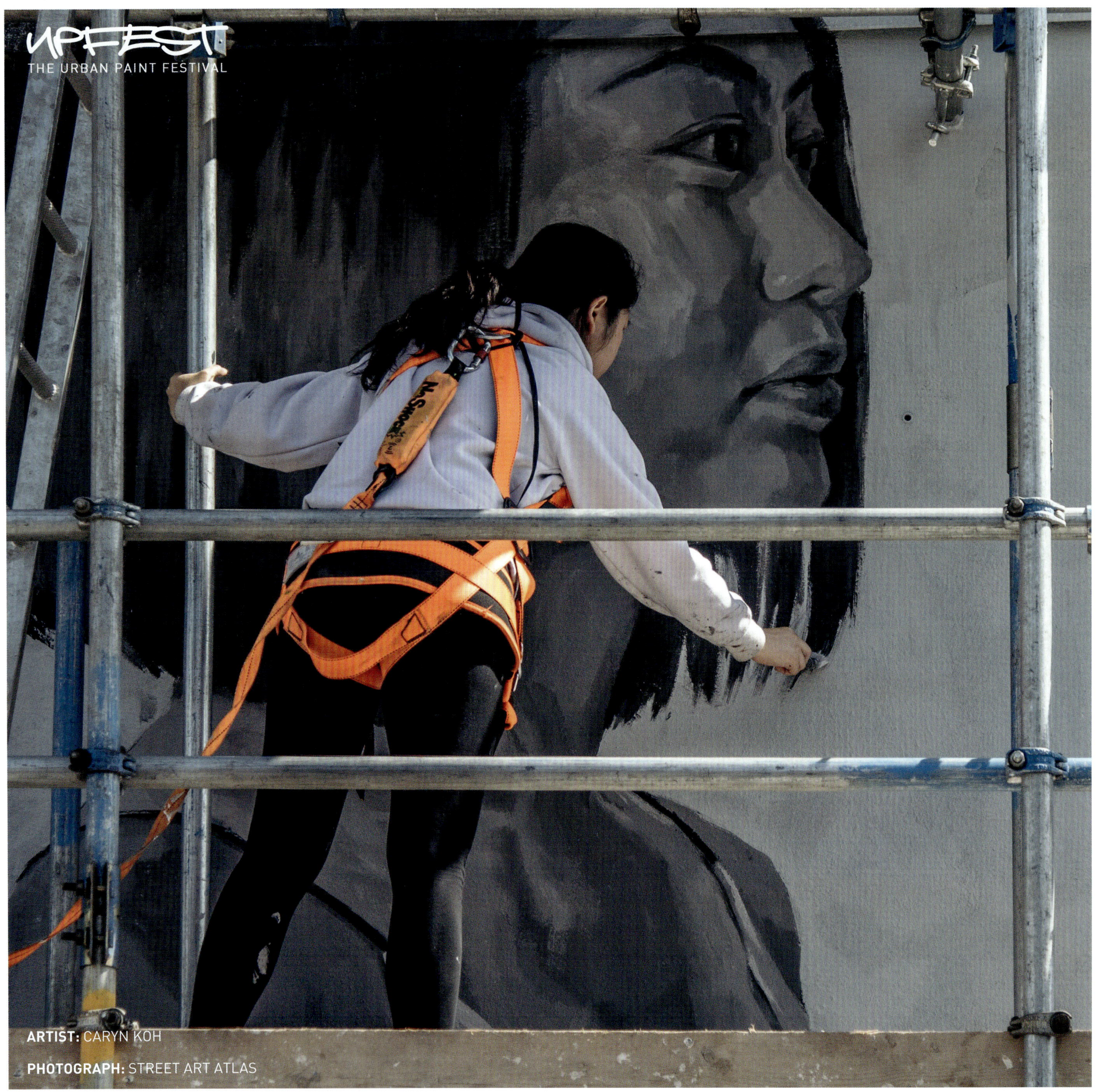

ARTIST: CARYN KOH

PHOTOGRAPH: STREET ART ATLAS

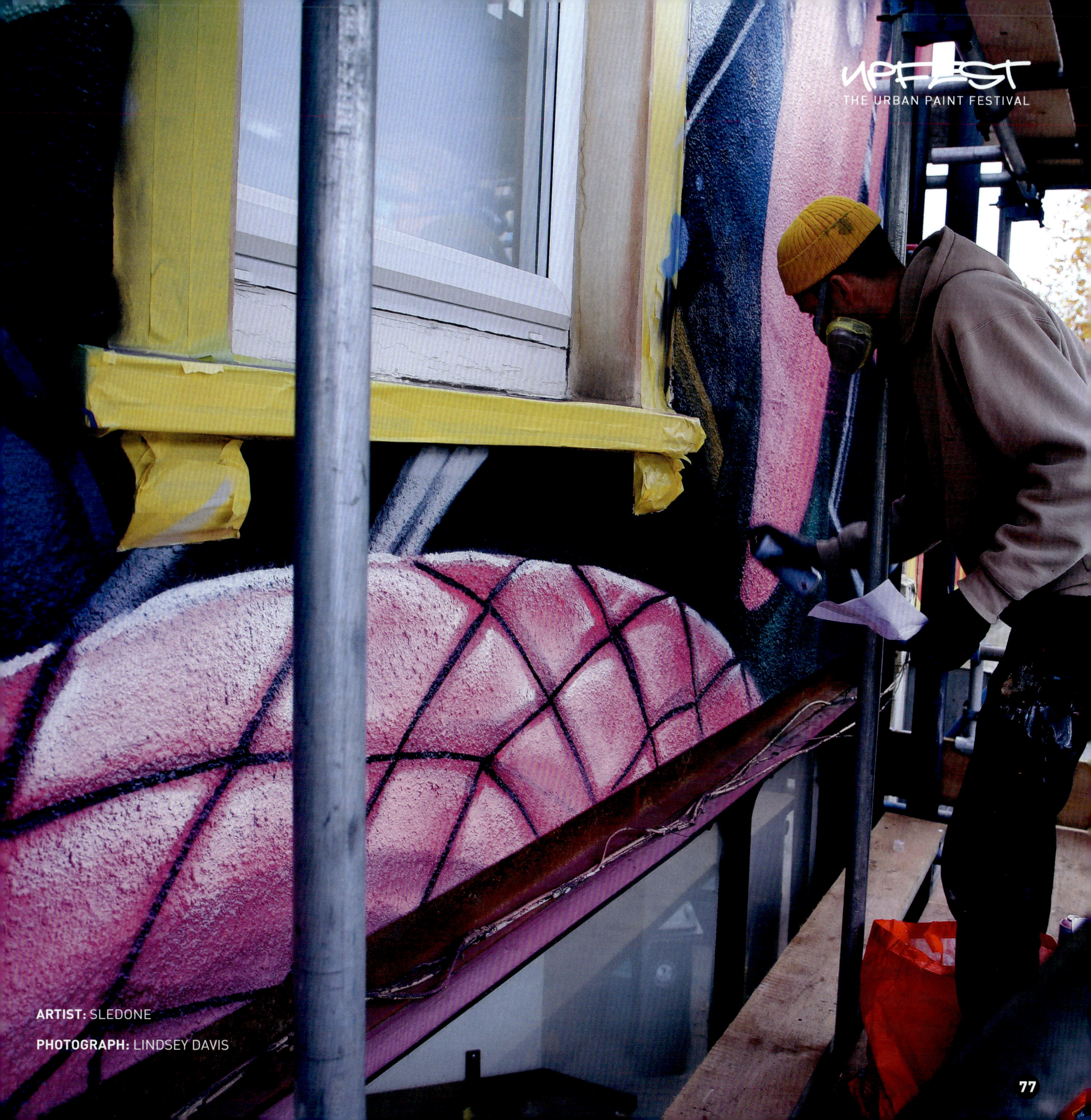

ARTIST: SLEDONE

PHOTOGRAPH: LINDSEY DAVIS

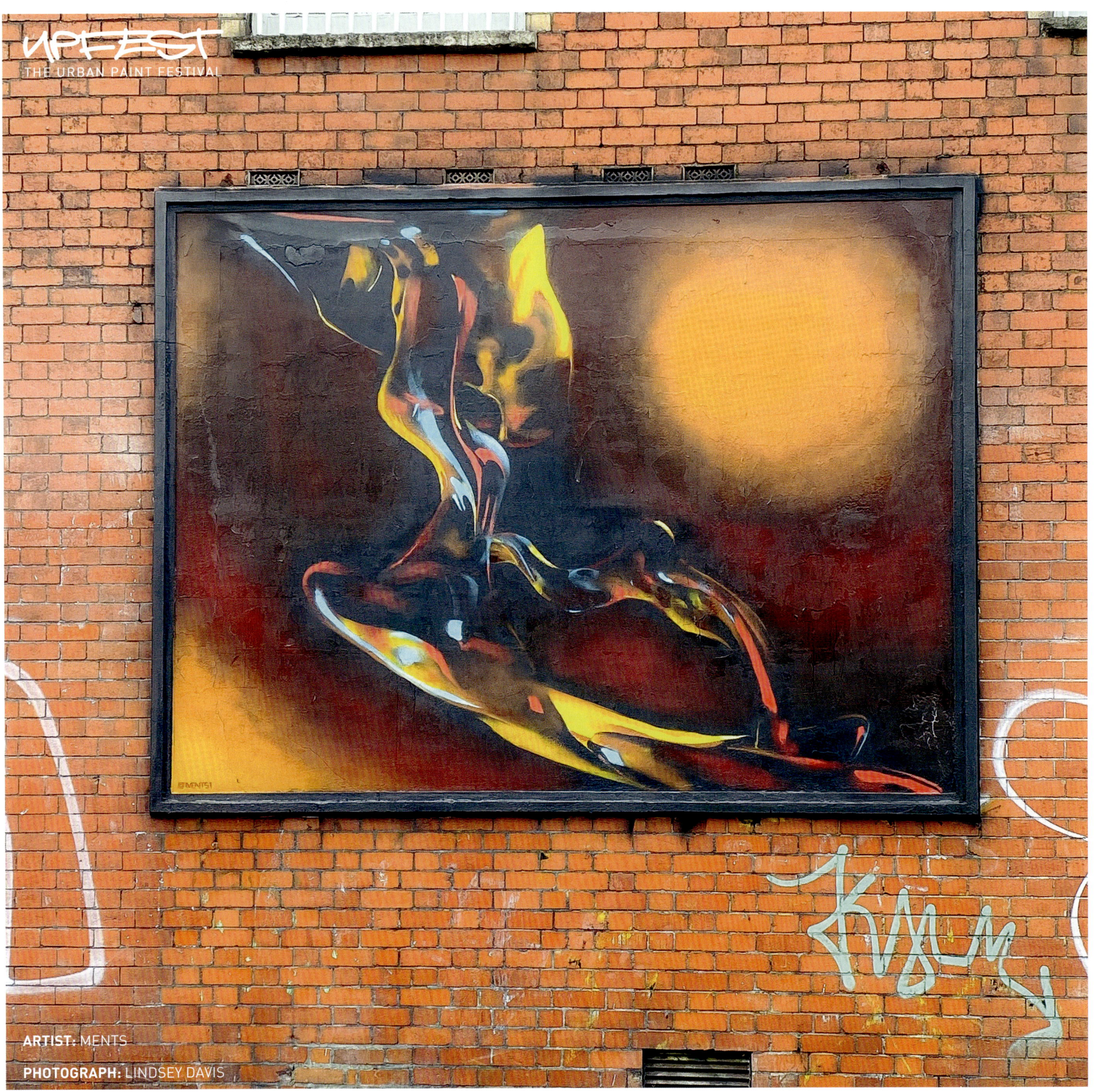

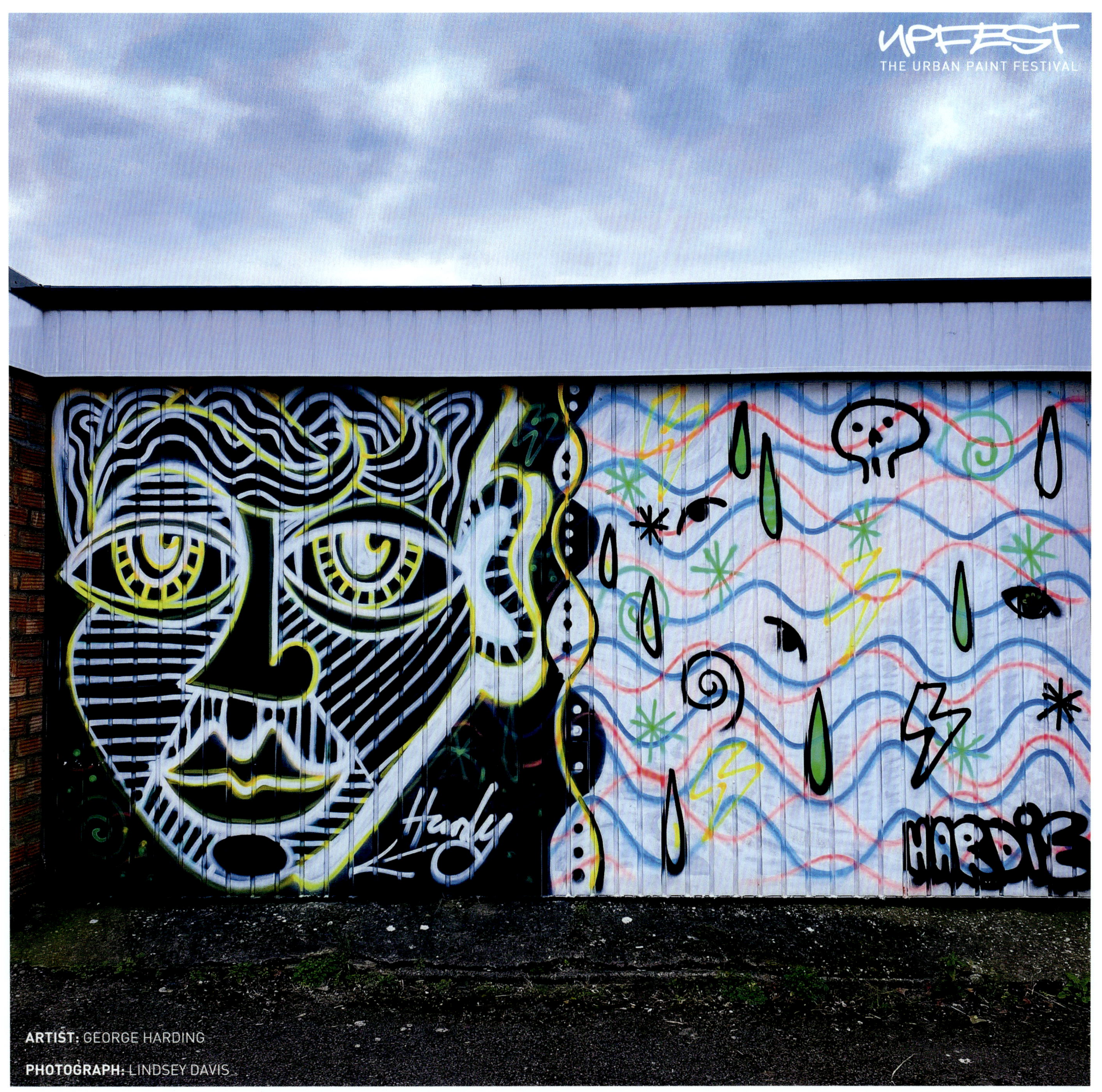

UPFEST
THE URBAN PAINT FESTIVAL

ARTIST: GEORGE HARDING

PHOTOGRAPH: LINDSEY DAVIS

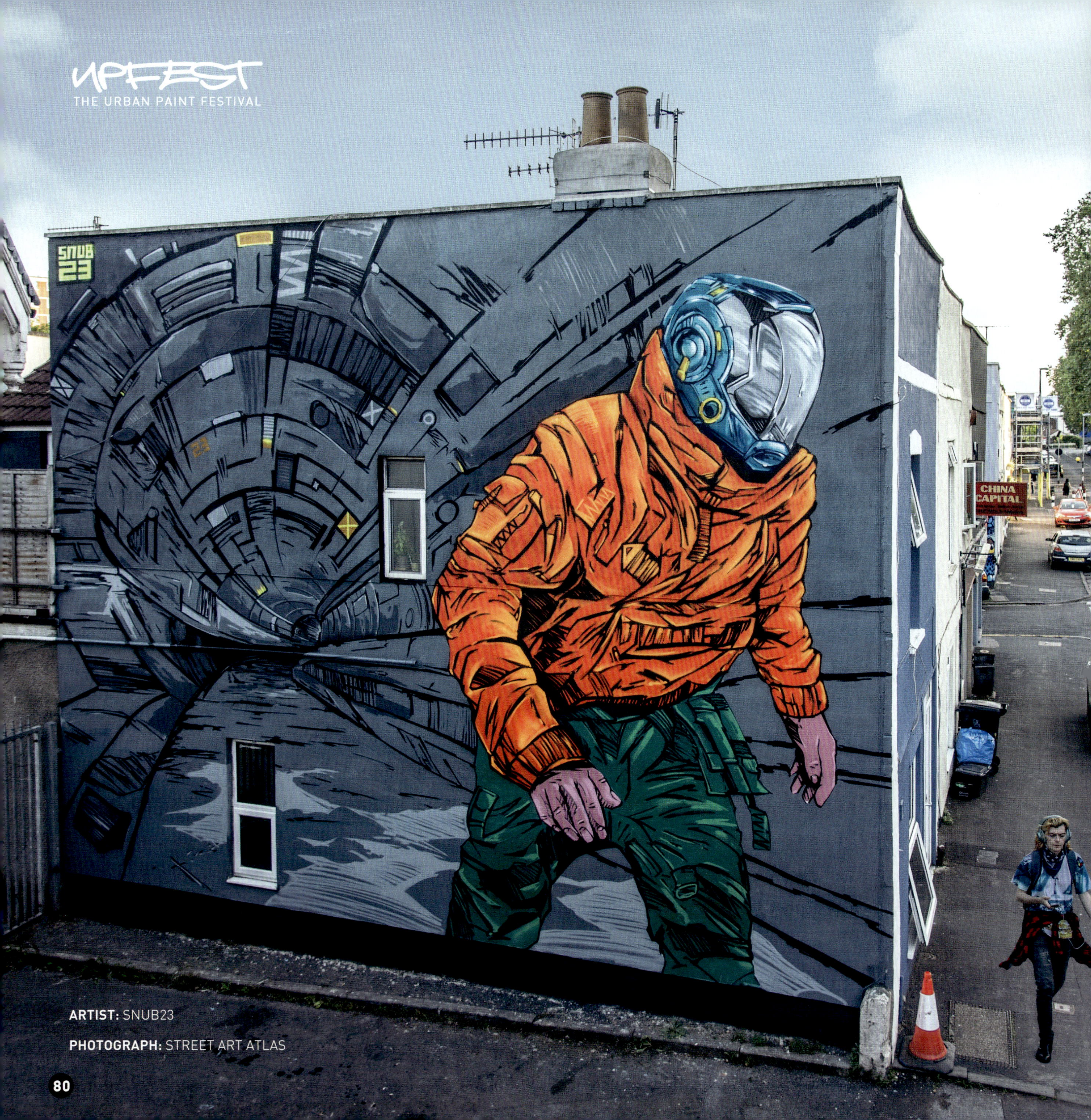

ARTIST: SNUB23

PHOTOGRAPH: STREET ART ATLAS

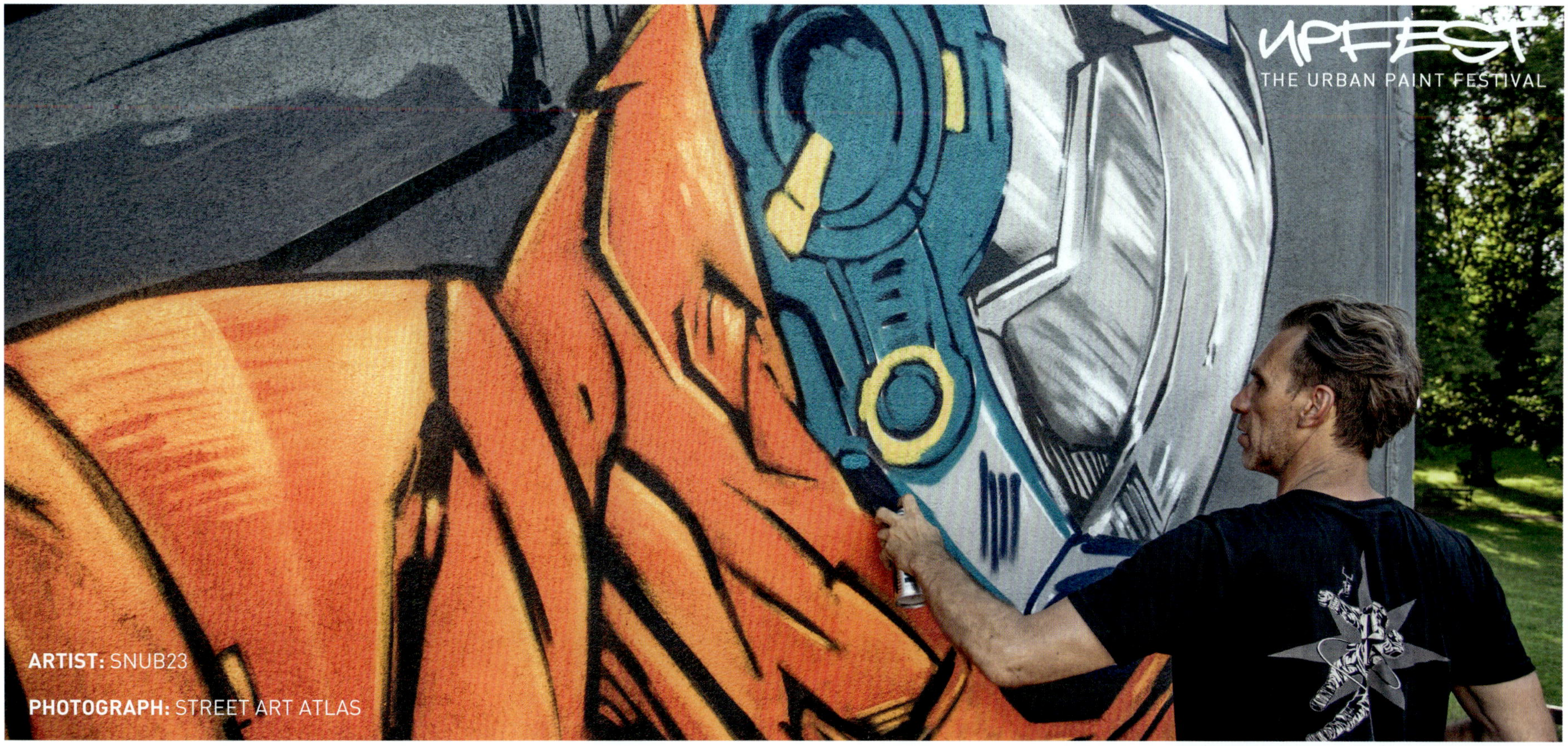

ARTIST: SNUB23

PHOTOGRAPH: STREET ART ATLAS

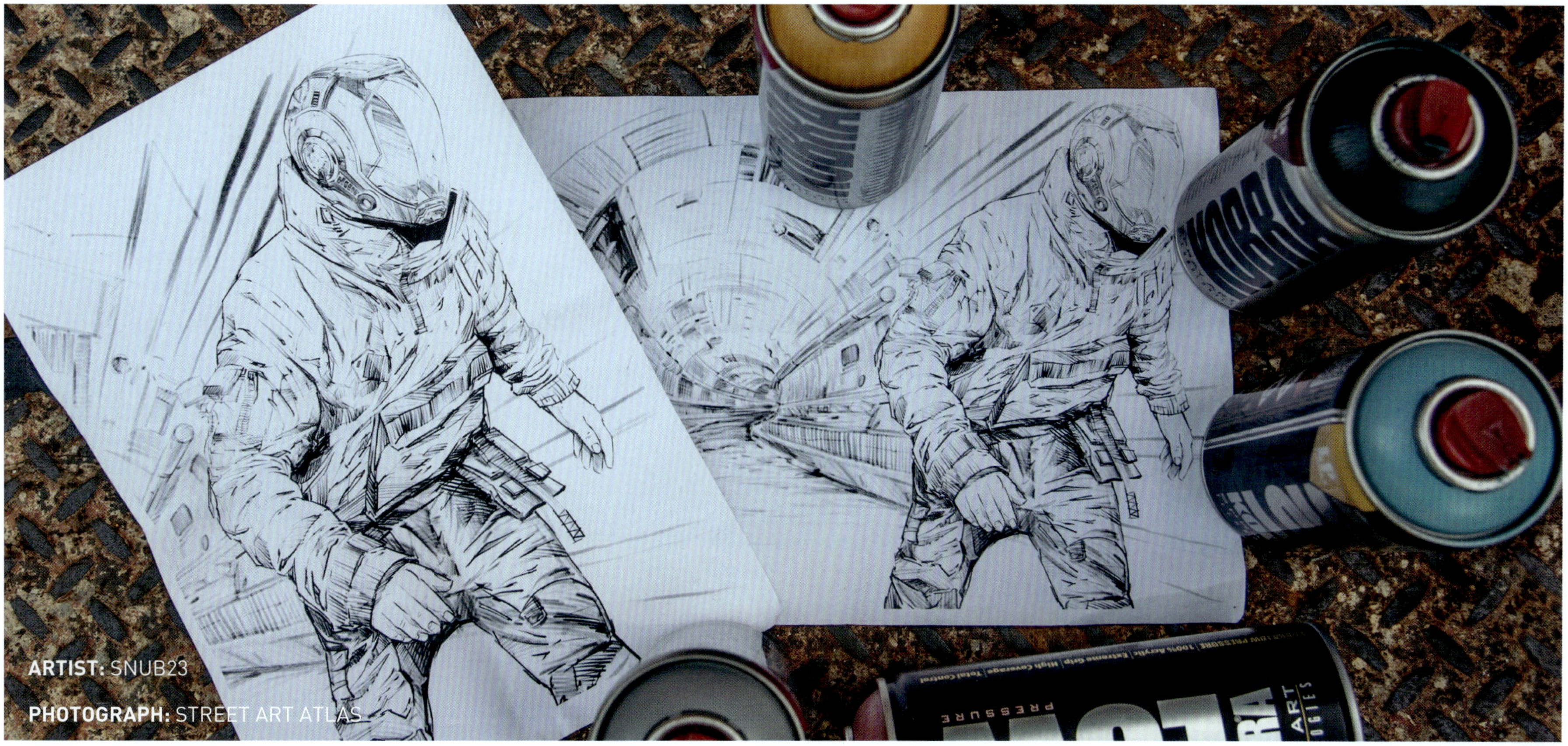

ARTIST: SNUB23

PHOTOGRAPH: STREET ART ATLAS

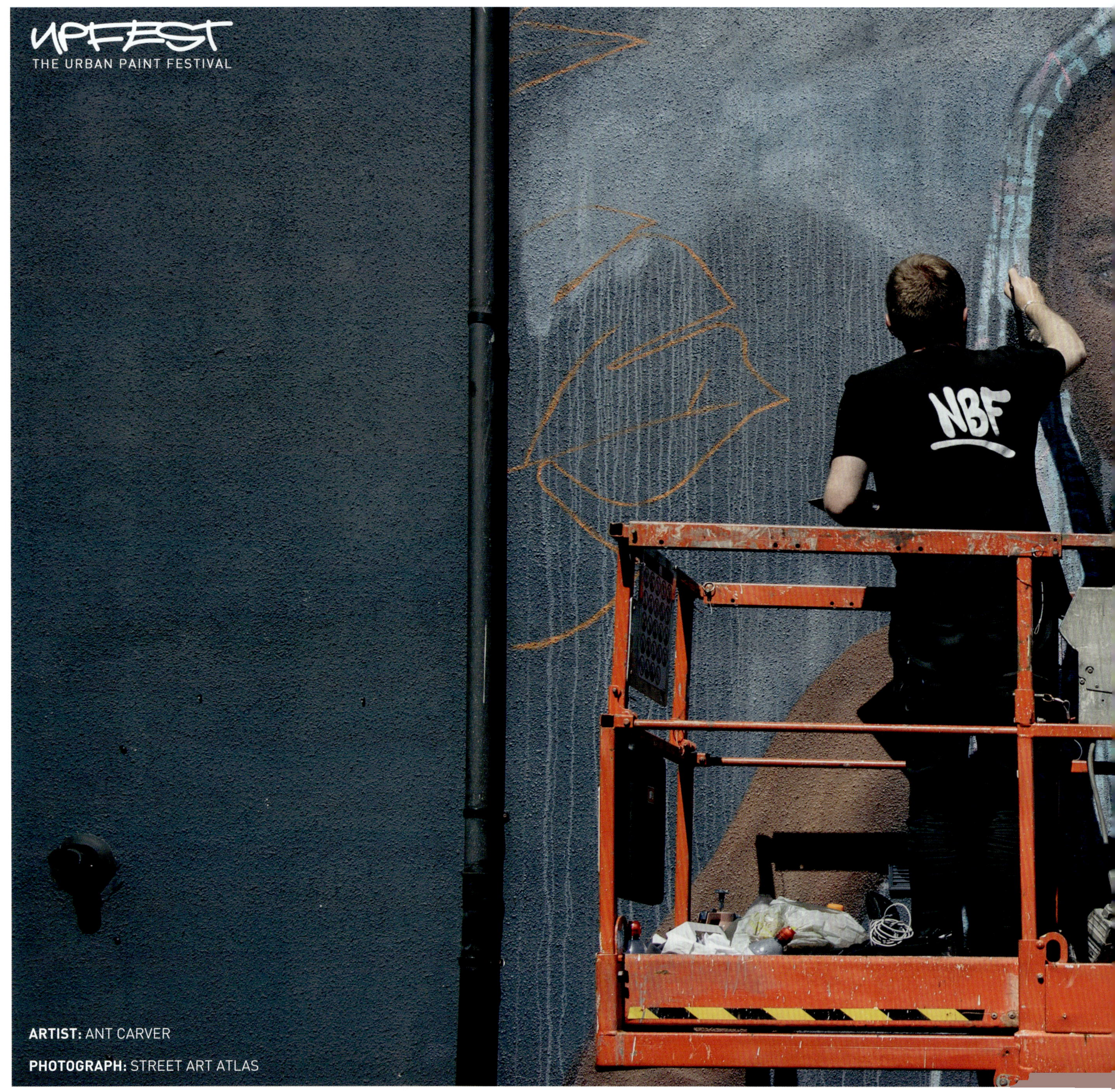

ARTIST: ANT CARVER

PHOTOGRAPH: STREET ART ATLAS

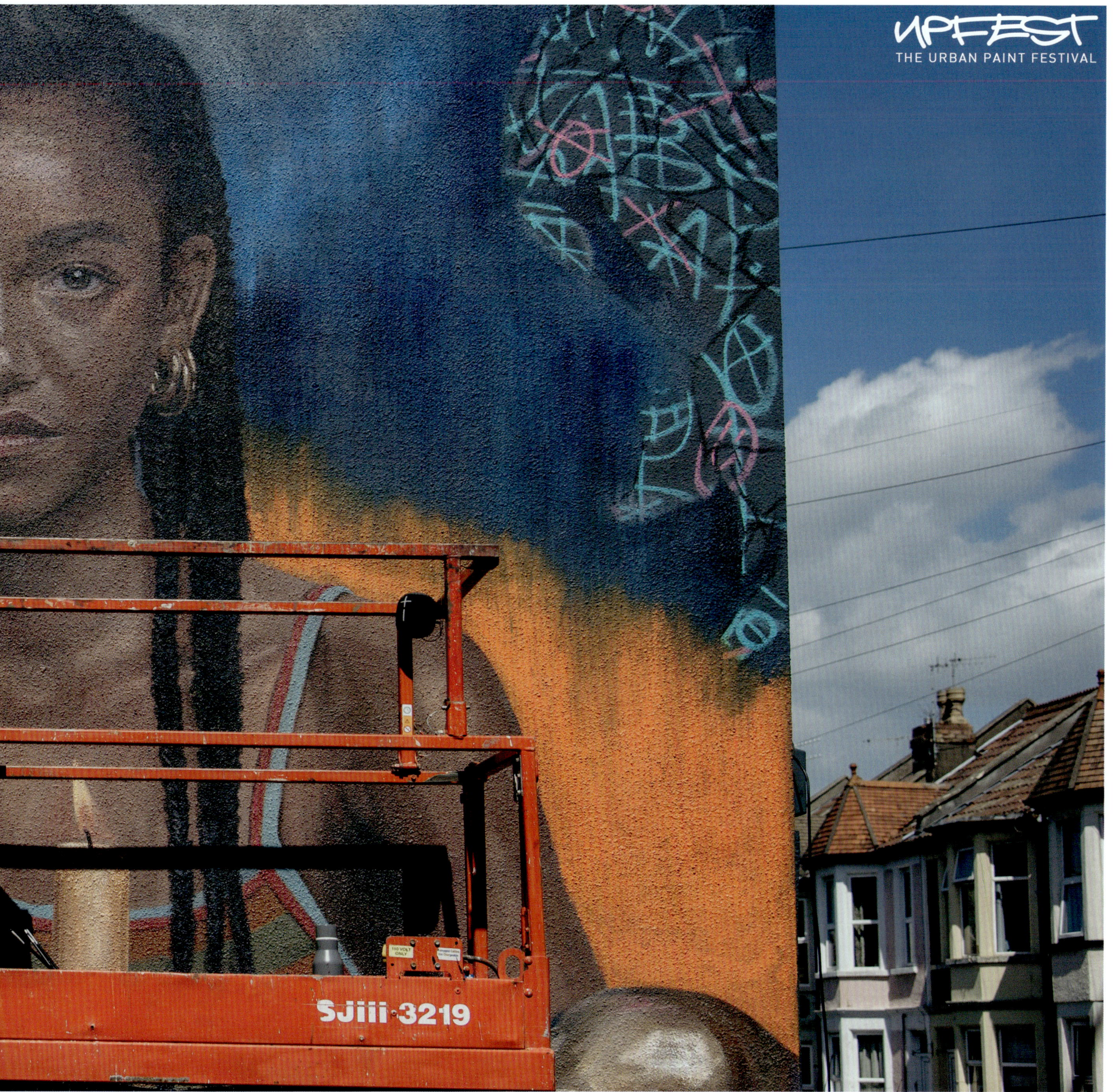
UPFEST
THE URBAN PAINT FESTIVAL
SJiii 3219

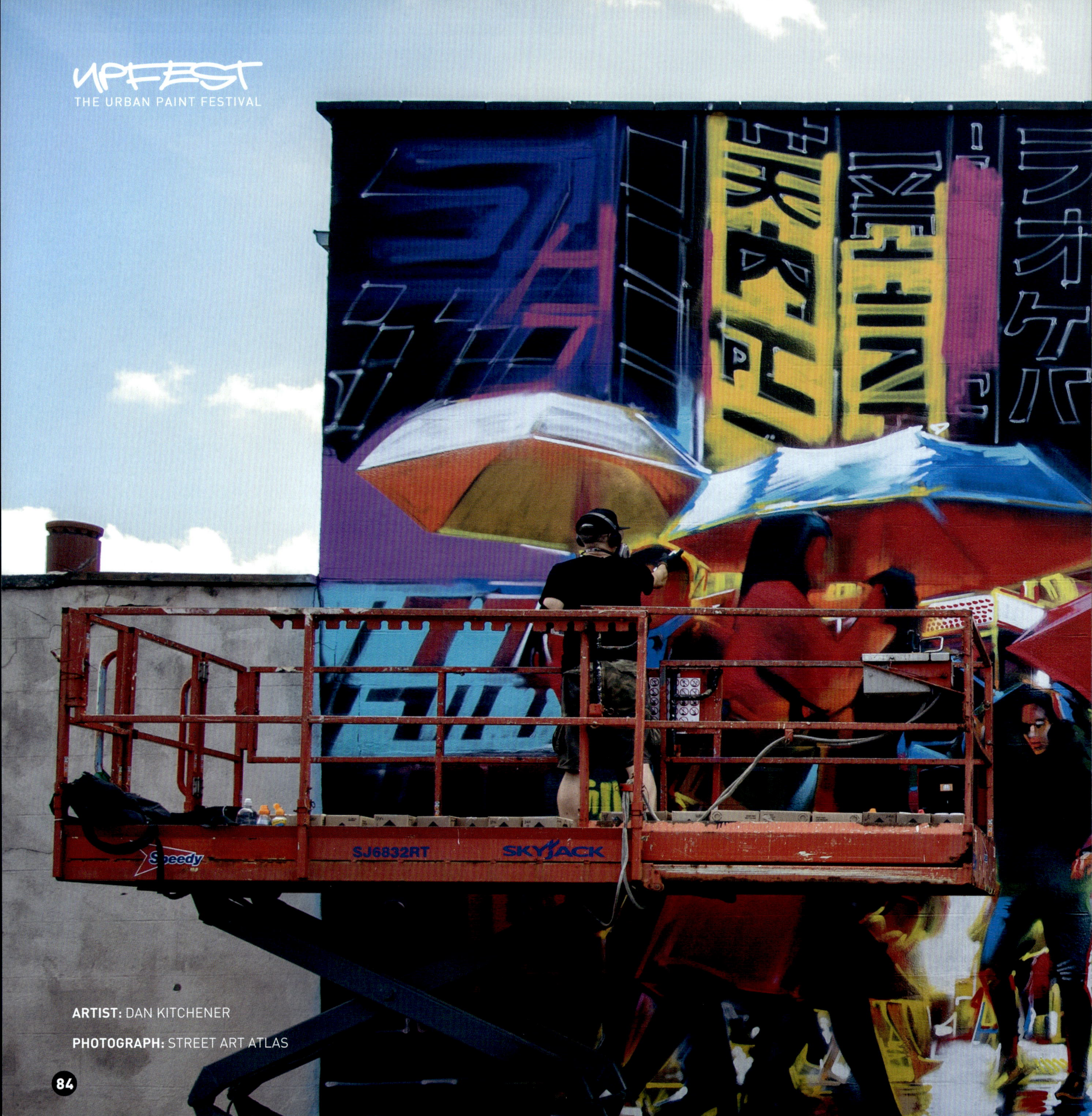

ARTIST: DAN KITCHENER

PHOTOGRAPH: STREET ART ATLAS

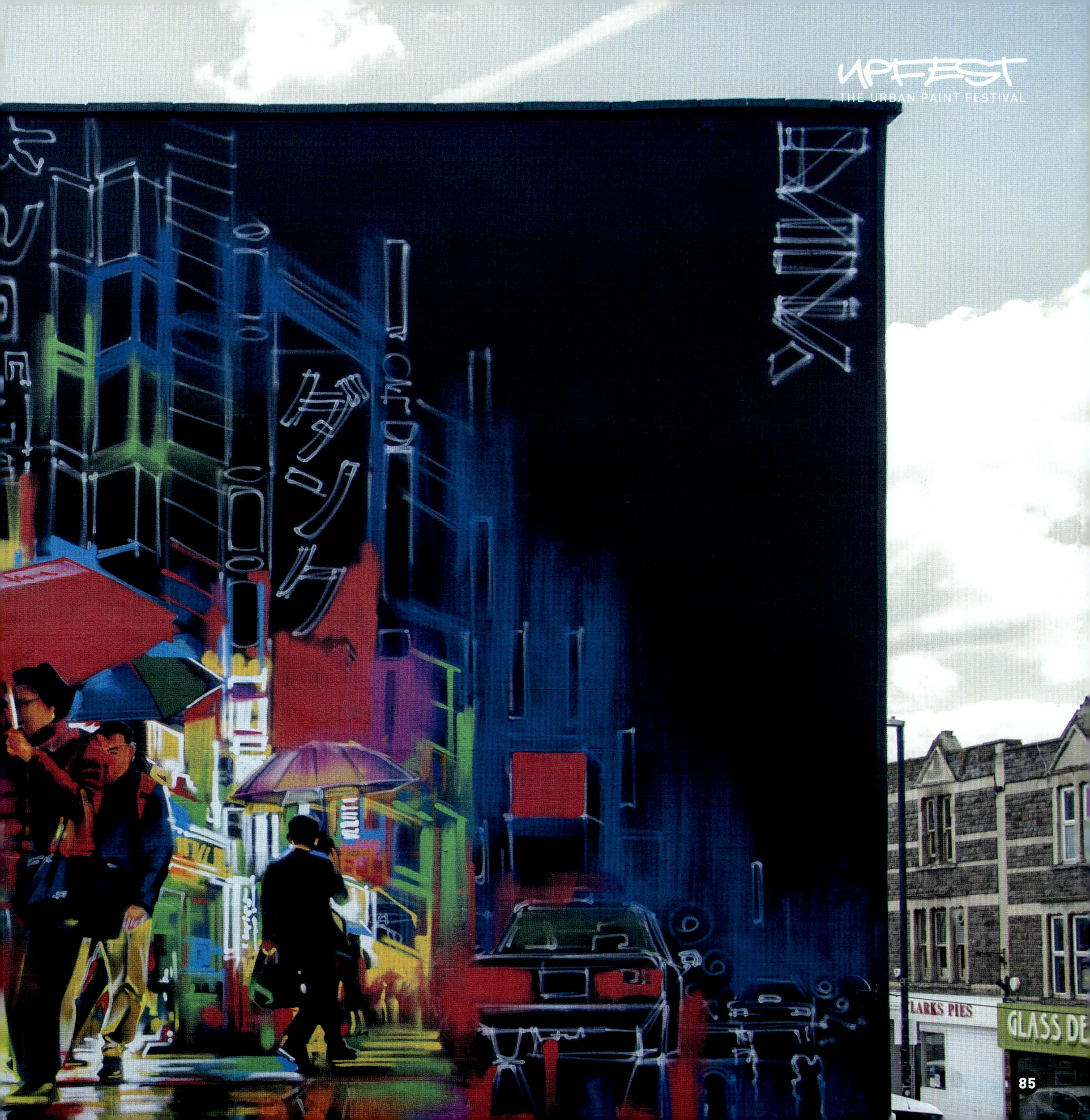

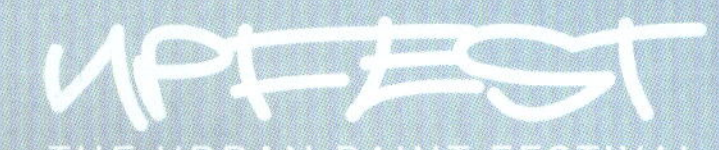

UPFEST
THE URBAN PAINT FESTIVAL

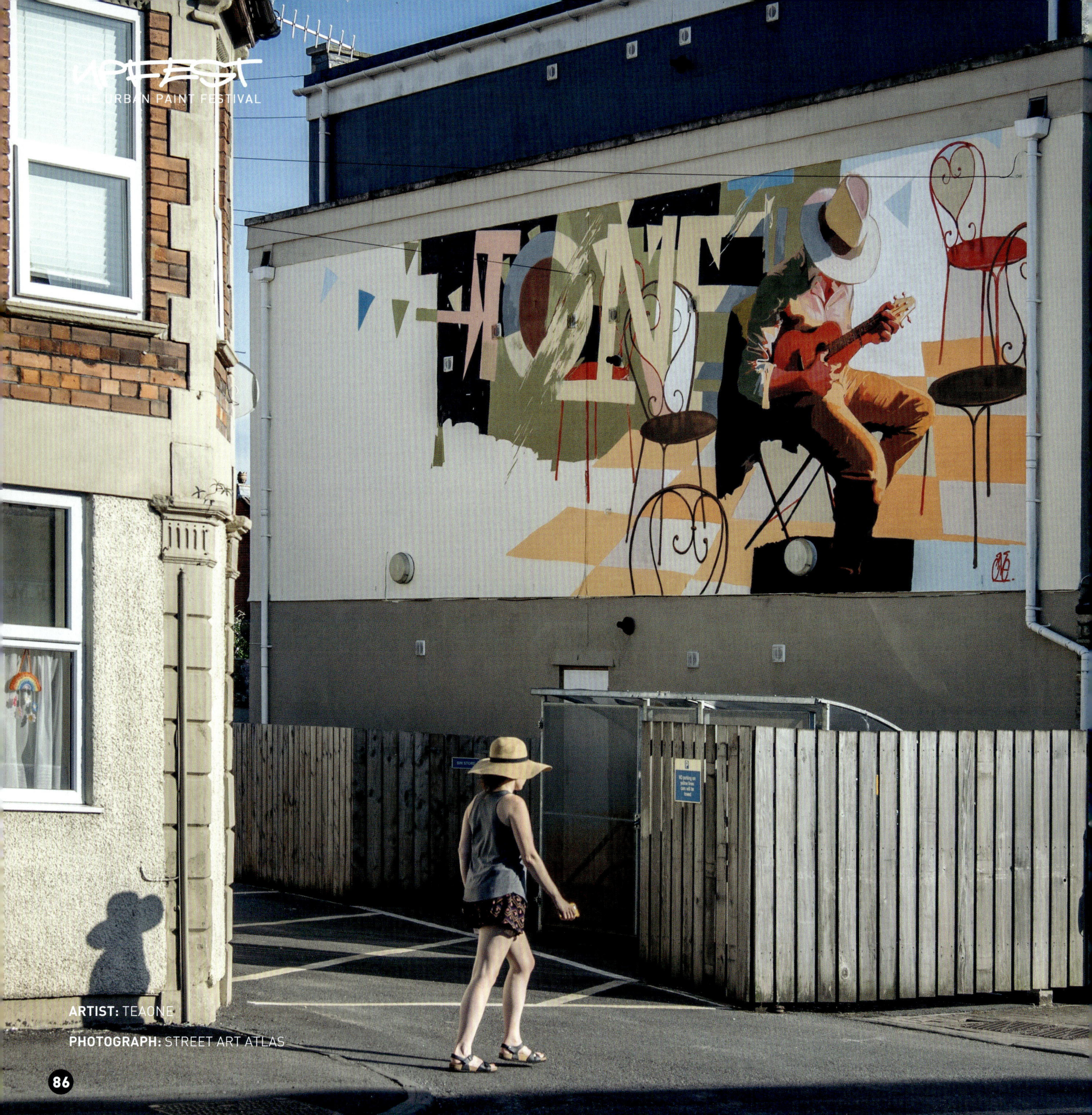

ARTIST: TEAONE

PHOTOGRAPH: STREET ART ATLAS

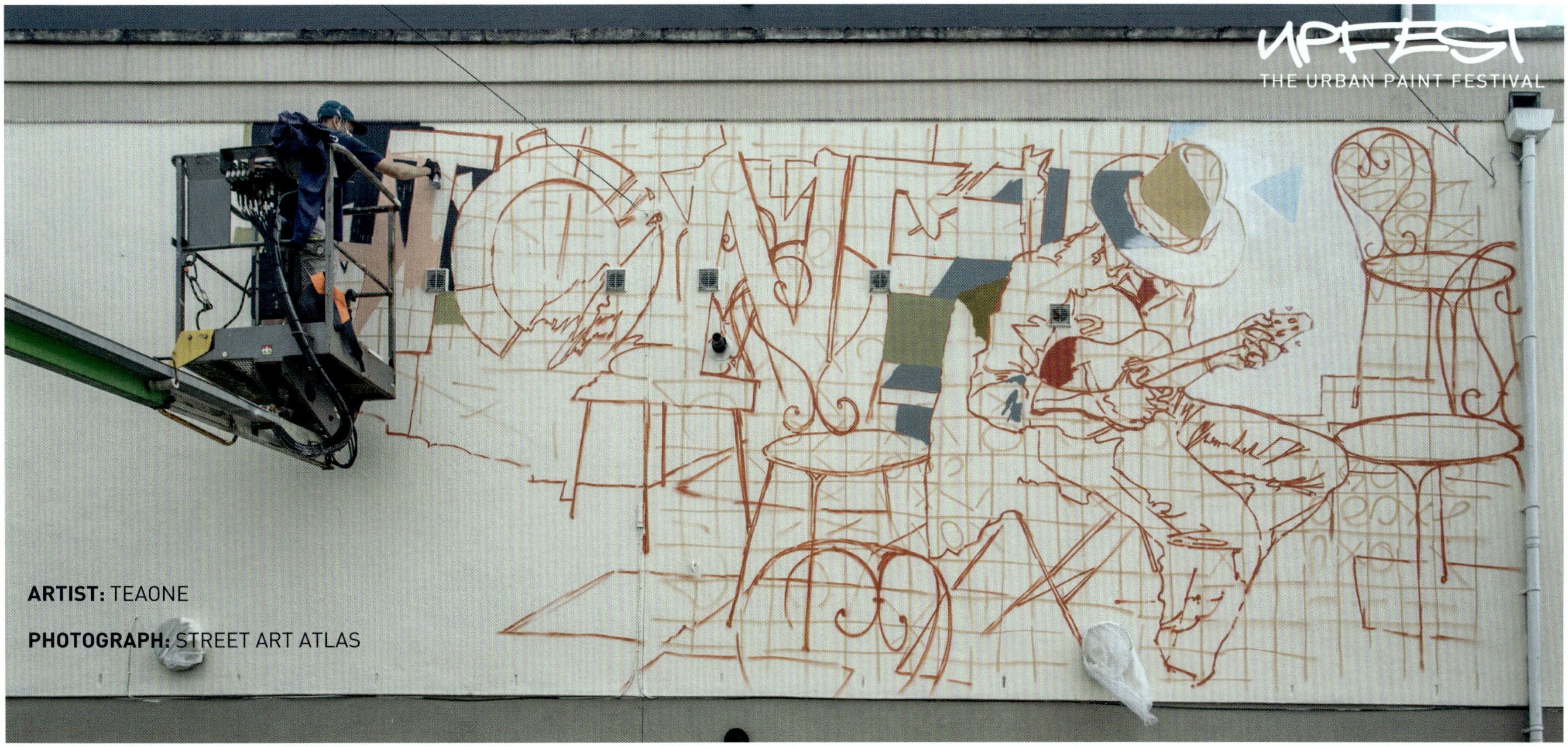

ARTIST: TEAONE

PHOTOGRAPH: STREET ART ATLAS

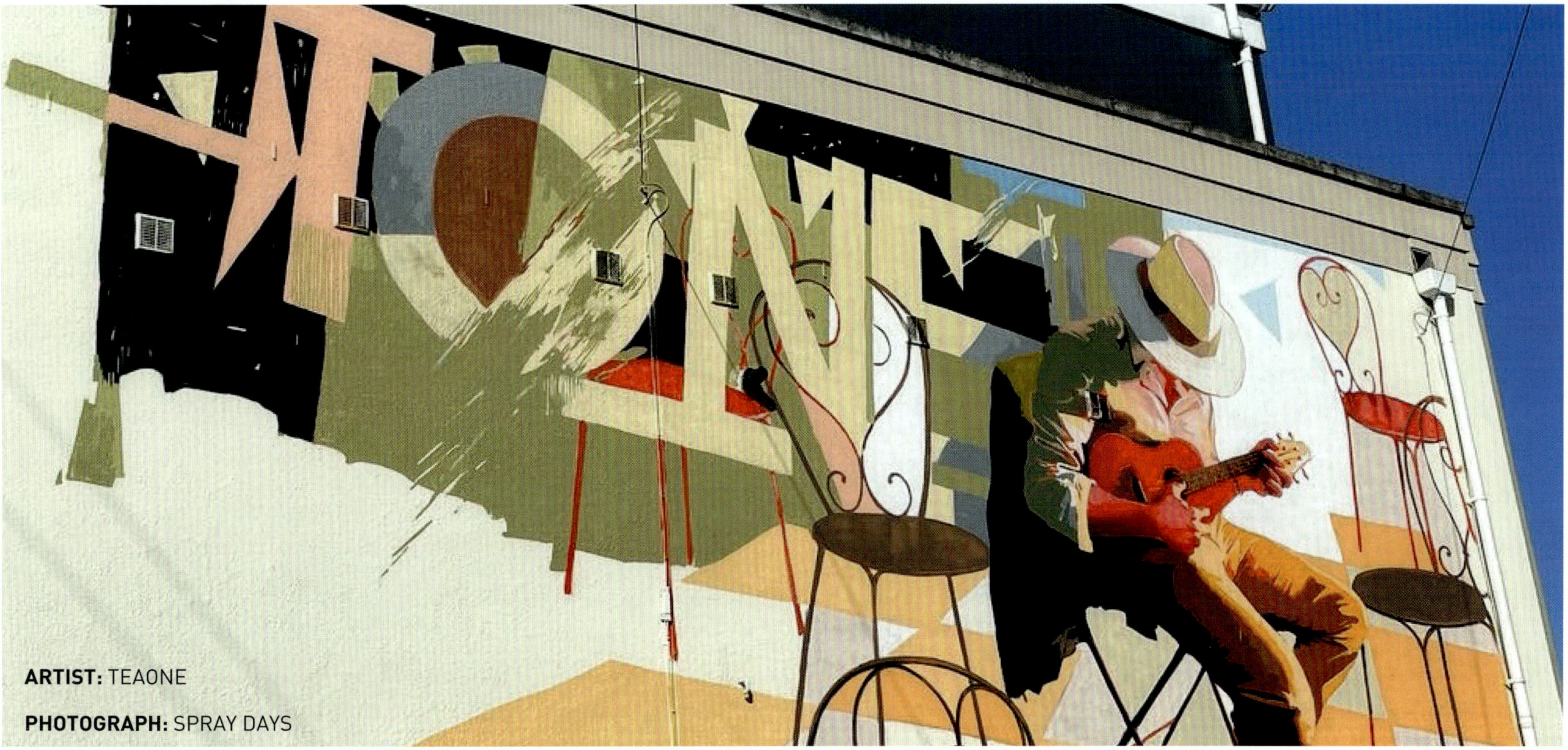

ARTIST: TEAONE

PHOTOGRAPH: SPRAY DAYS

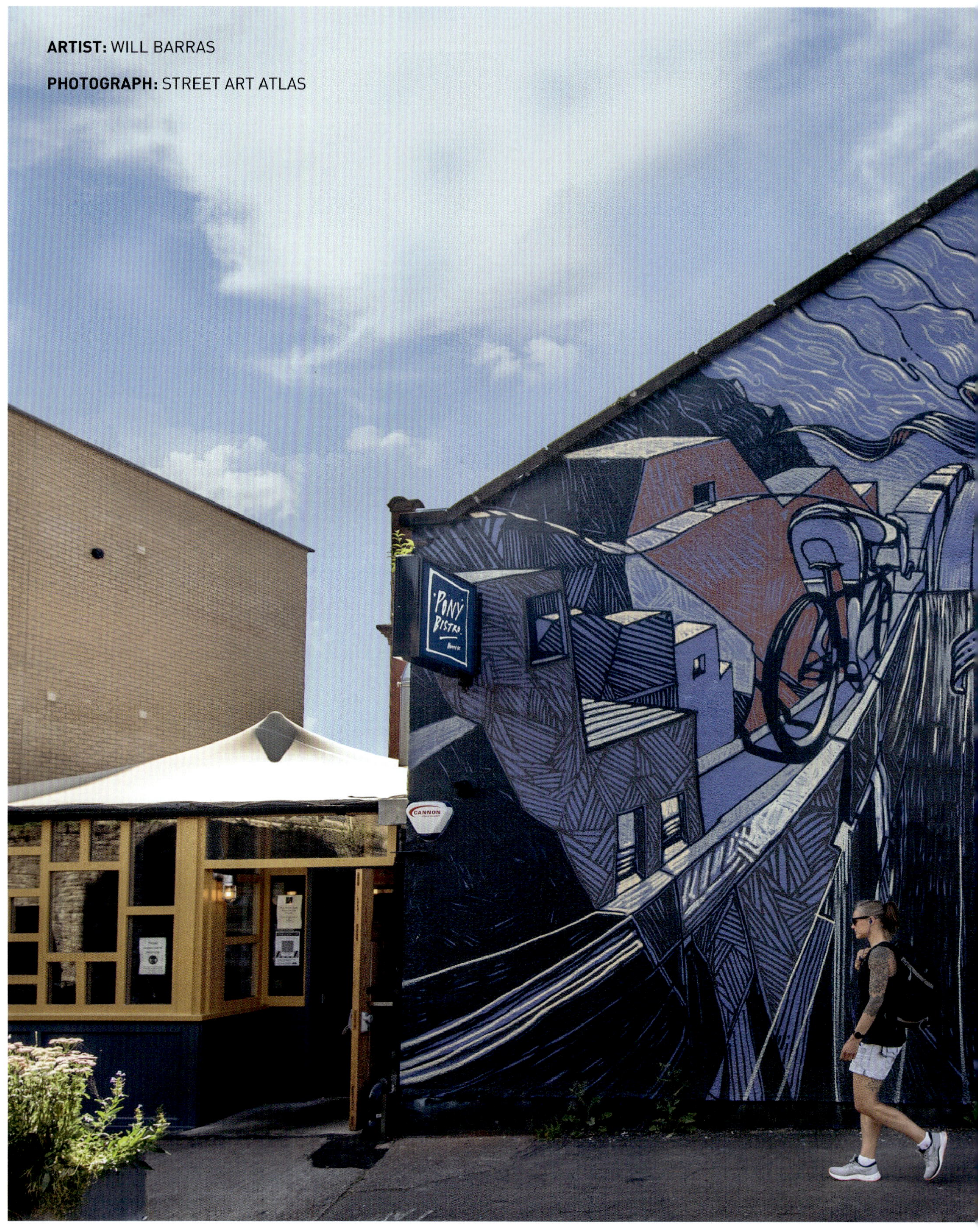

ARTIST: WILL BARRAS

PHOTOGRAPH: STREET ART ATLAS

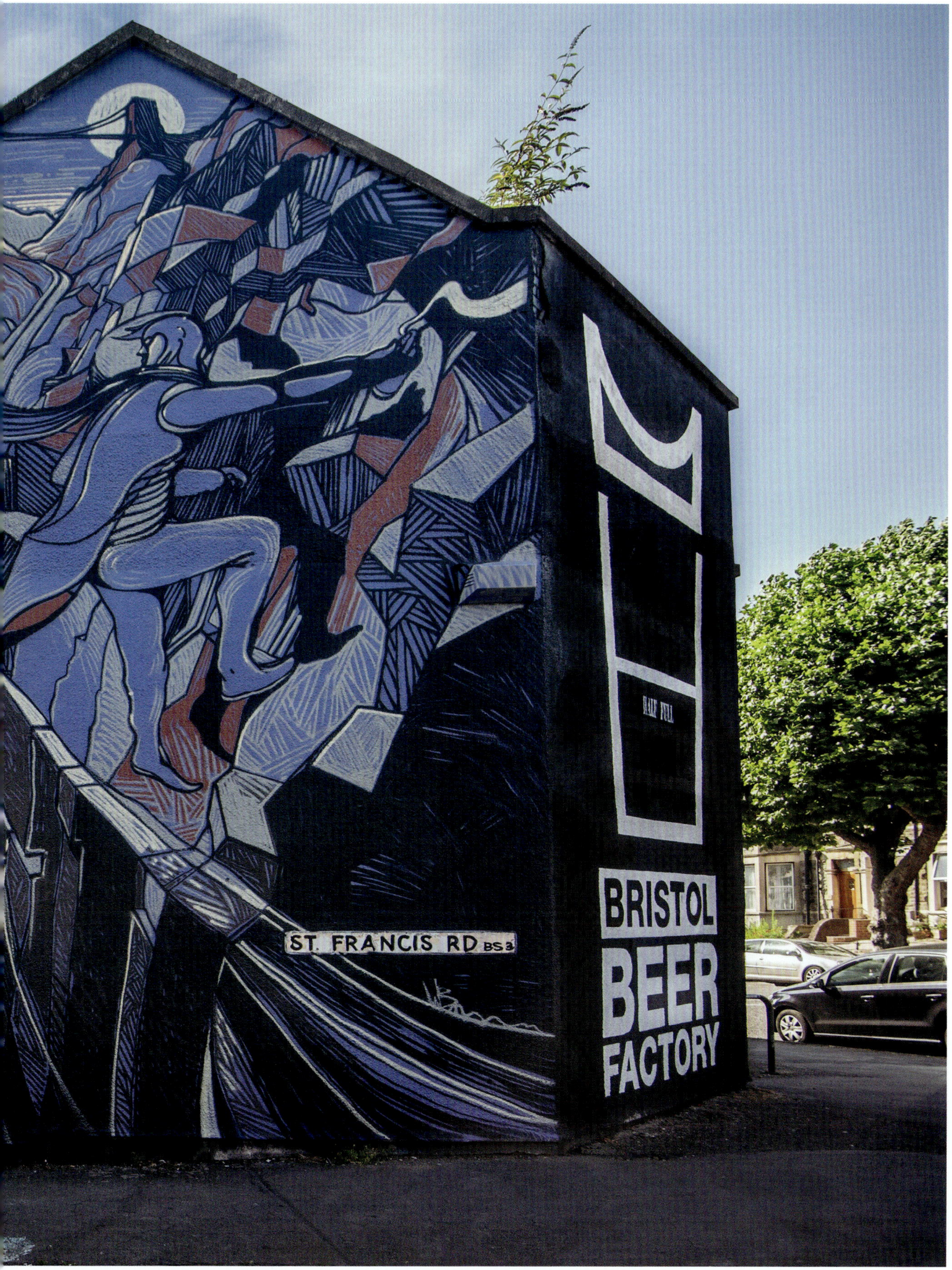

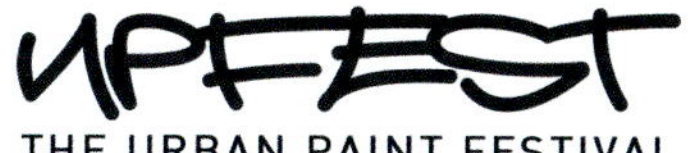

HALF FULL
BRISTOL
BEER
FACTORY
ST. FRANCIS RD BS3

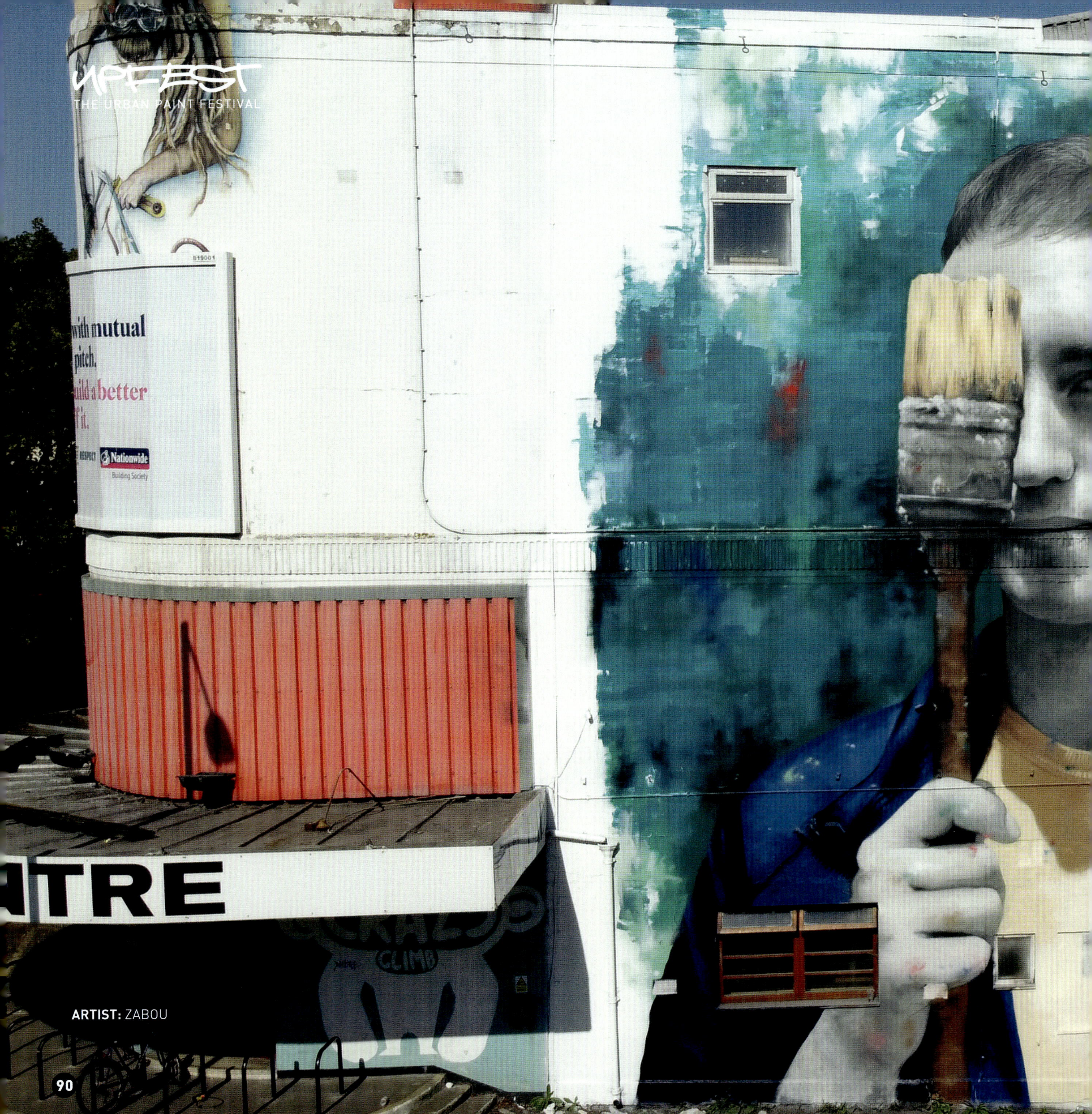

ARTIST: ZABOU

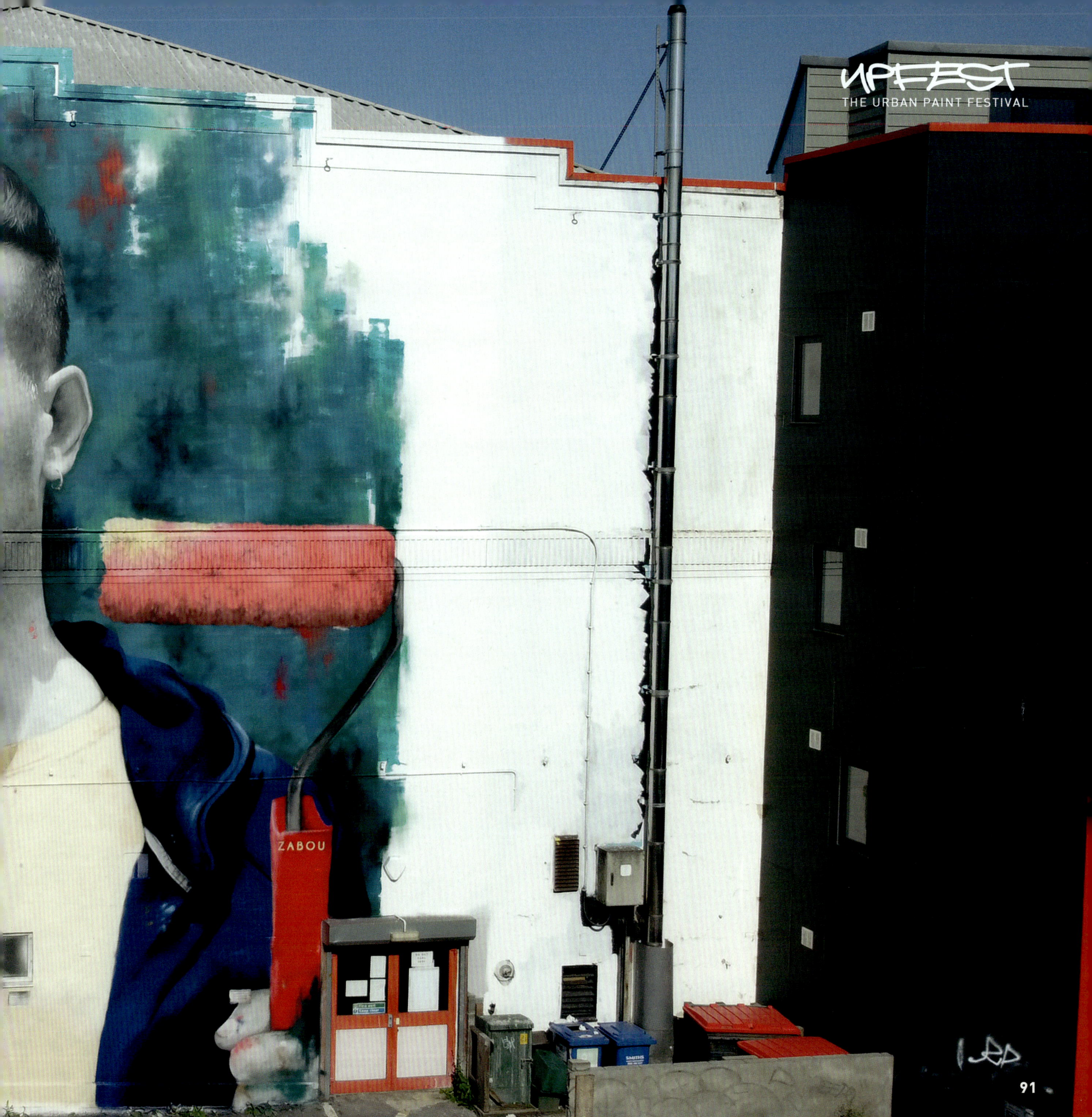
UPFEST
THE URBAN PAINT FESTIVAL
ZABOU

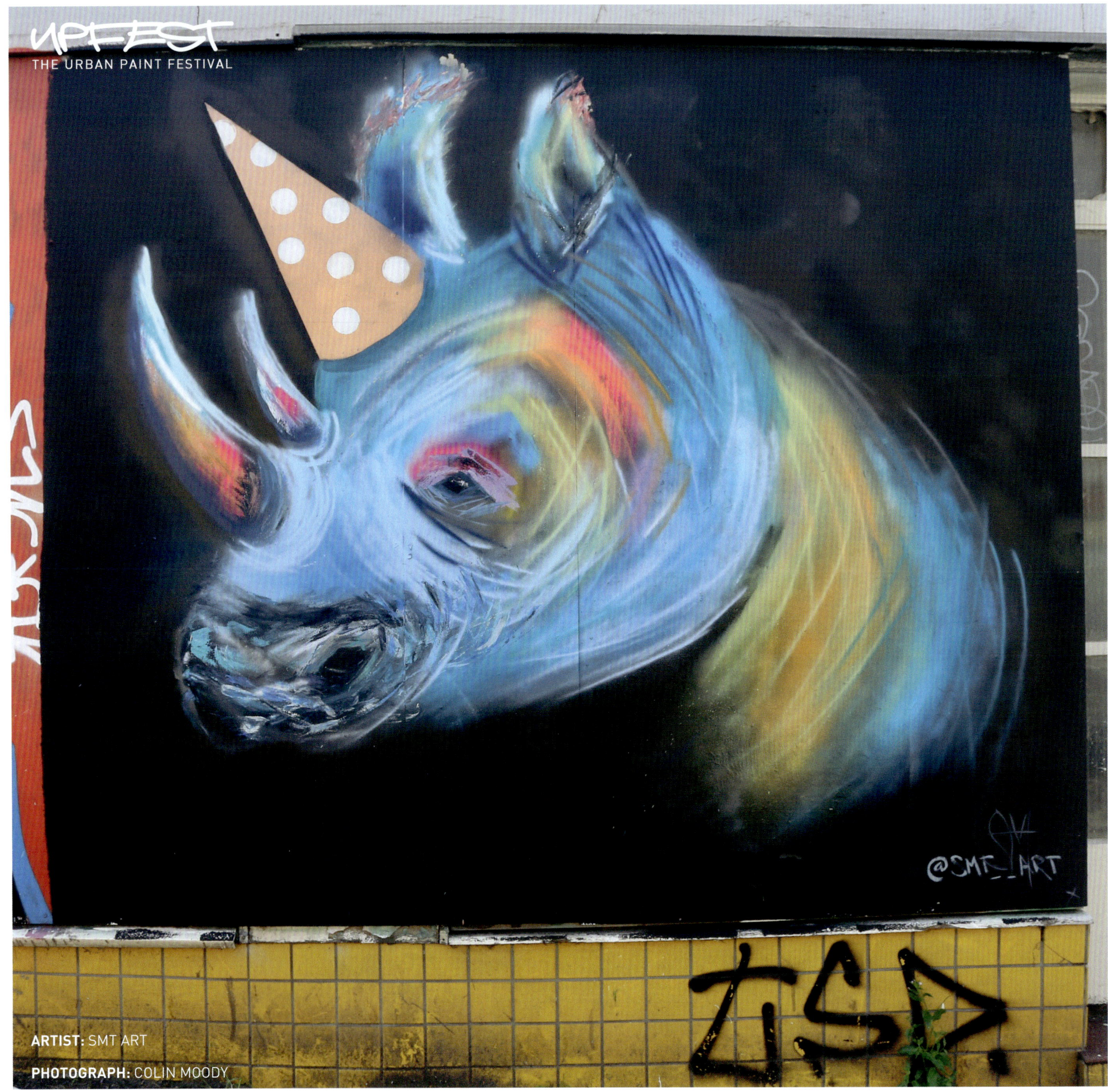

ARTIST: SMT ART

PHOTOGRAPH: COLIN MOODY

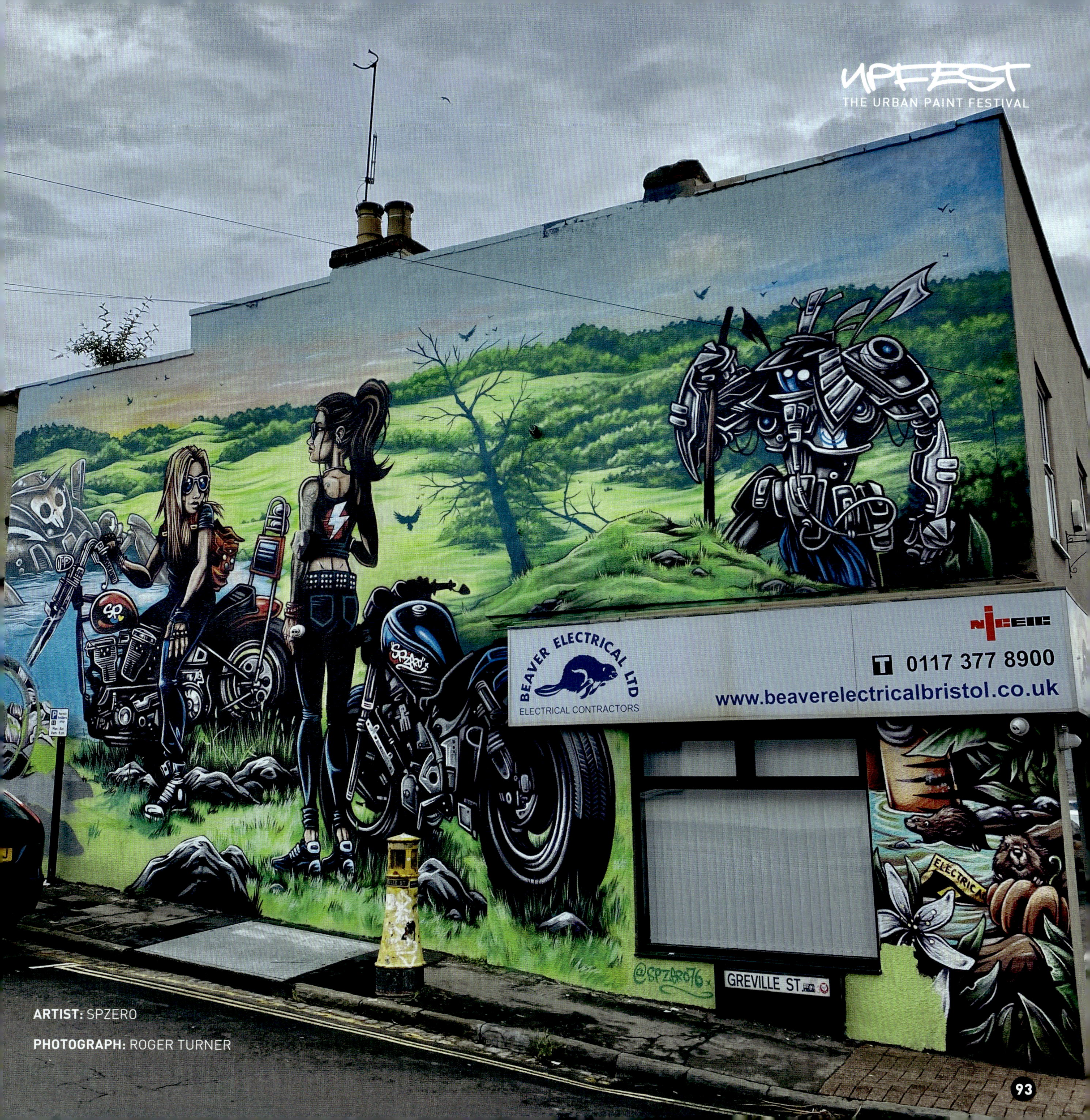

UPFEST
THE URBAN PAINT FESTIVAL
BEAVER ELECTRICAL LTD
ELECTRICAL CONTRACTORS
NICEIC
T 0117 377 8900
www.beaverelectricalbristol.co.uk
@SPZERO76
GREVILLE ST

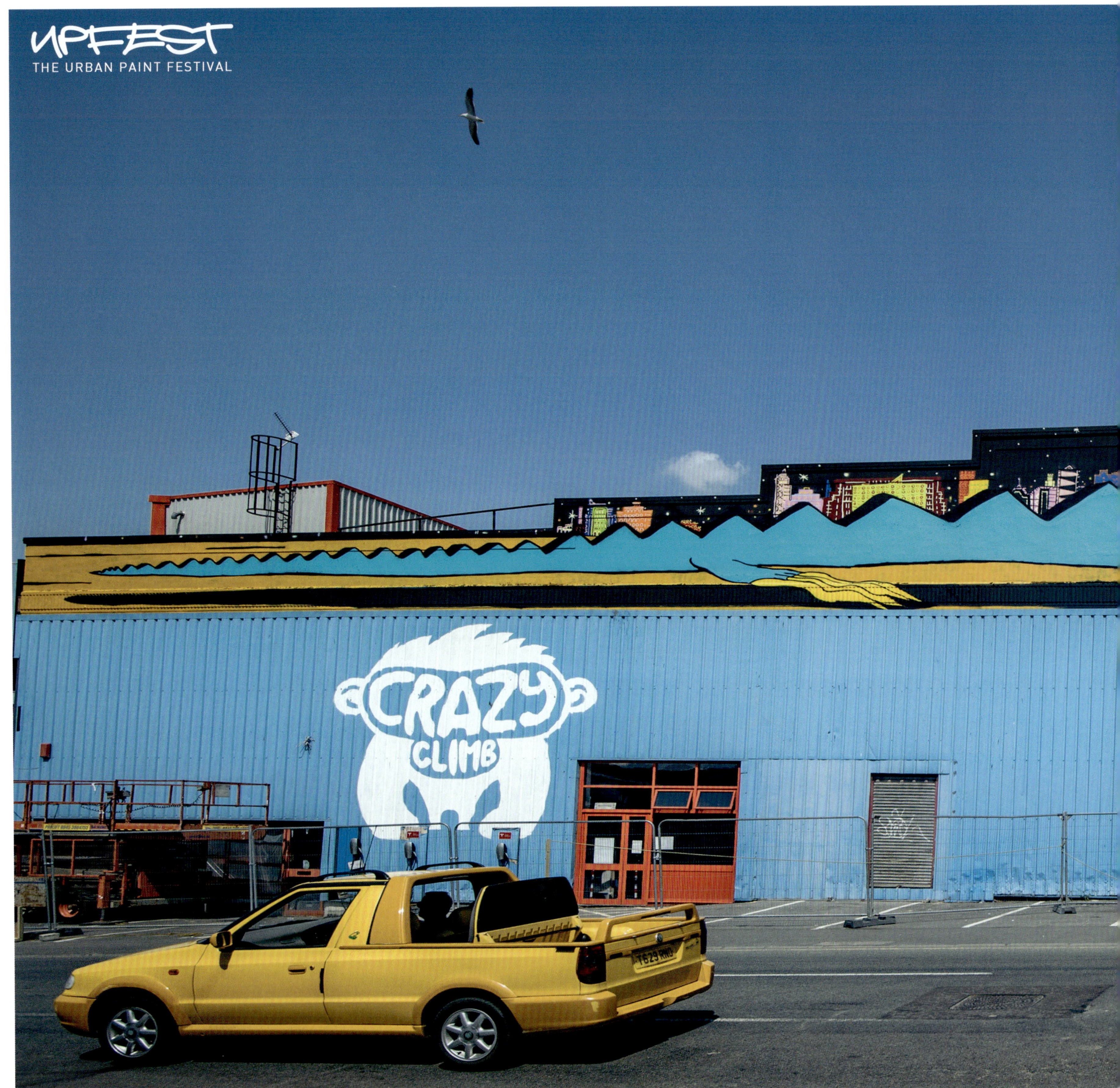
UPFEST
THE URBAN PAINT FESTIVAL
CRAZY
CLIMB

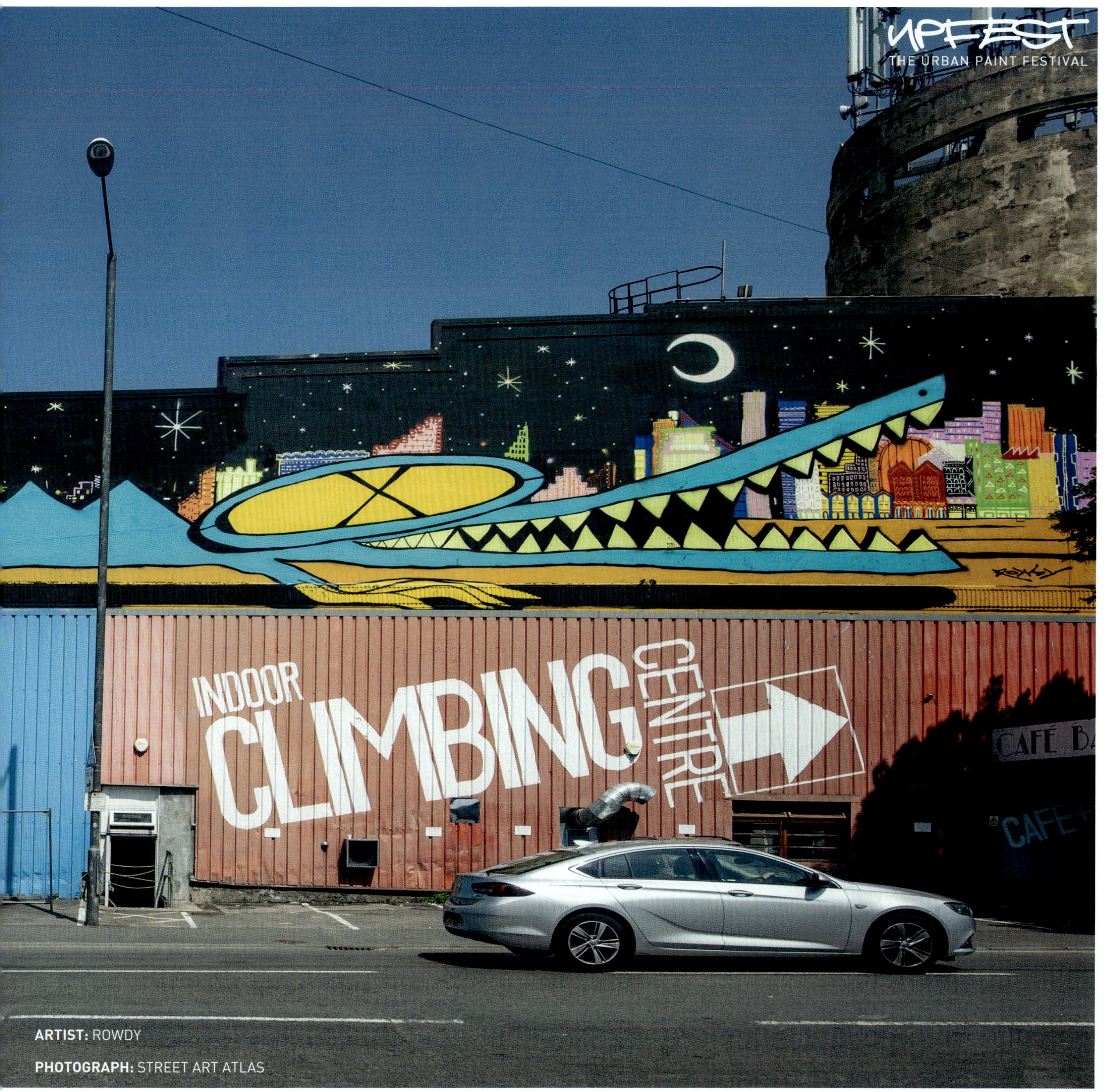

ARTIST: ROWDY

PHOTOGRAPH: STREET ART ATLAS

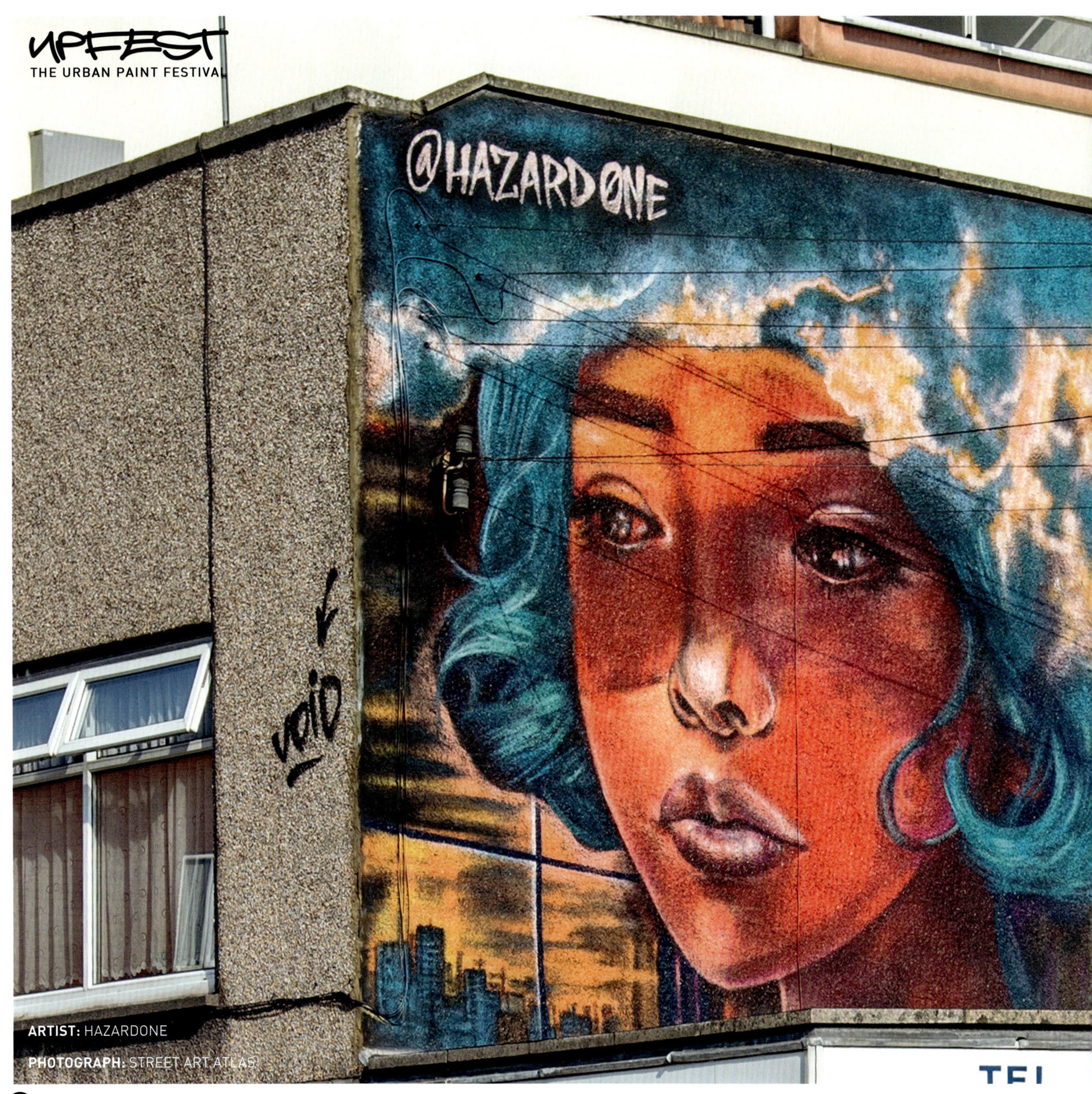

ARTIST: HAZARDONE

PHOTOGRAPH: STREET ART ATLAS

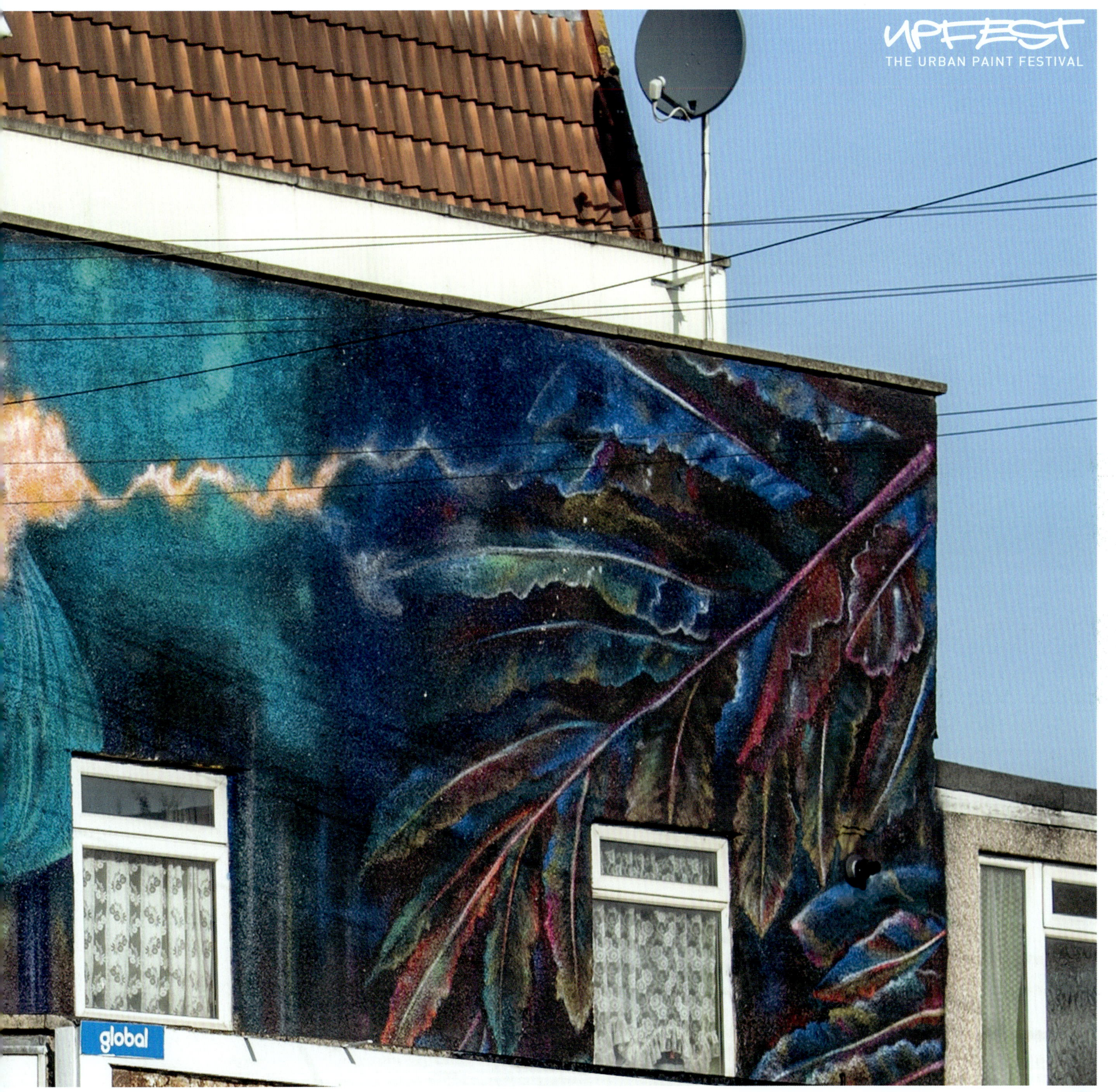
UPFEST
THE URBAN PAINT FESTIVAL
global

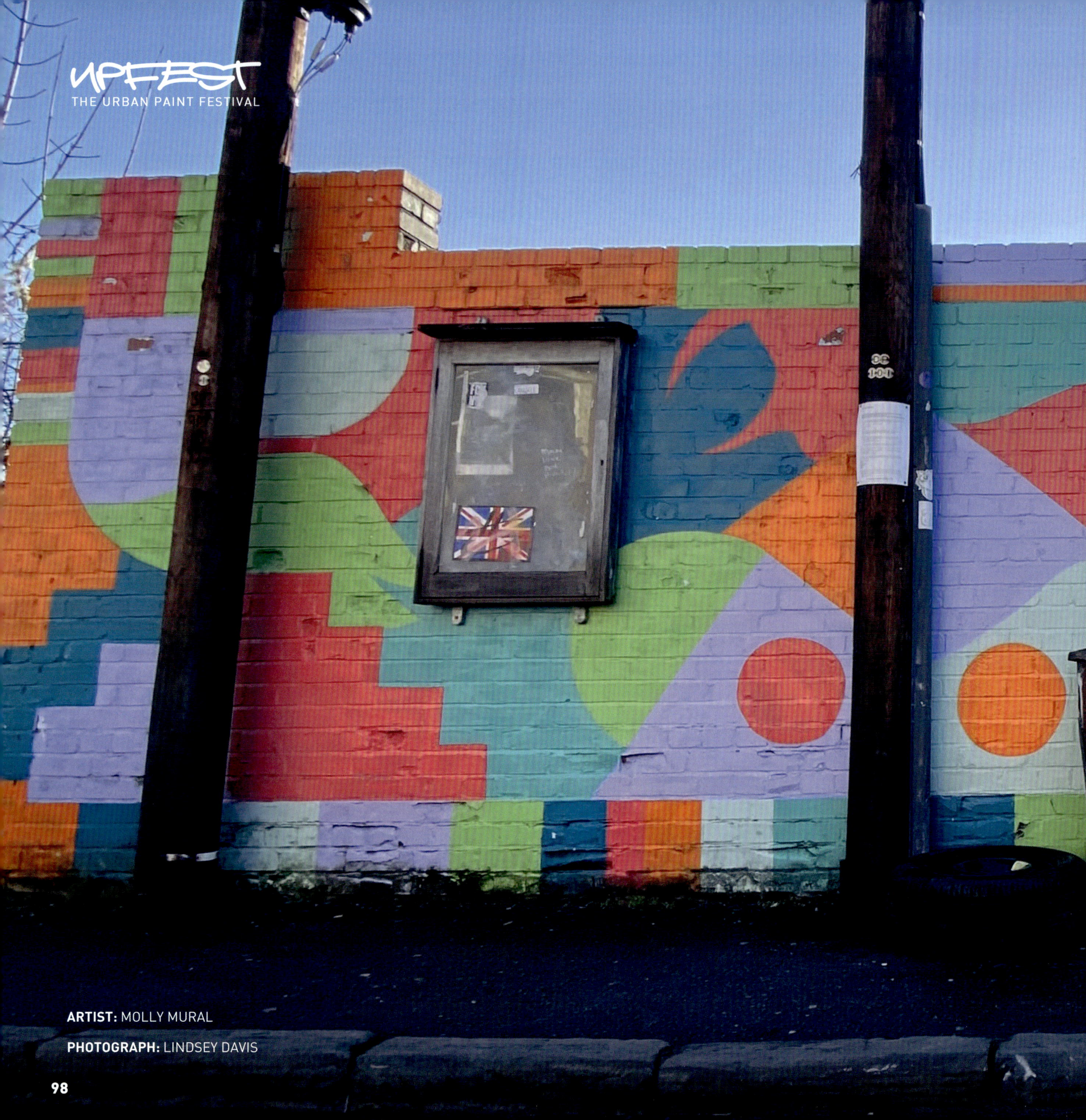
UPFEST
THE URBAN PAINT FESTIVAL

ARTIST: MOLLY MURAL

PHOTOGRAPH: LINDSEY DAVIS

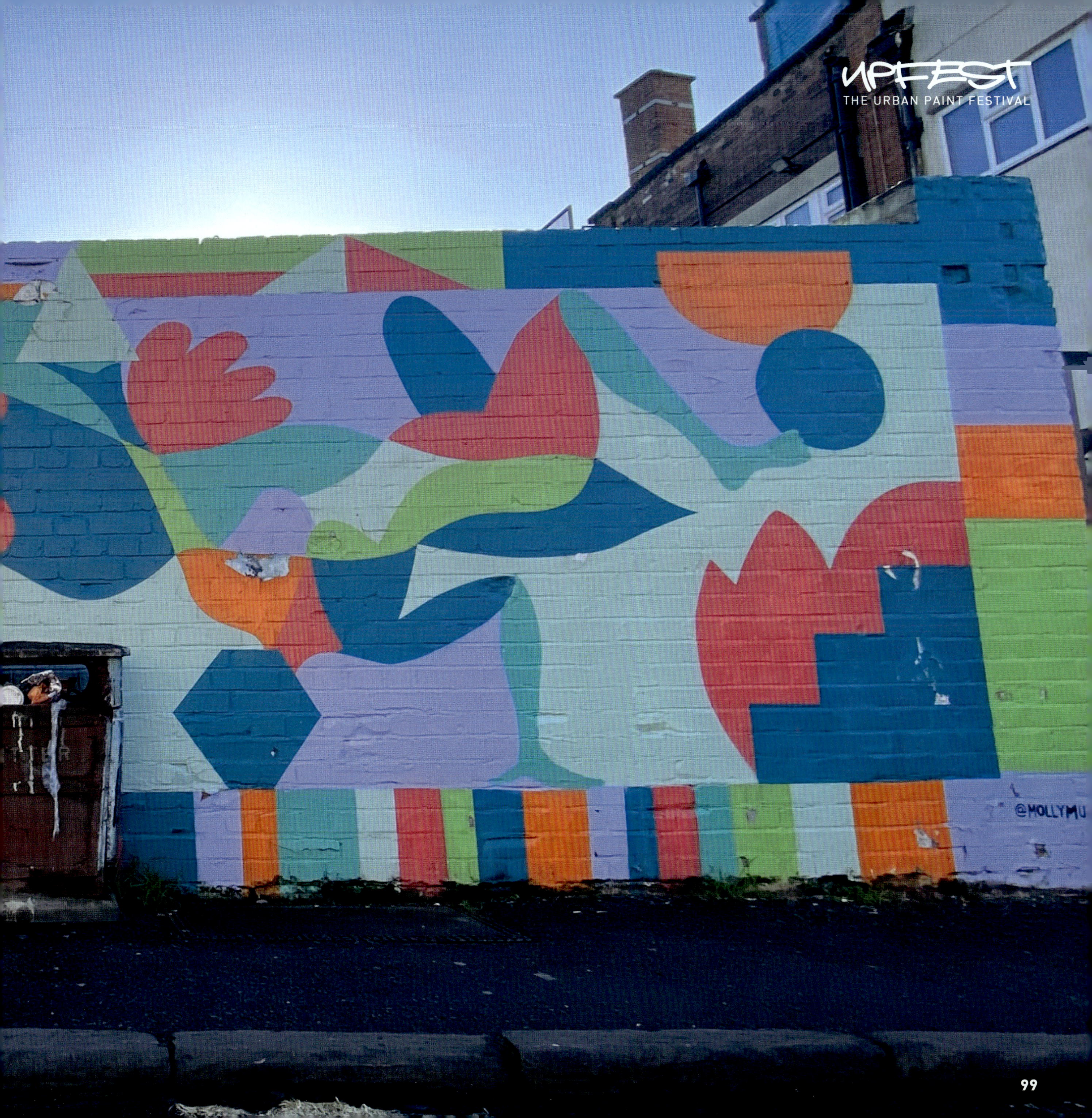

UPFEST
THE URBAN PAINT FESTIVAL
@MOLLYMU

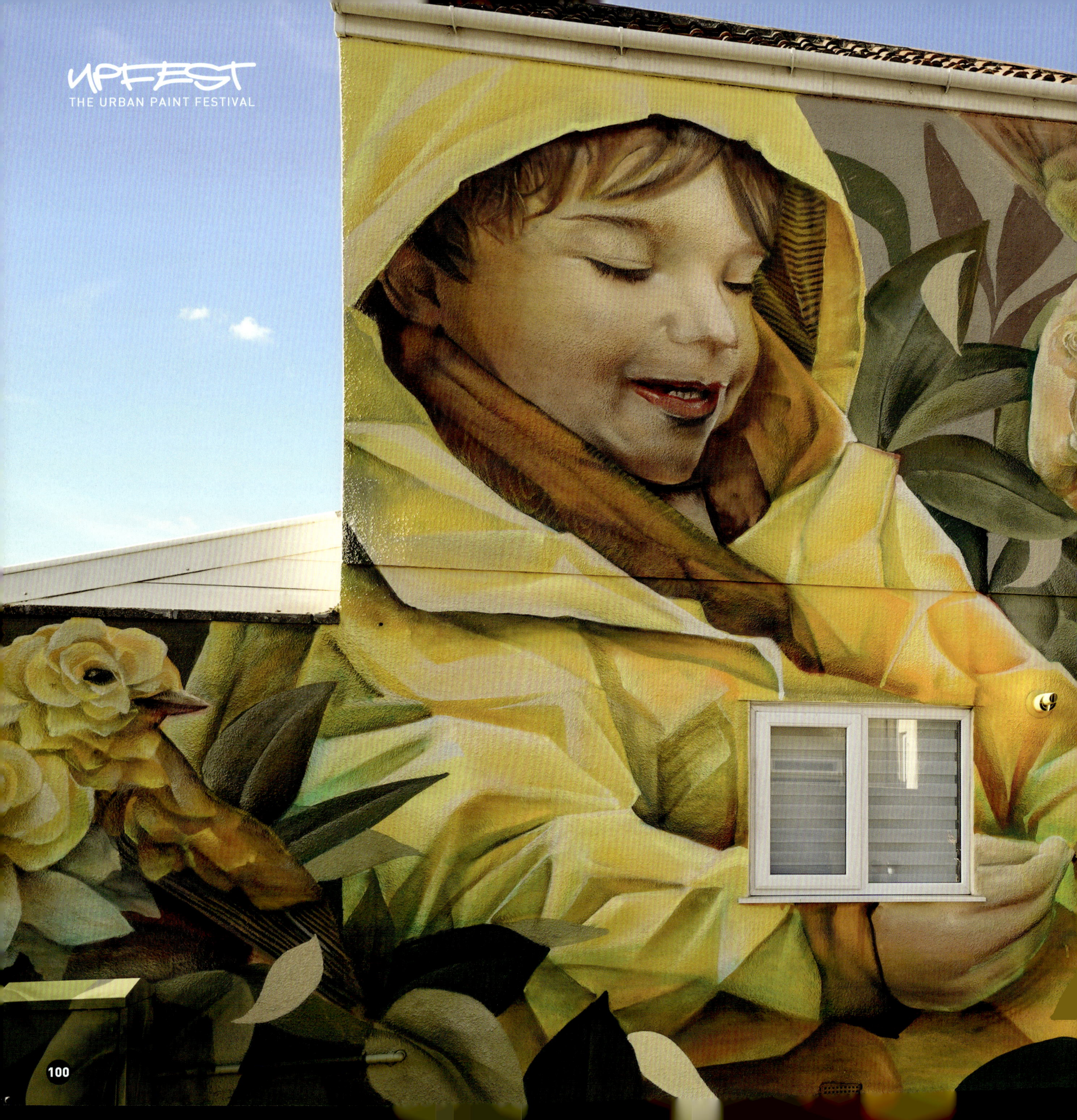
UPFEST
THE URBAN PAINT FESTIVAL

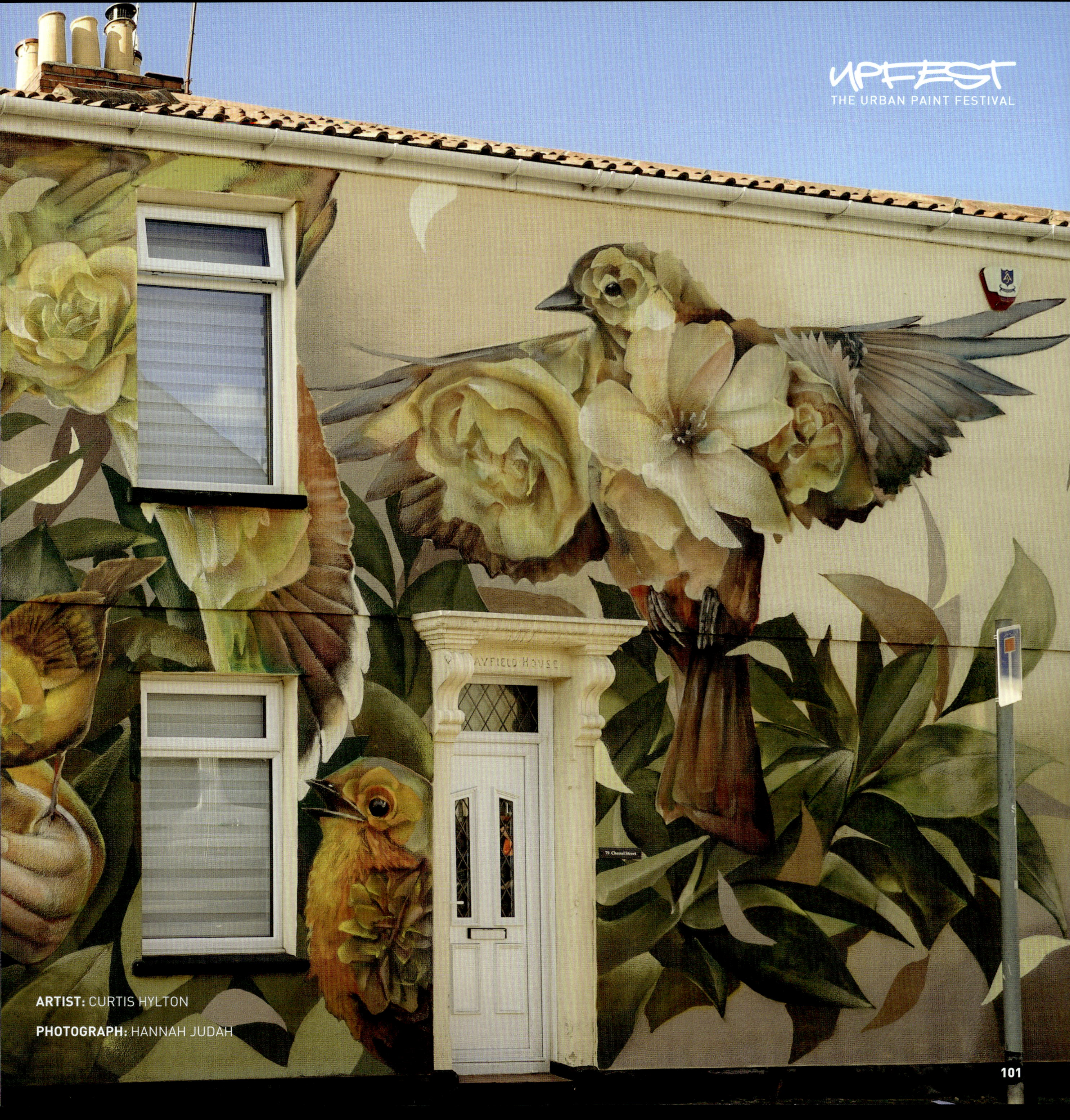

ARTIST: CURTIS HYLTON

PHOTOGRAPH: HANNAH JUDAH

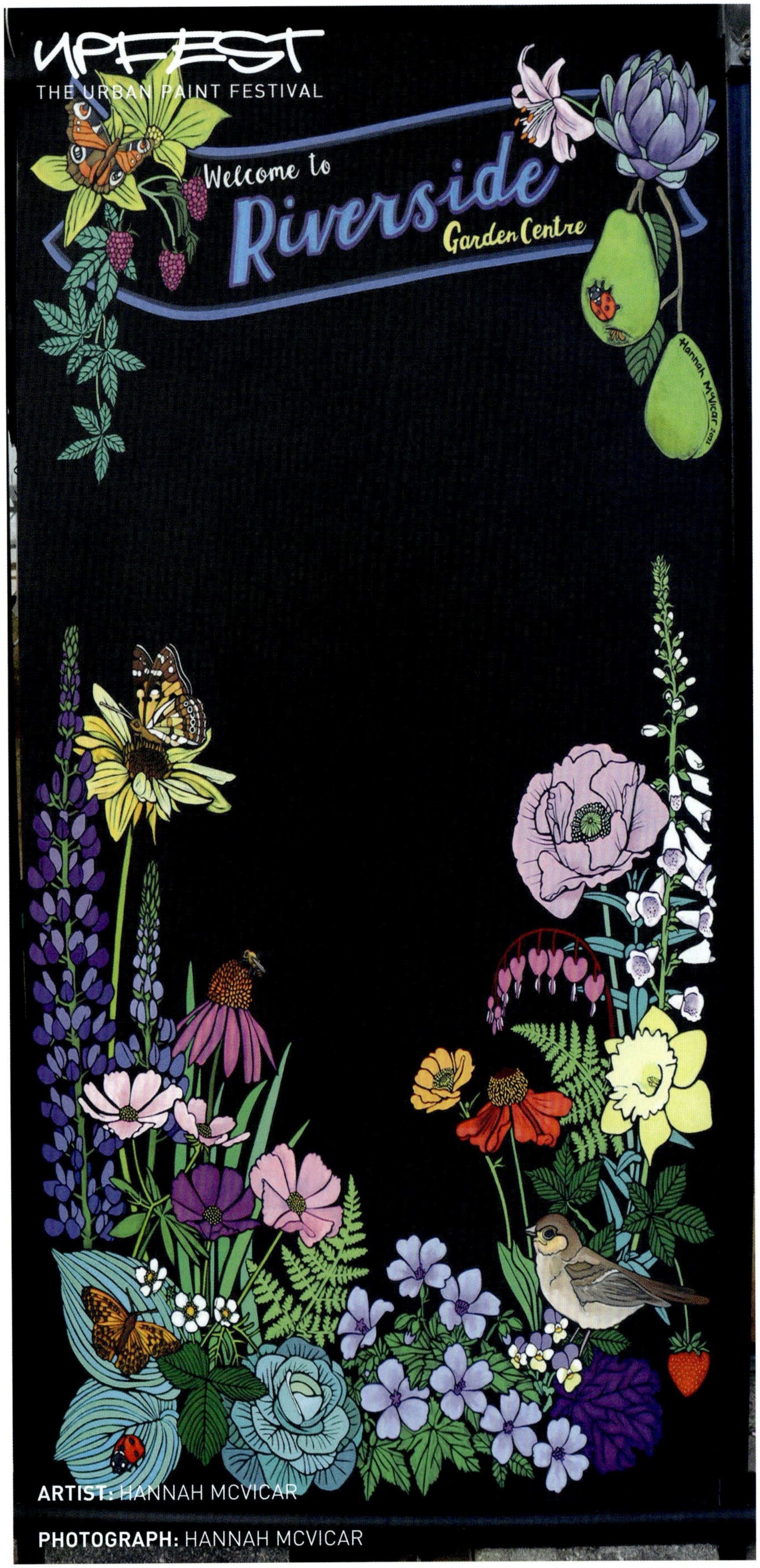

ARTIST: HANNAH MCVICAR

PHOTOGRAPH: HANNAH MCVICAR

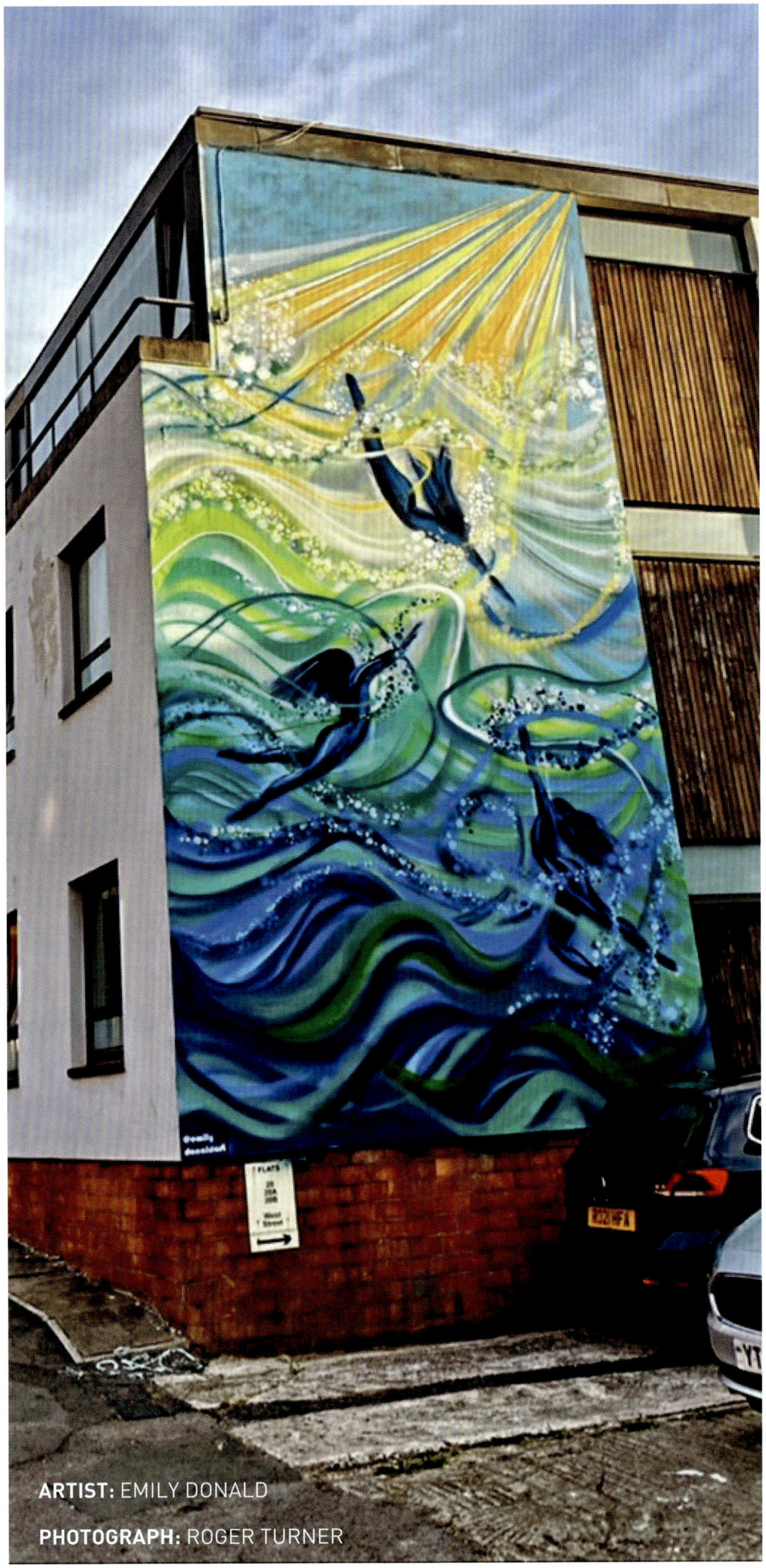

ARTIST: EMILY DONALD

PHOTOGRAPH: ROGER TURNER

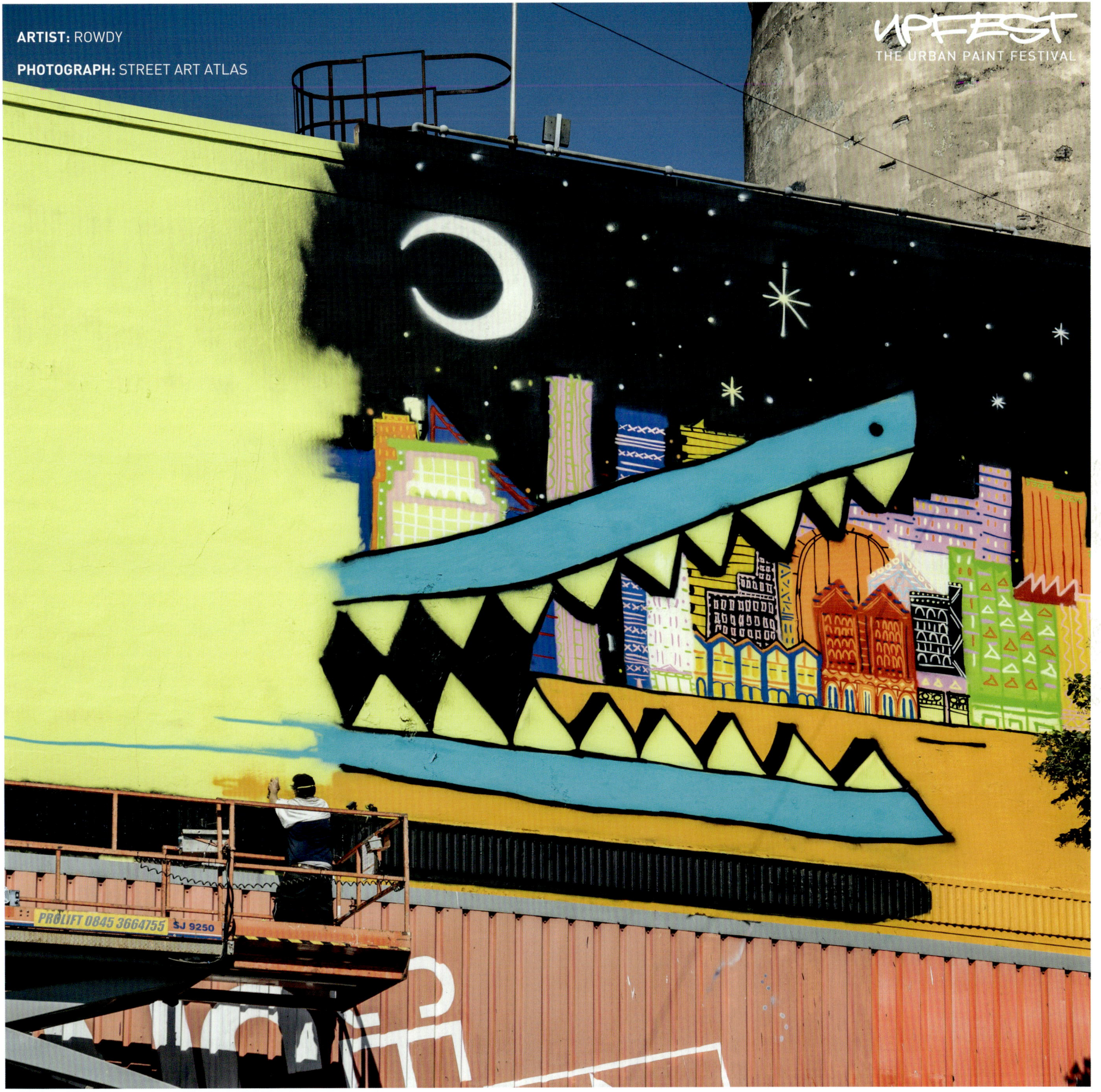
UPFEST
THE URBAN PAINT FESTIVAL
PROLIFT 0845 3664755 SJ 9250

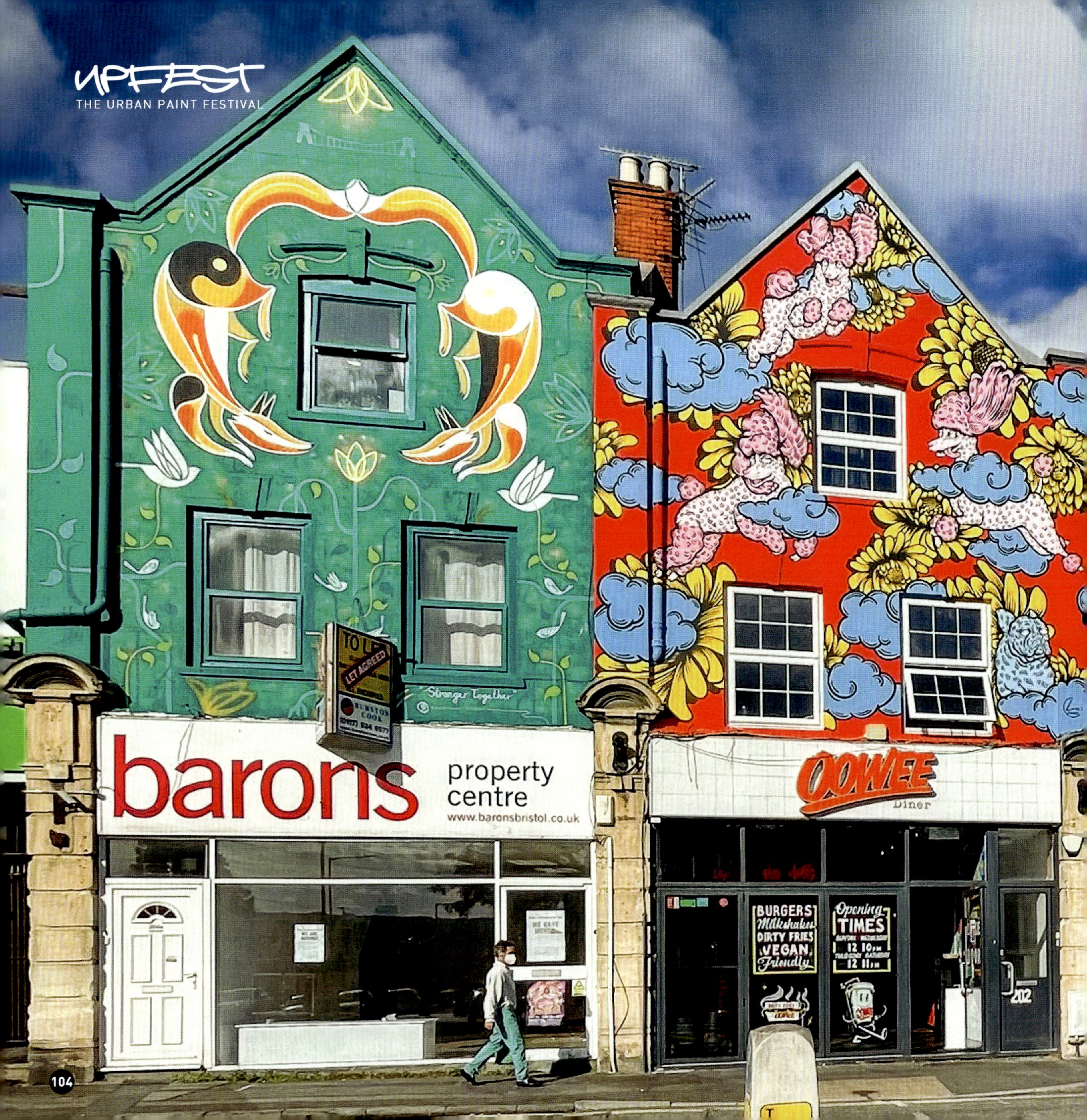
UPFEST
THE URBAN PAINT FESTIVAL
Stronger Together
TO LET
LET AGREED
BURSTON COOK
barons
property
centre
www.baronsbristol.co.uk
OOWEE
Diner
BURGERS
Milkshakes
DIRTY FRIES
VEGAN
Friendly
Opening
TIMES
202

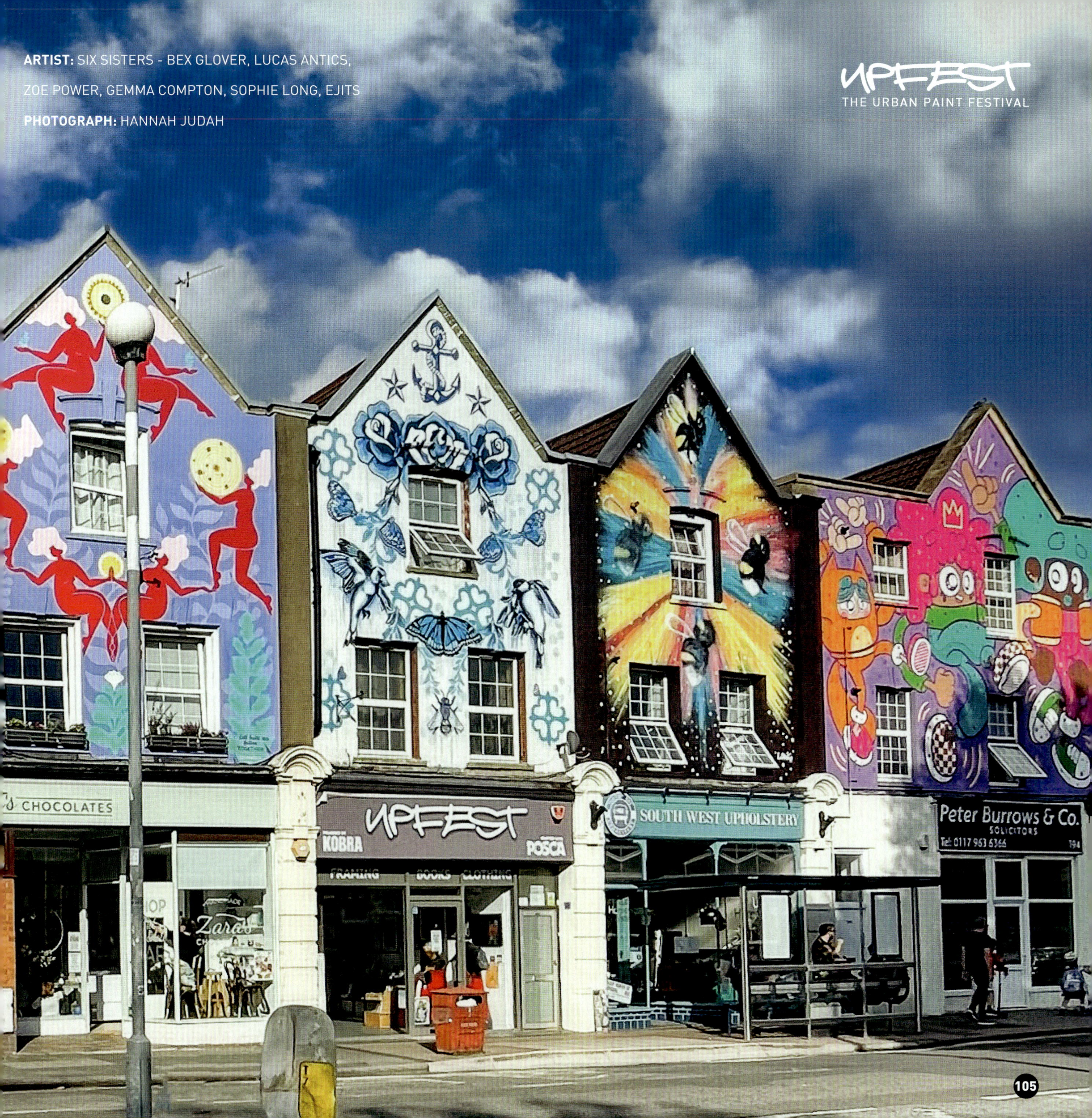

ARTIST: SIX SISTERS - BEX GLOVER, LUCAS ANTICS,
ZOE POWER, GEMMA COMPTON, SOPHIE LONG, EJITS
PHOTOGRAPH: HANNAH JUDAH
UPFEST
THE URBAN PAINT FESTIVAL
CHOCOLATES
KOBRA
UPFEST
POSCA
FRAMING
BOOKS
CLOTHING
SOUTH WEST UPHOLSTERY
Peter Burrows & Co.
SOLICITORS
Tel: 0117 963 6366
Zaras

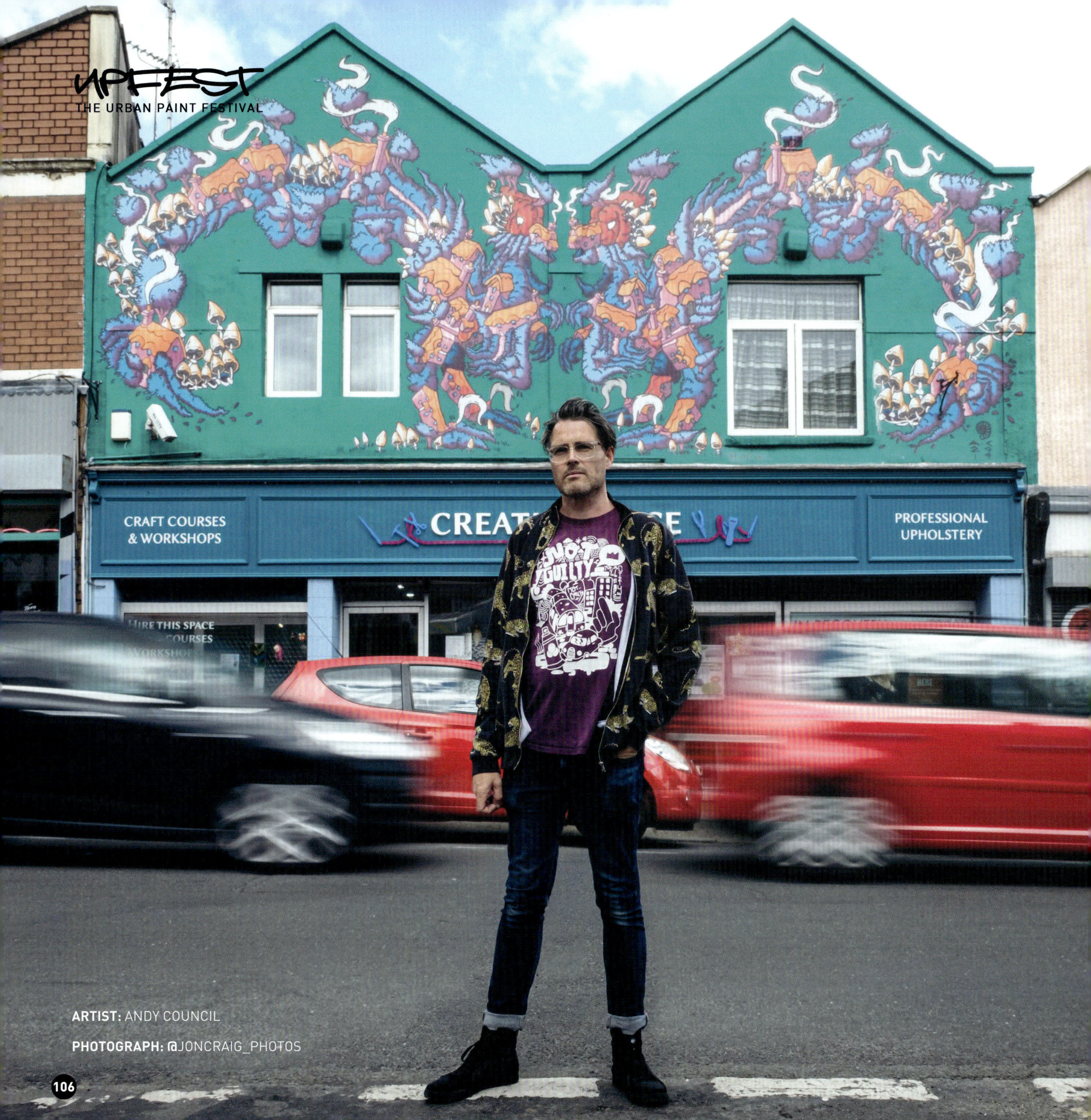

ARTIST: ANDY COUNCIL

PHOTOGRAPH: @JONCRAIG_PHOTOS

SUMMER EDITIONS.

Upfest Summer Editions kicked off in 2019, driven by the need for the Crew to take a fallow year and have a break from the festival yet wanting to keep the walls changing. Selfishly having artists in town that the team could spend proper time with and maybe the odd beer was a real highlight for us making it feel like 2008 once again.

With the Upfest Summer Editions extending into 2020 due to the dreaded C word we were just thankful for being able to get back outside and bring even more colour to the streets of South Bristol. Speaking to many members of our community, they're grateful for the efforts of all the artists who continue to help change the visual landscape of our amazing city, this motivates us no end to keep on getting out and getting UP!

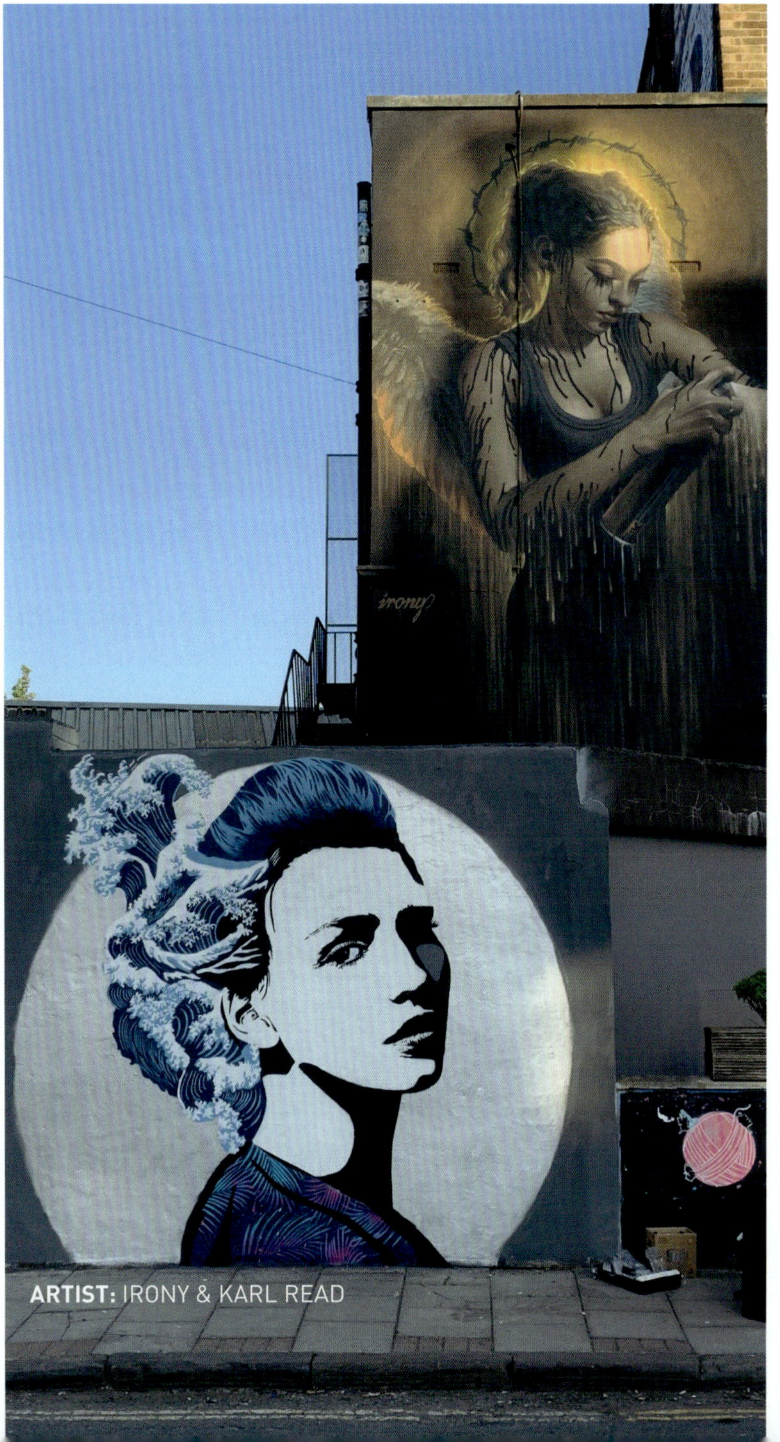

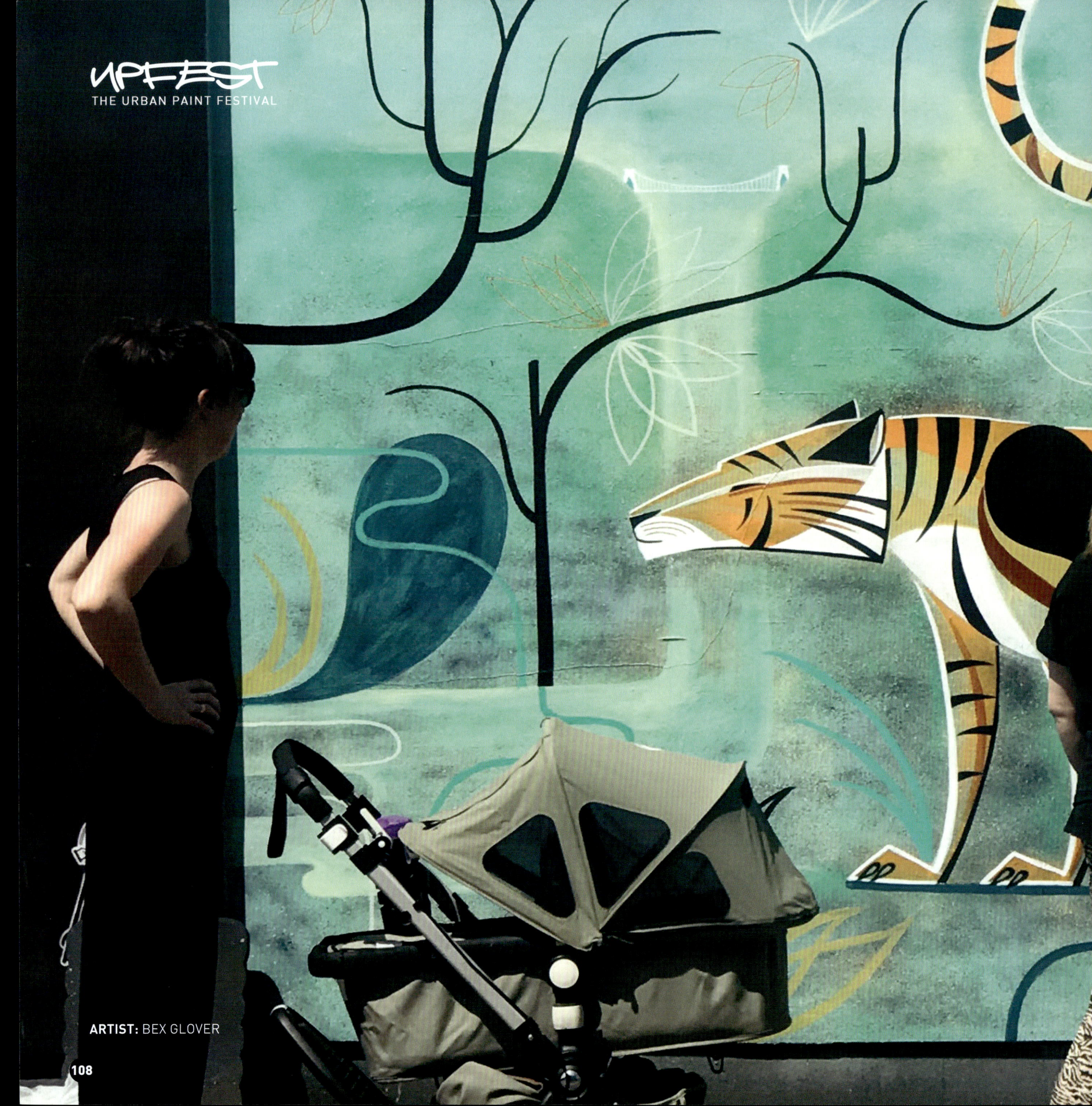

ARTIST: BEX GLOVER

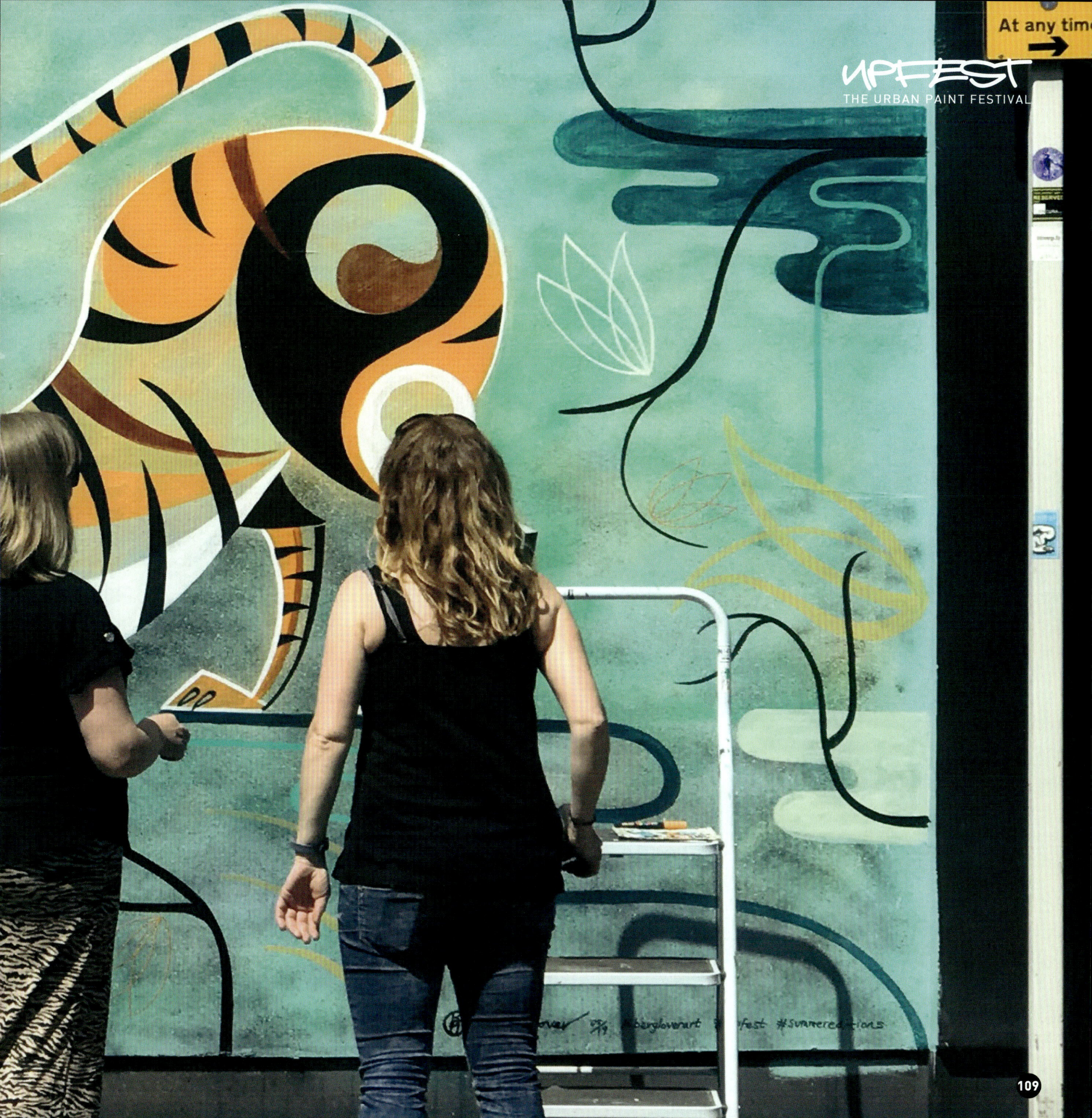

At any time
UPFEST
THE URBAN PAINT FESTIVAL

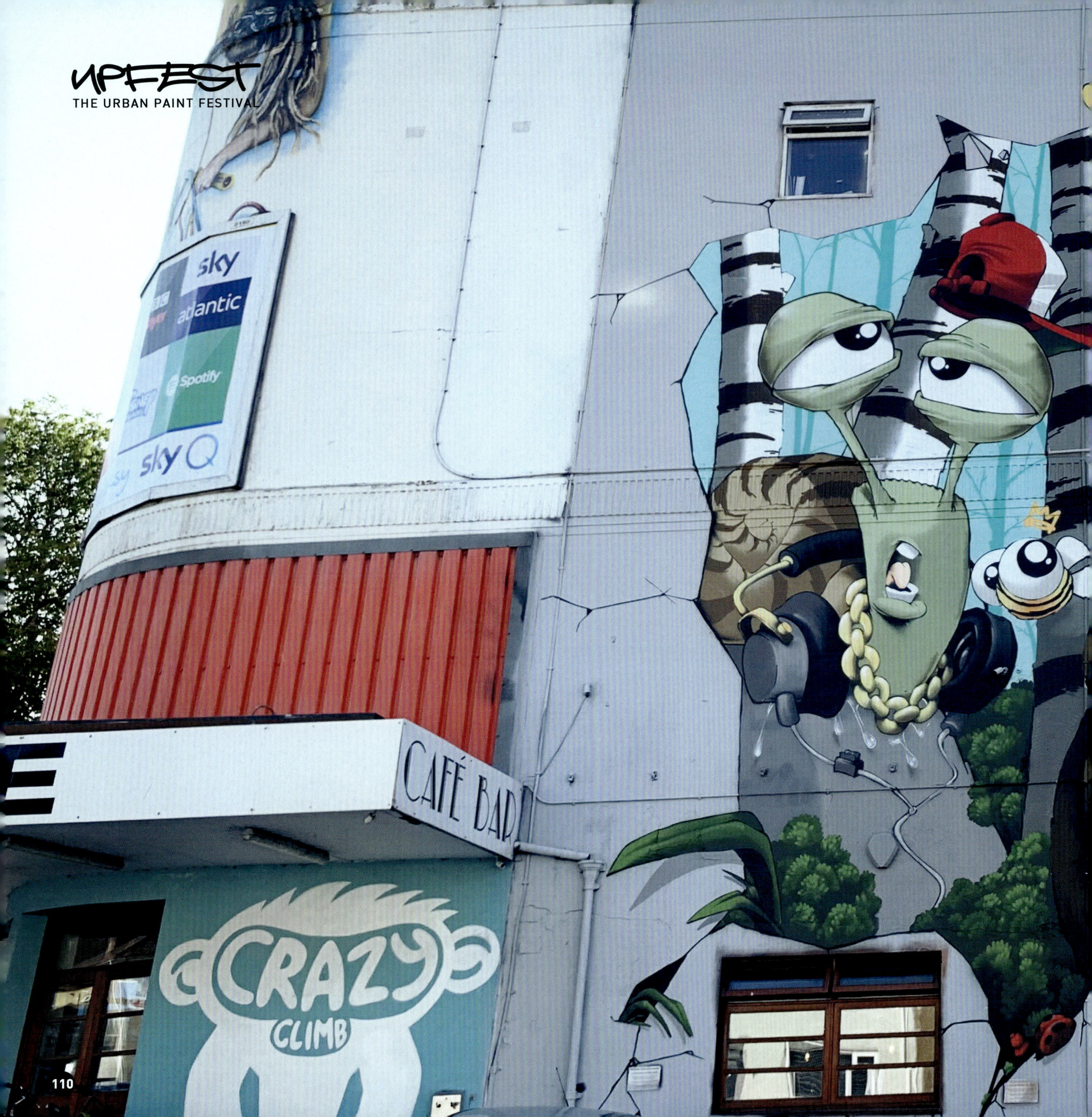
UPFEST
THE URBAN PAINT FESTIVAL
sky
atlantic
Spotify
sky Q
sky
CAFÉ BAR
CRAZY
CLIMB

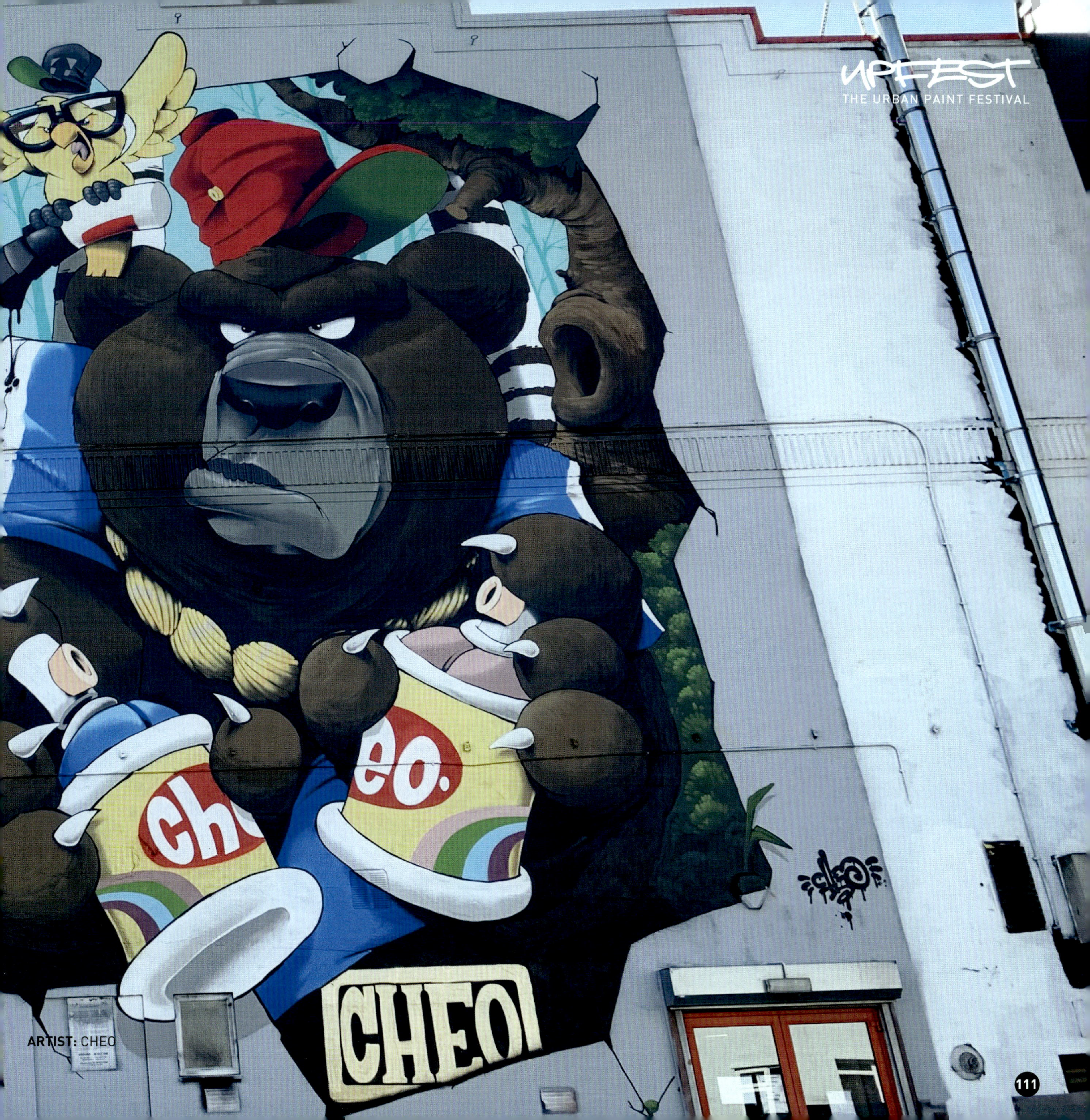

UPFEST
THE URBAN PAINT FESTIVAL
cho
eo.
CHEO

ARTIST: CHEO

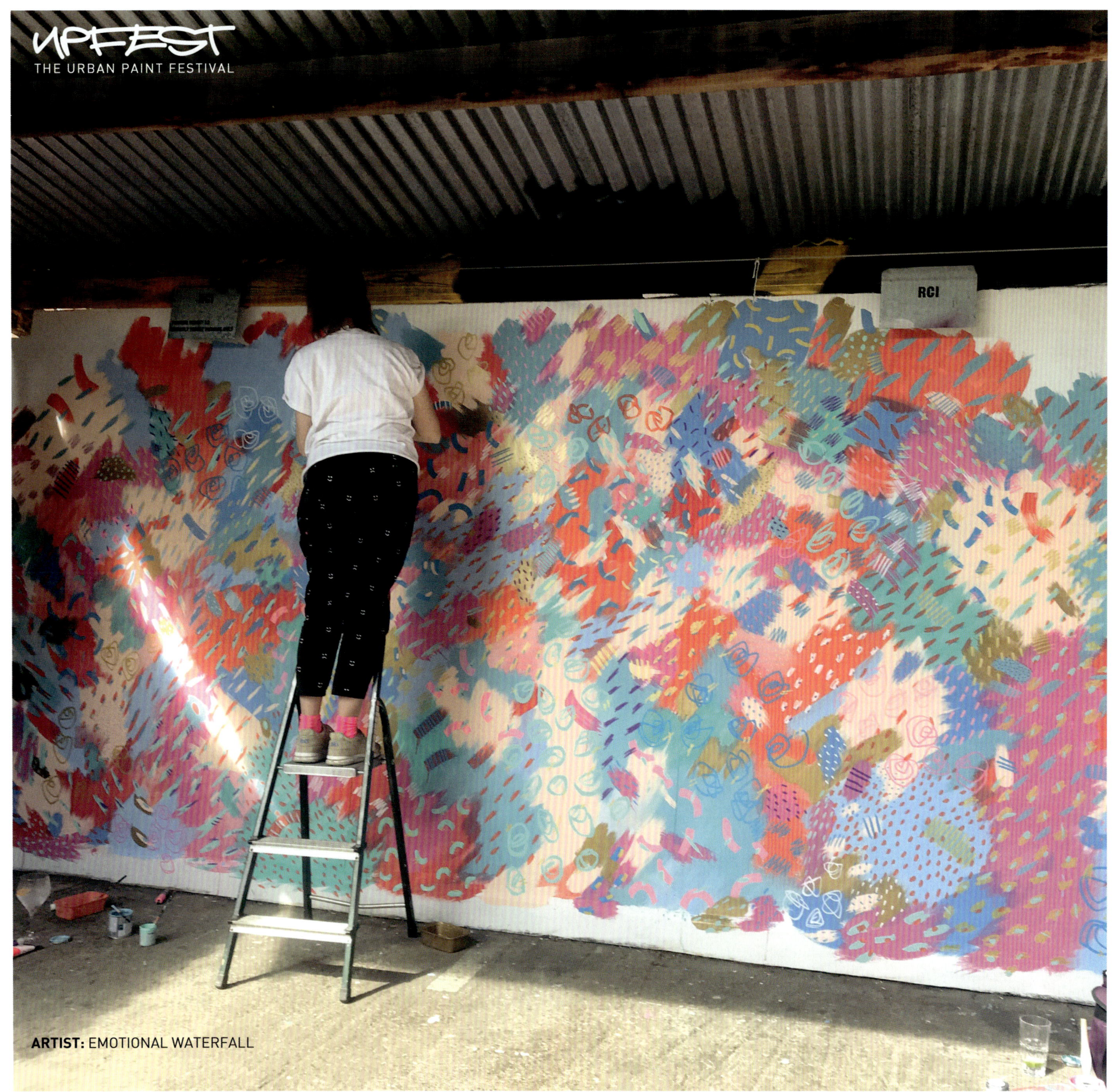

ARTIST: EMOTIONAL WATERFALL

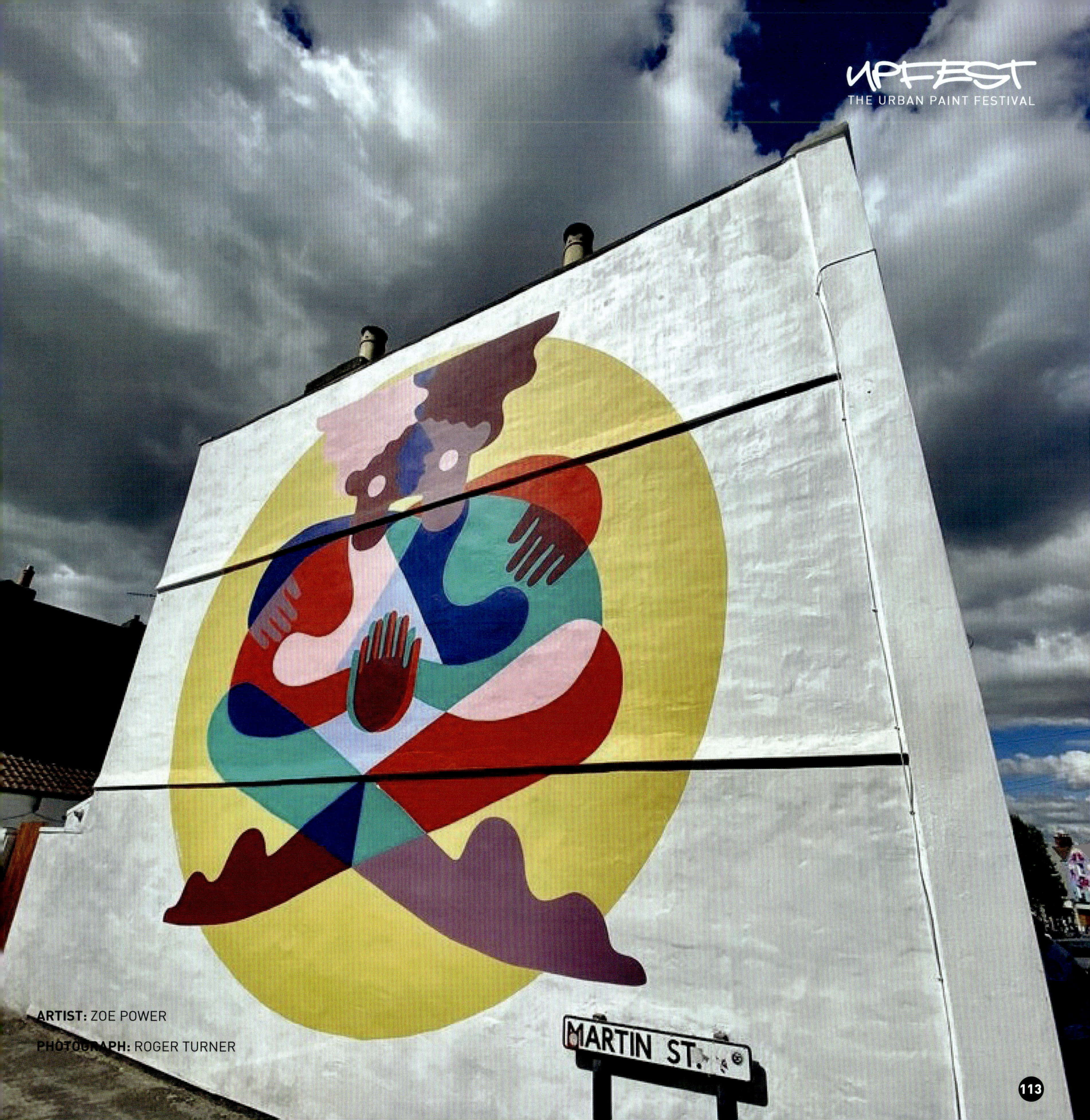
UPFEST
THE URBAN PAINT FESTIVAL
MARTIN ST.
ARTIST: ZOE POWER
PHOTOGRAPH: ROGER TURNER
113

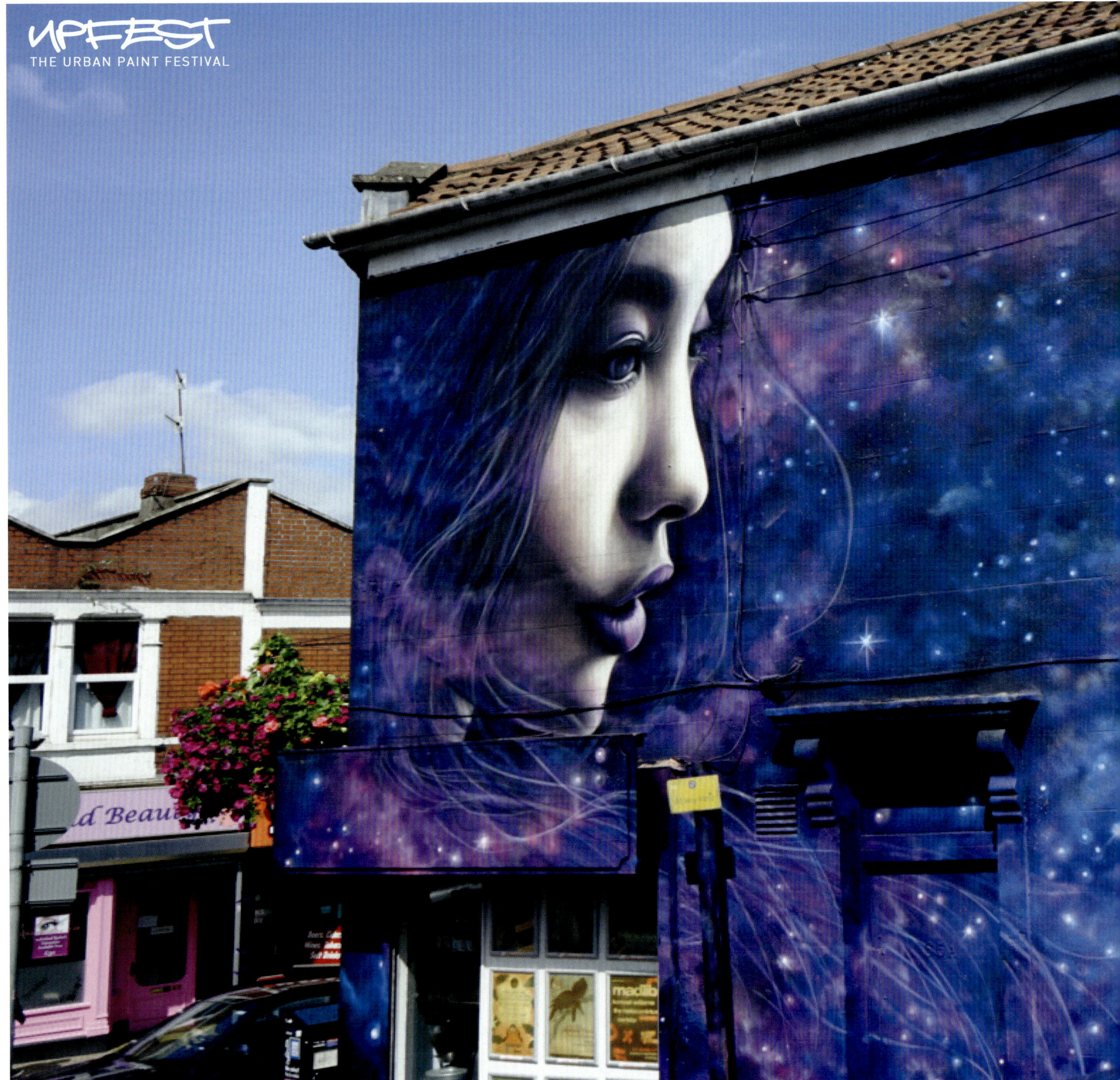

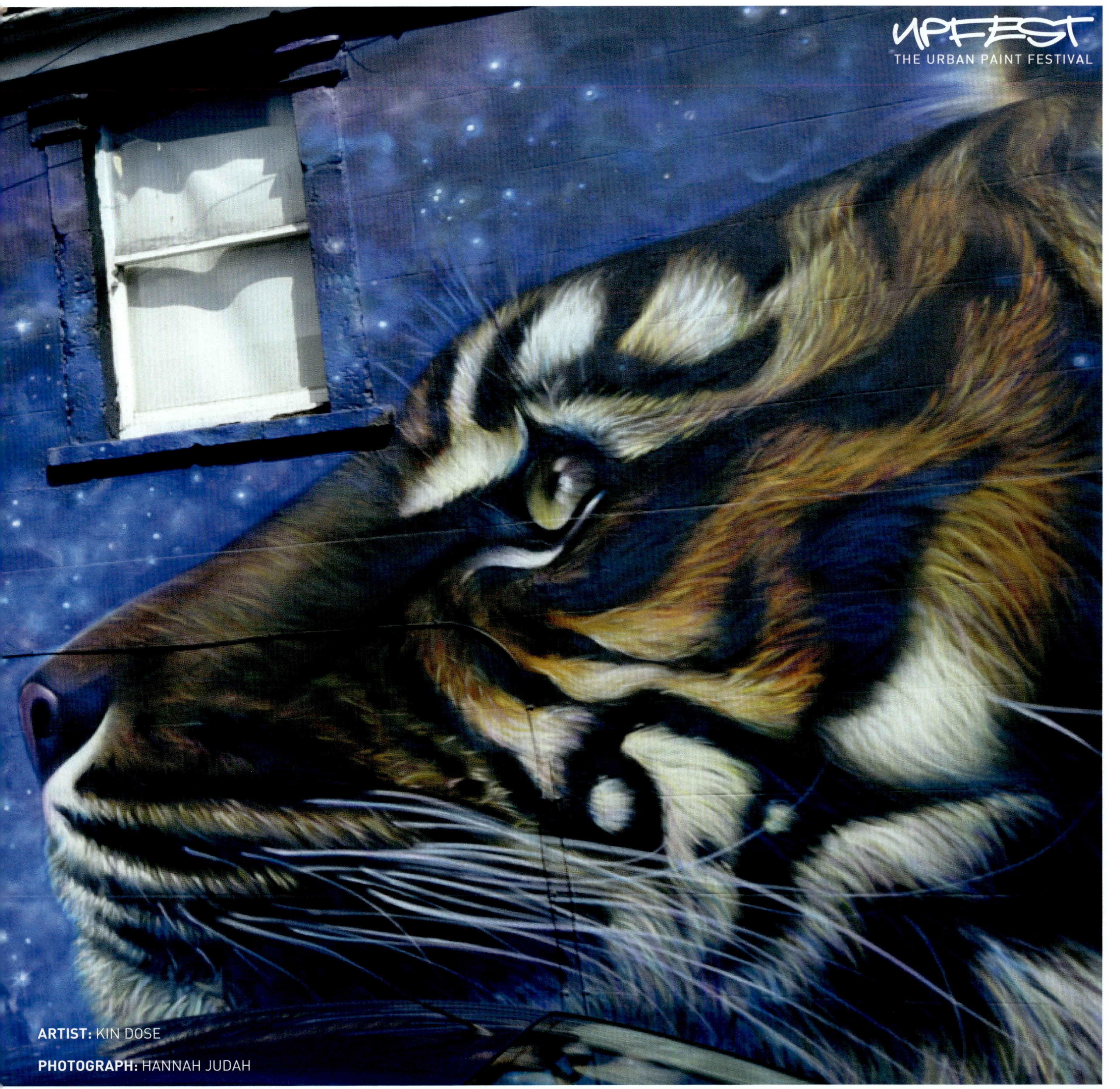

ARTIST: KIN DOSE

PHOTOGRAPH: HANNAH JUDAH

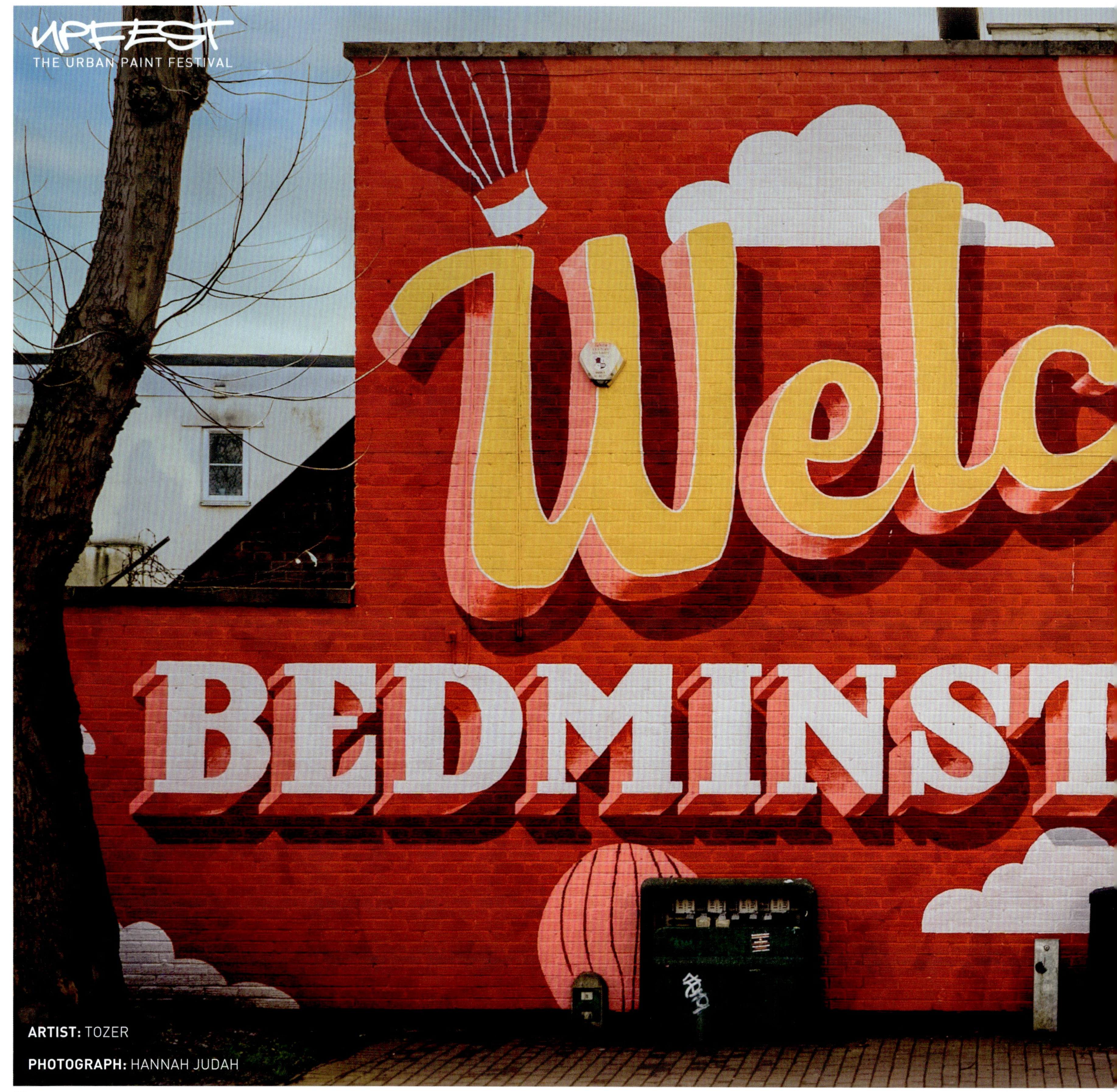

ARTIST: TOZER

PHOTOGRAPH: HANNAH JUDAH

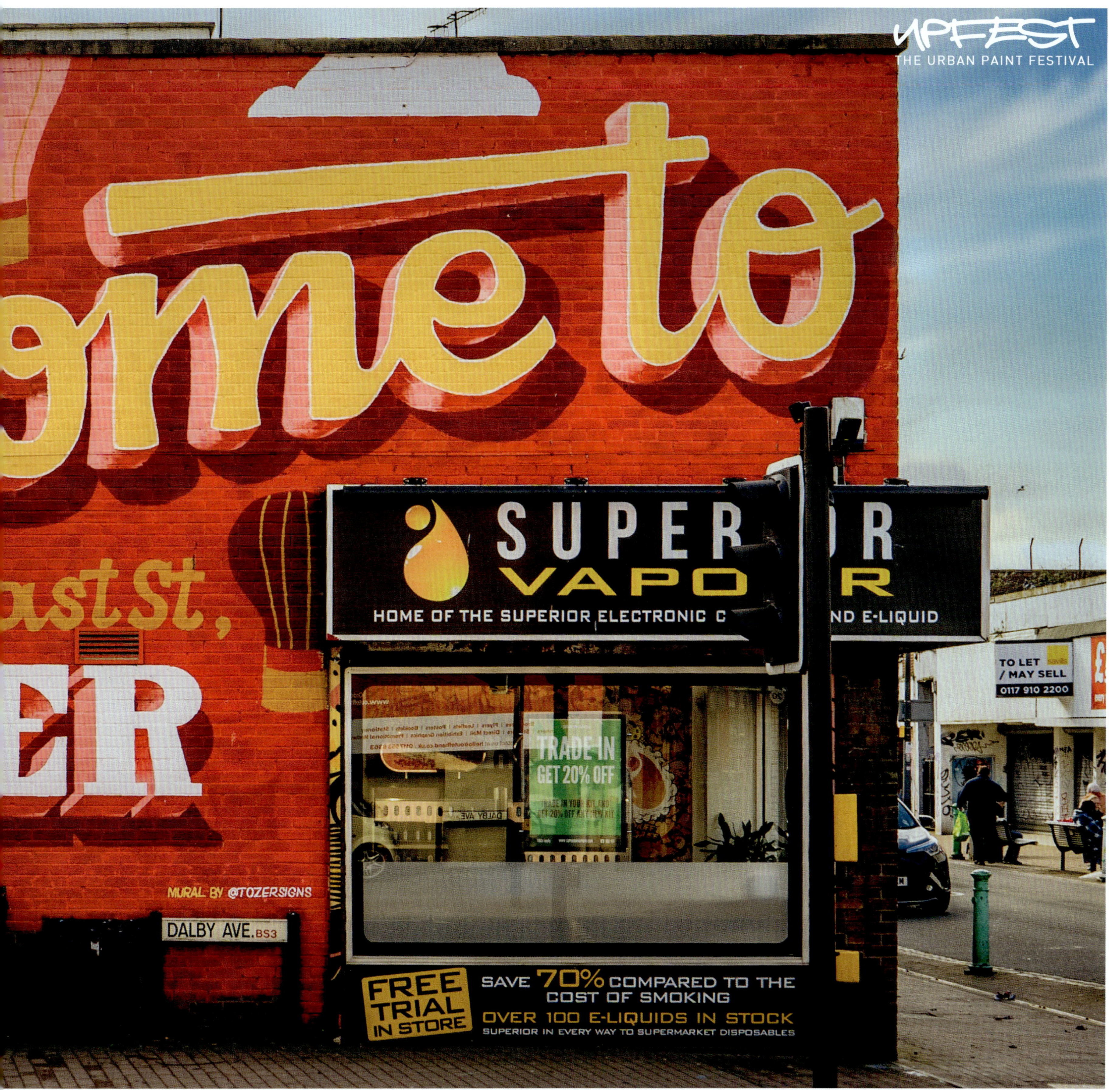
UPFEST
THE URBAN PAINT FESTIVAL
me to
to
ome
ast St,
ER
ER
SUPER
VAPO
R
HOME OF THE SUPERIOR ELECTRONIC C
ND E-LIQUID
TRADE IN
GET 20% OFF
TO LET
/ MAY SELL
0117 910 2200
MURAL BY @TOZERSIGNS
DALBY AVE. BS3
FREE
TRIAL
IN STORE
SAVE 70% COMPARED TO THE
COST OF SMOKING
OVER 100 E-LIQUIDS IN STOCK
SUPERIOR IN EVERY WAY TO SUPERMARKET DISPOSABLES

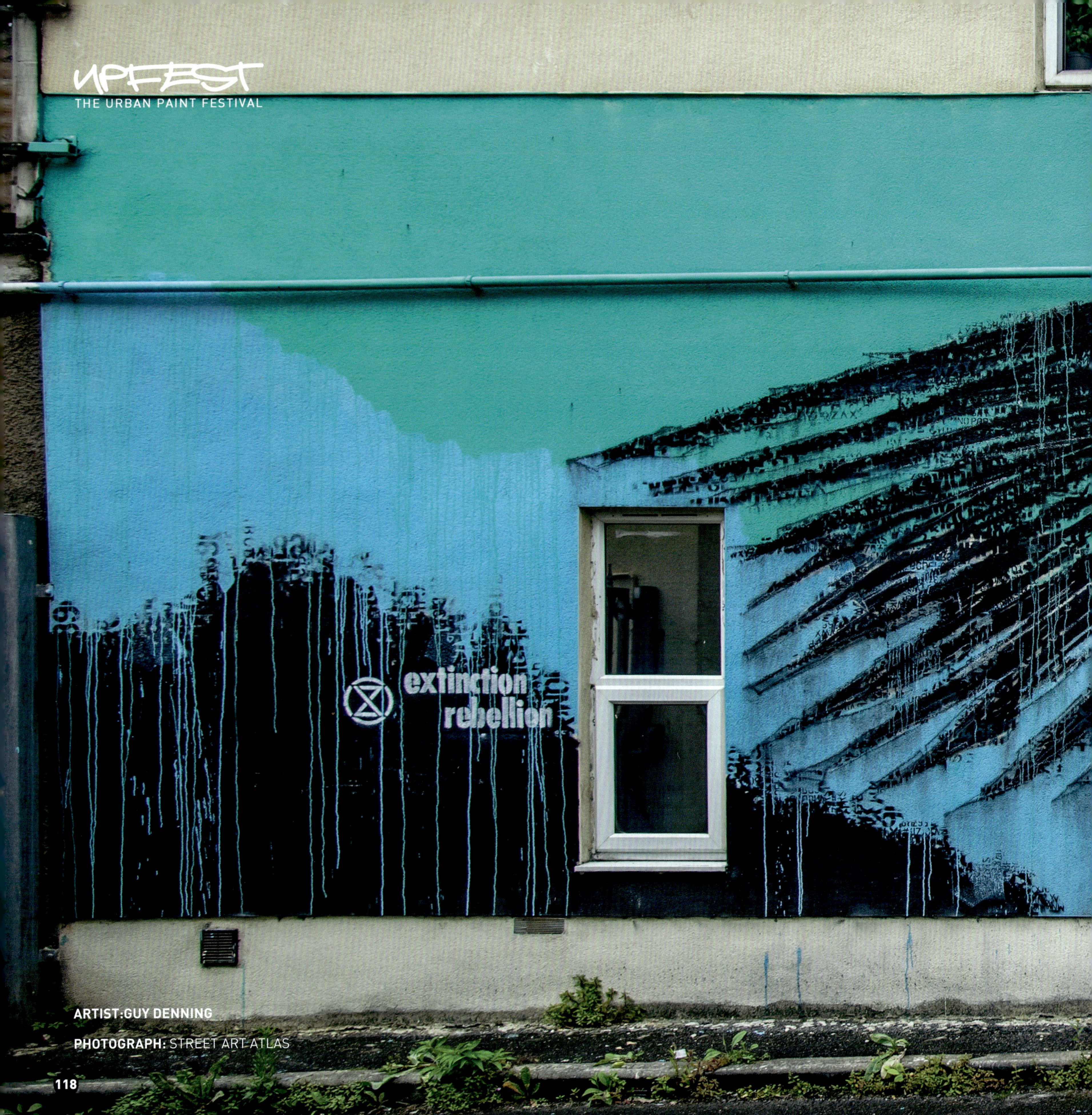

ARTIST: GUY DENNING

PHOTOGRAPH: STREET ART ATLAS

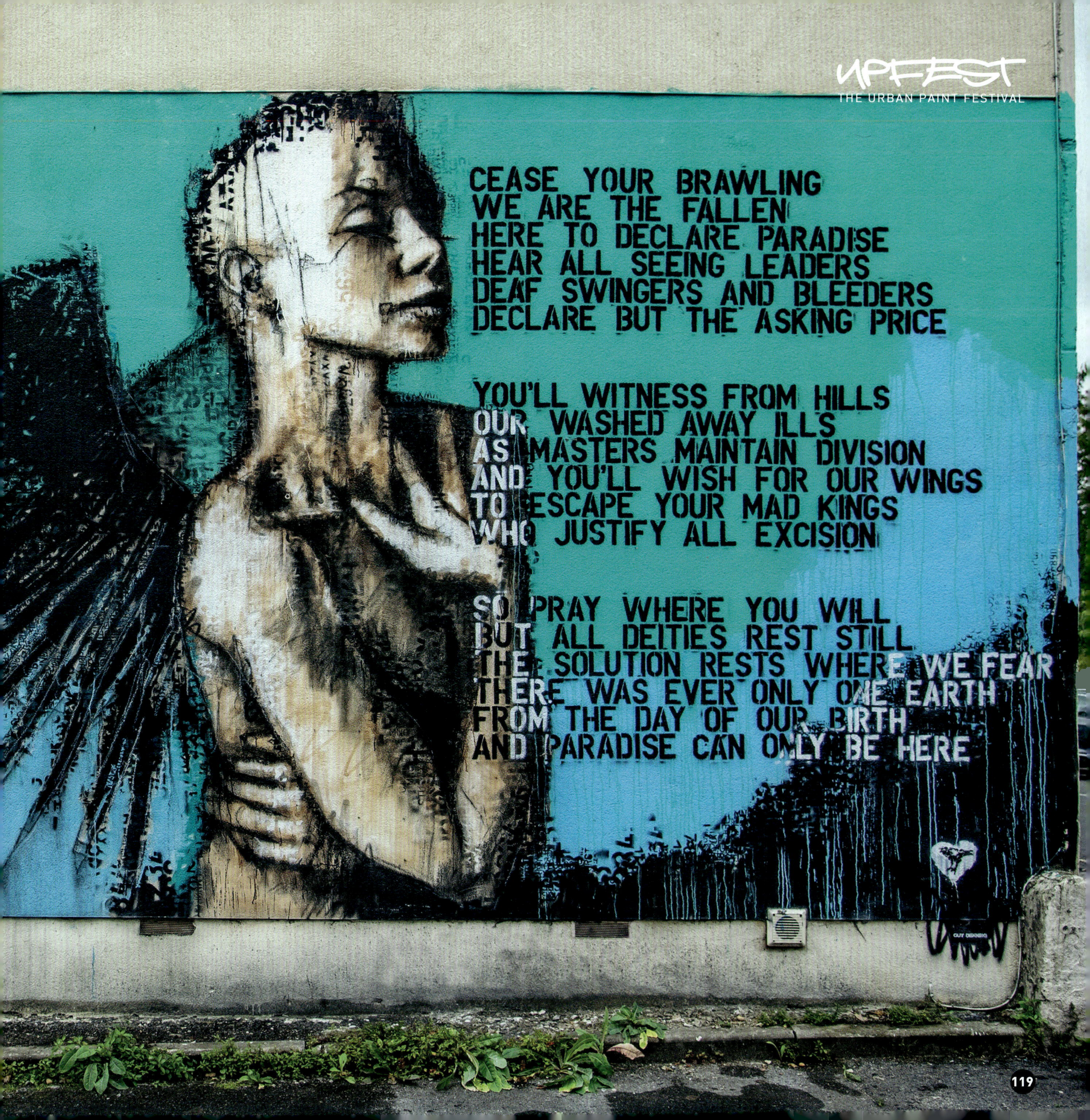

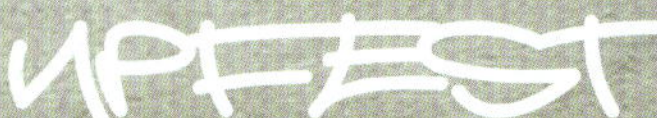
UPFEST
THE URBAN PAINT FESTIVAL

CEASE YOUR BRAWLING
WE ARE THE FALLEN
HERE TO DECLARE PARADISE
HEAR ALL SEEING LEADERS
DEAF SWINGERS AND BLEEDERS
DECLARE BUT THE ASKING PRICE

YOU'LL WITNESS FROM HILLS
OUR WASHED AWAY ILLS
AS MASTERS MAINTAIN DIVISION
AND YOU'LL WISH FOR OUR WINGS
TO ESCAPE YOUR MAD KINGS
WHO JUSTIFY ALL EXCISION

SO PRAY WHERE YOU WILL
BUT ALL DEITIES REST STILL
THE SOLUTION RESTS WHERE WE FEAR
THERE WAS EVER ONLY ONE EARTH
FROM THE DAY OF OUR BIRTH
AND PARADISE CAN ONLY BE HERE

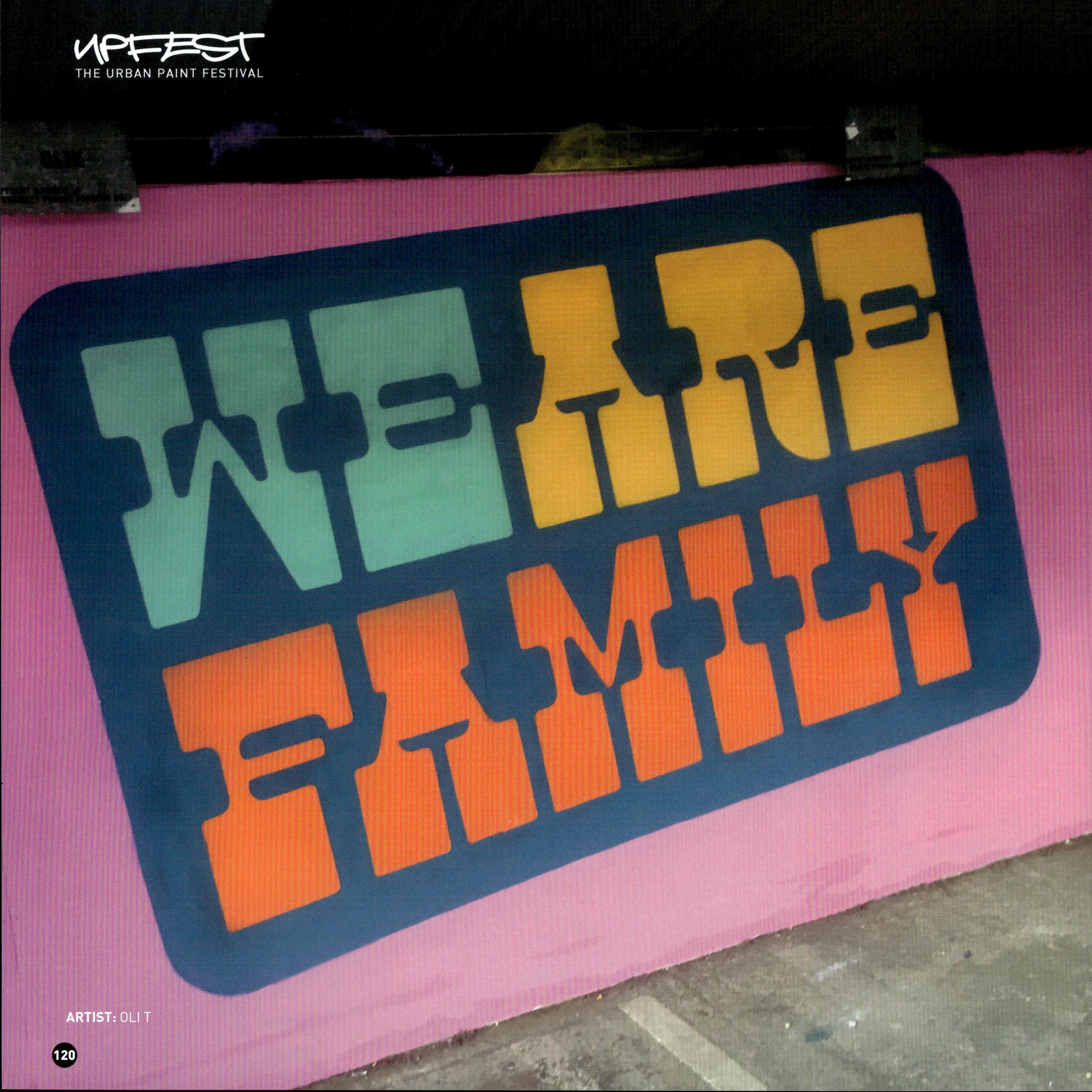

UPFEST
THE URBAN PAINT FESTIVAL
WE ARE FAMILY

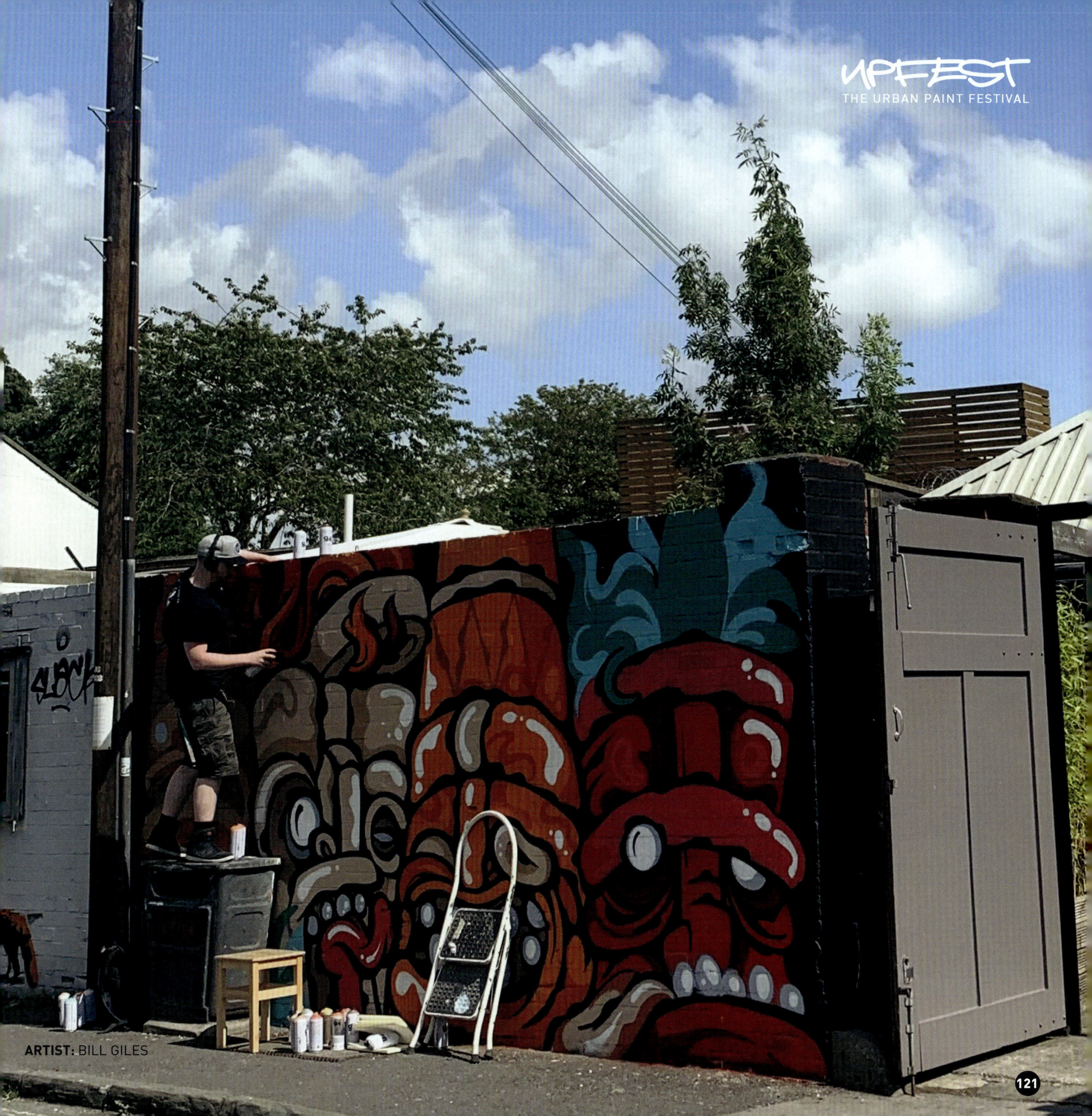

ARTIST: BILL GILES

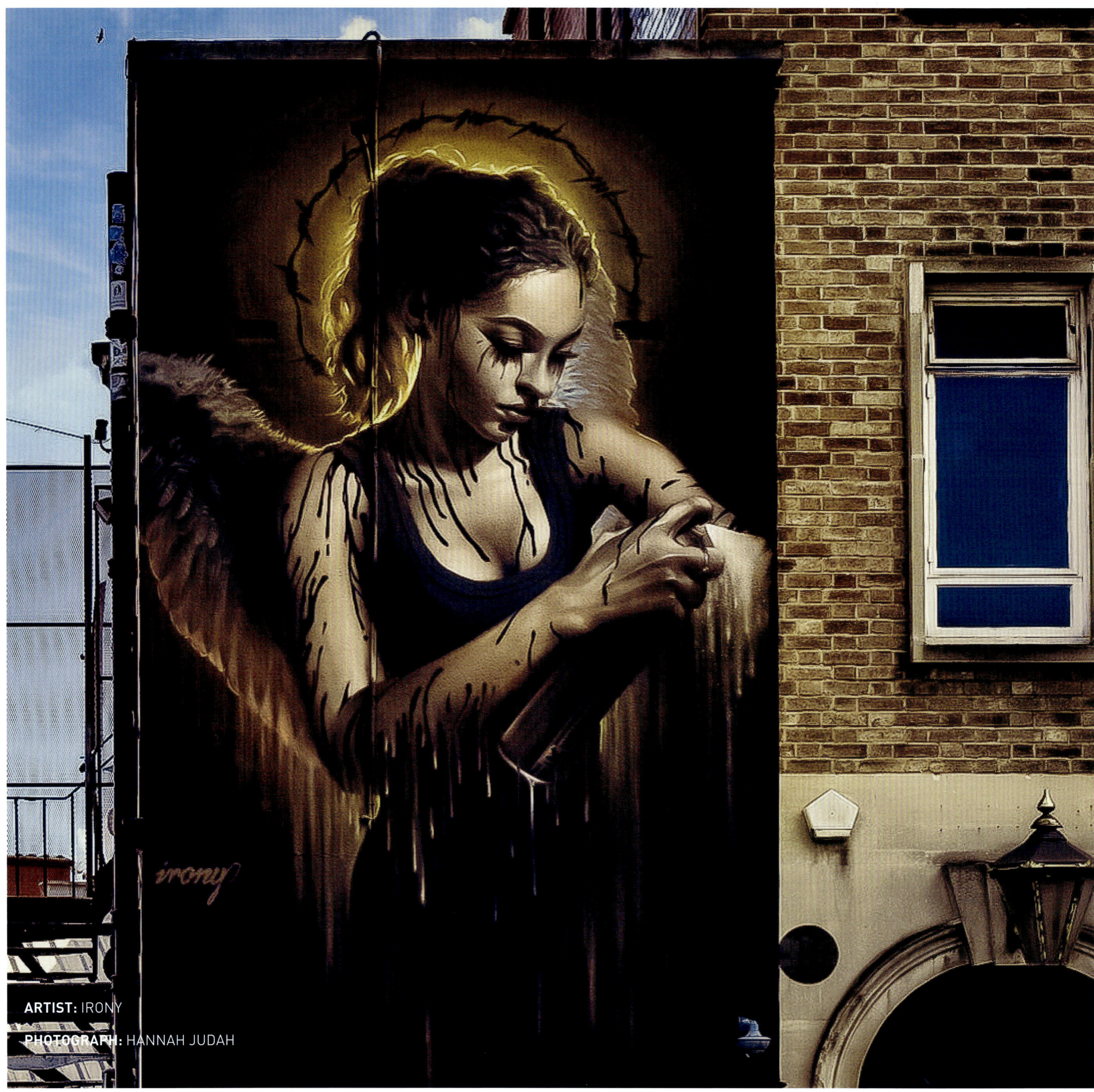

ARTIST: *IRONY*

PHOTOGRAPH: HANNAH JUDAH

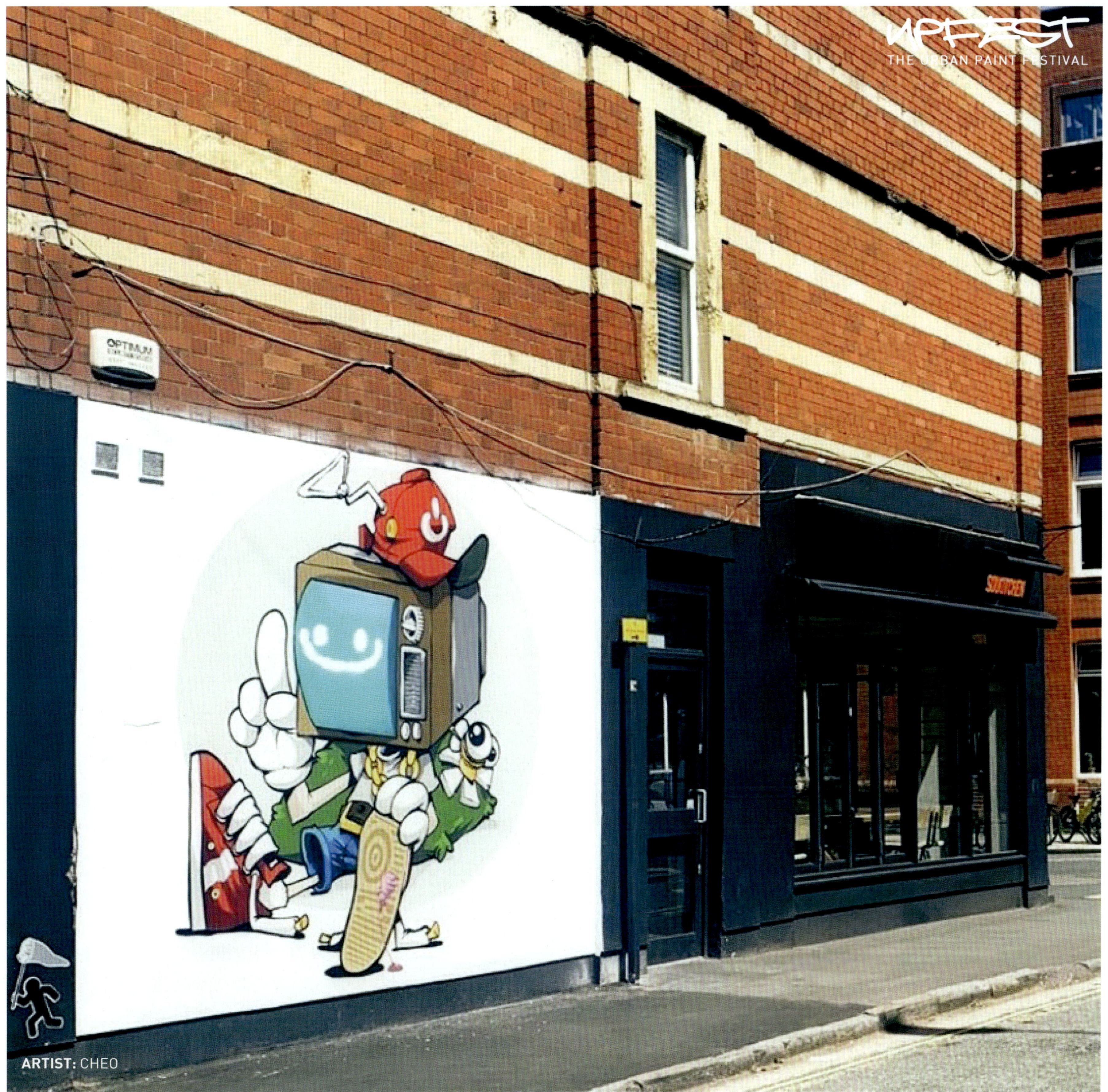

ARTIST: CHEO

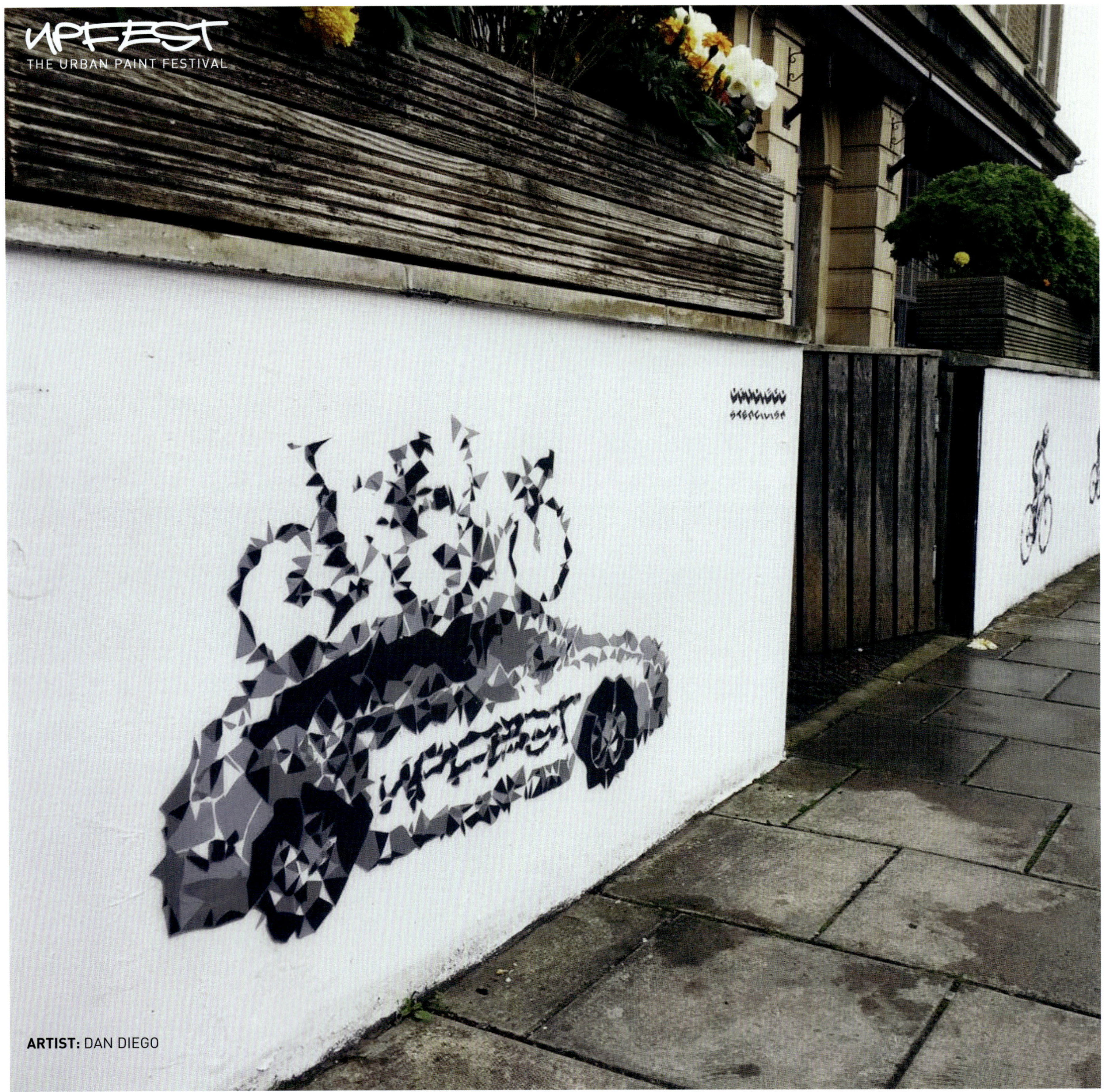

UPFEST
THE URBAN PAINT FESTIVAL

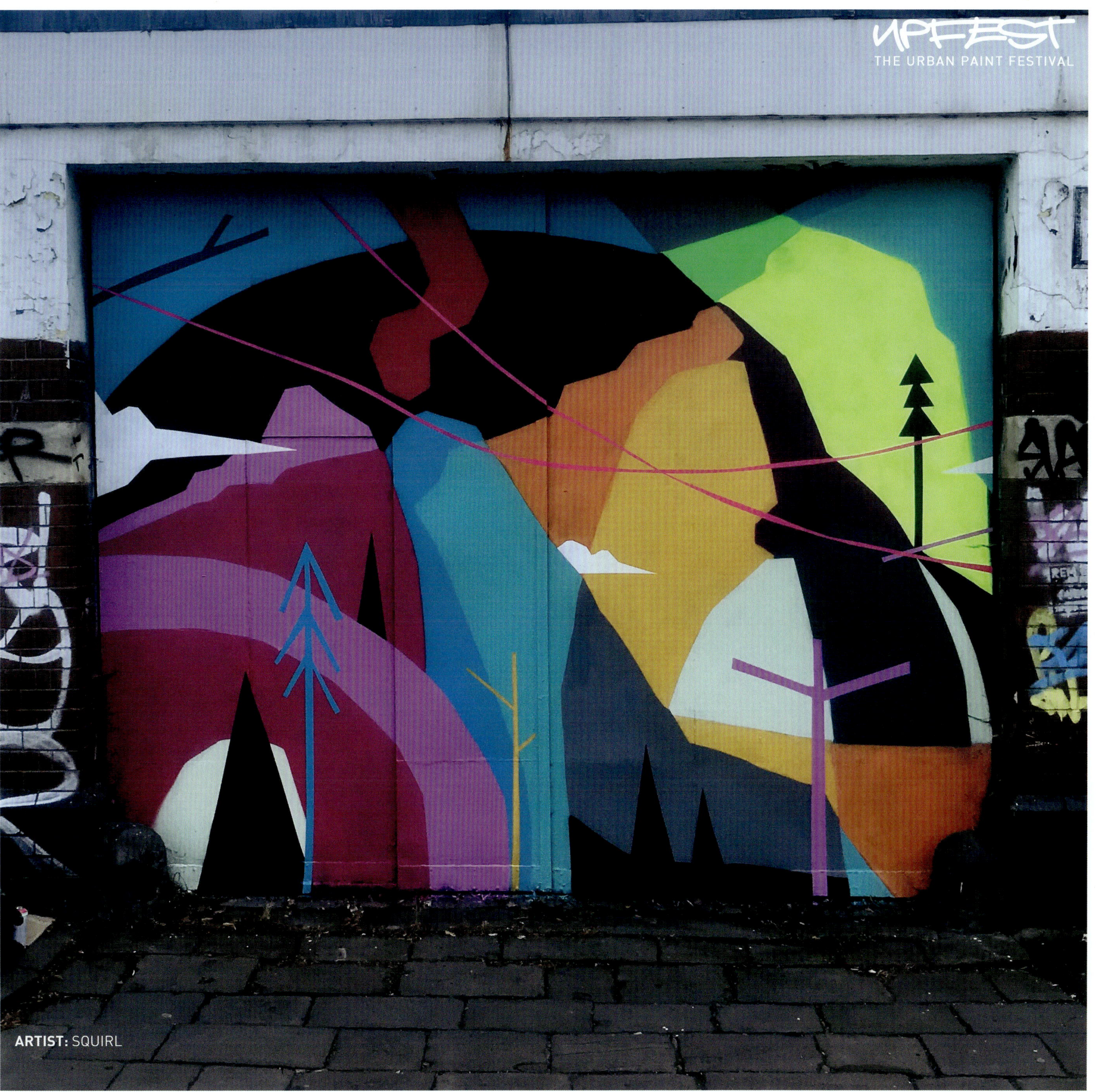
UPFEST
THE URBAN PAINT FESTIVAL
ARTIST: SQUIRL

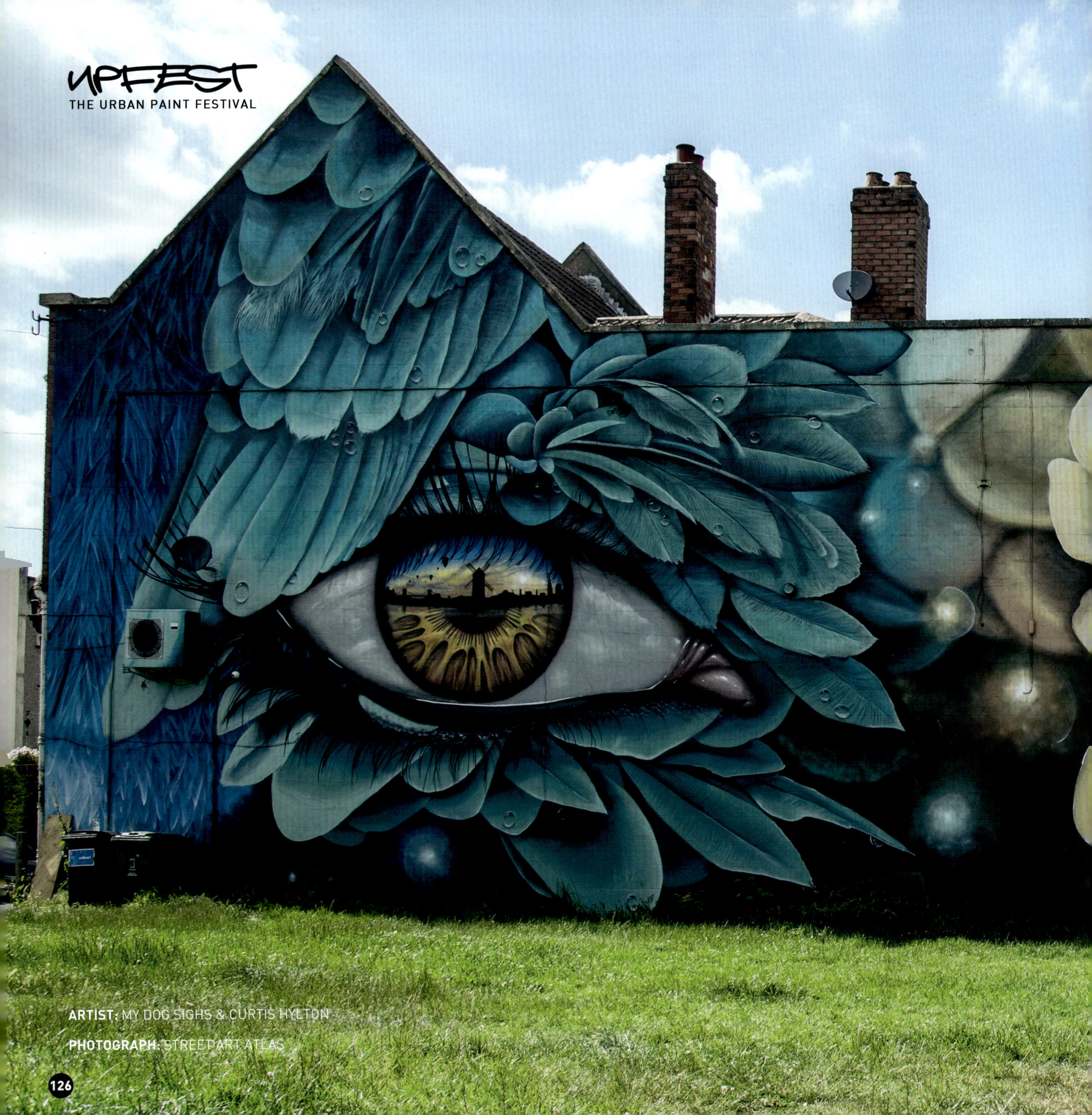

ARTIST: MY DOG SIGHS & CURTIS HYLTON

PHOTOGRAPH: STREETART ATLAS

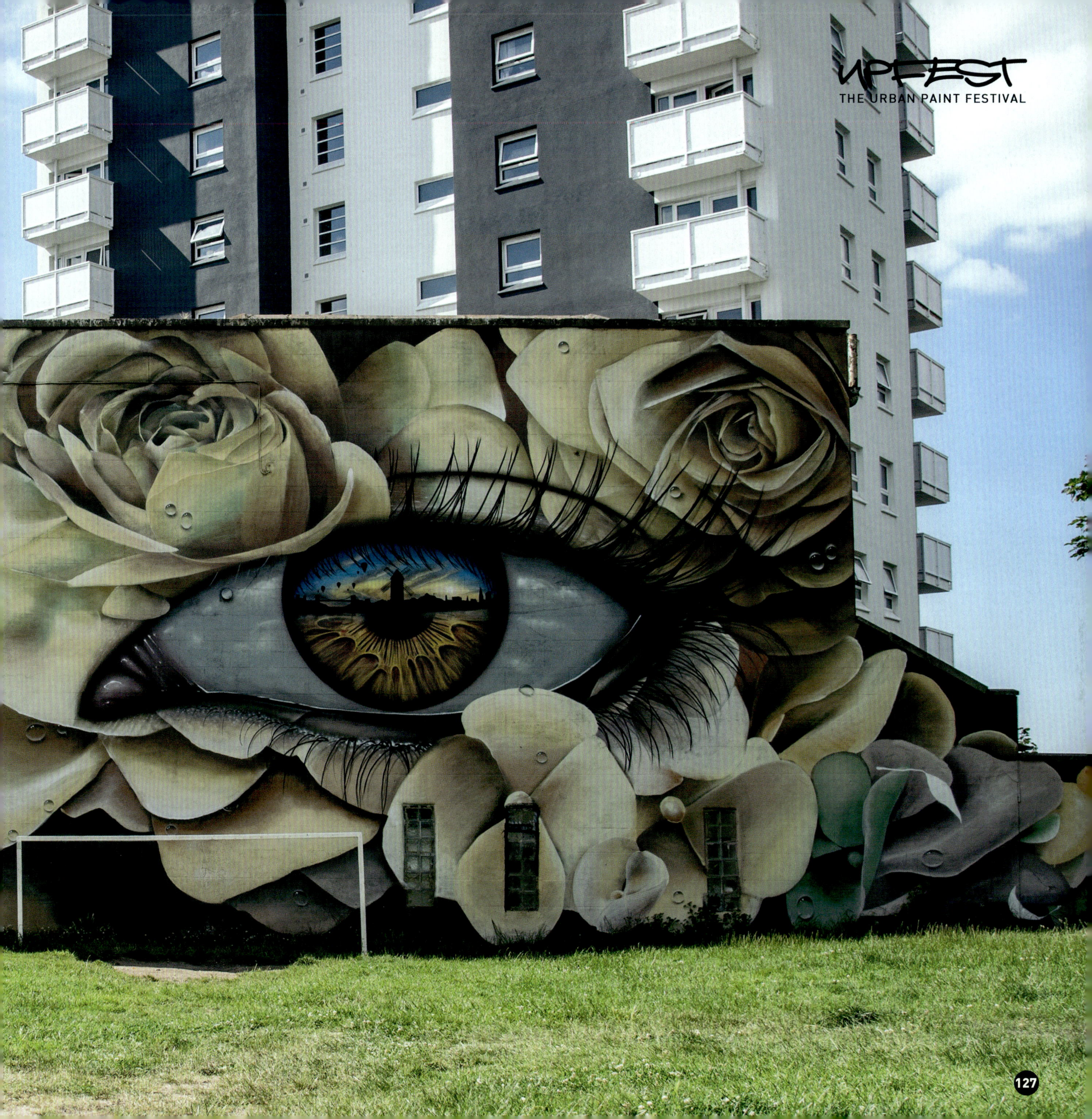

UPFEST
THE URBAN PAINT FESTIVAL

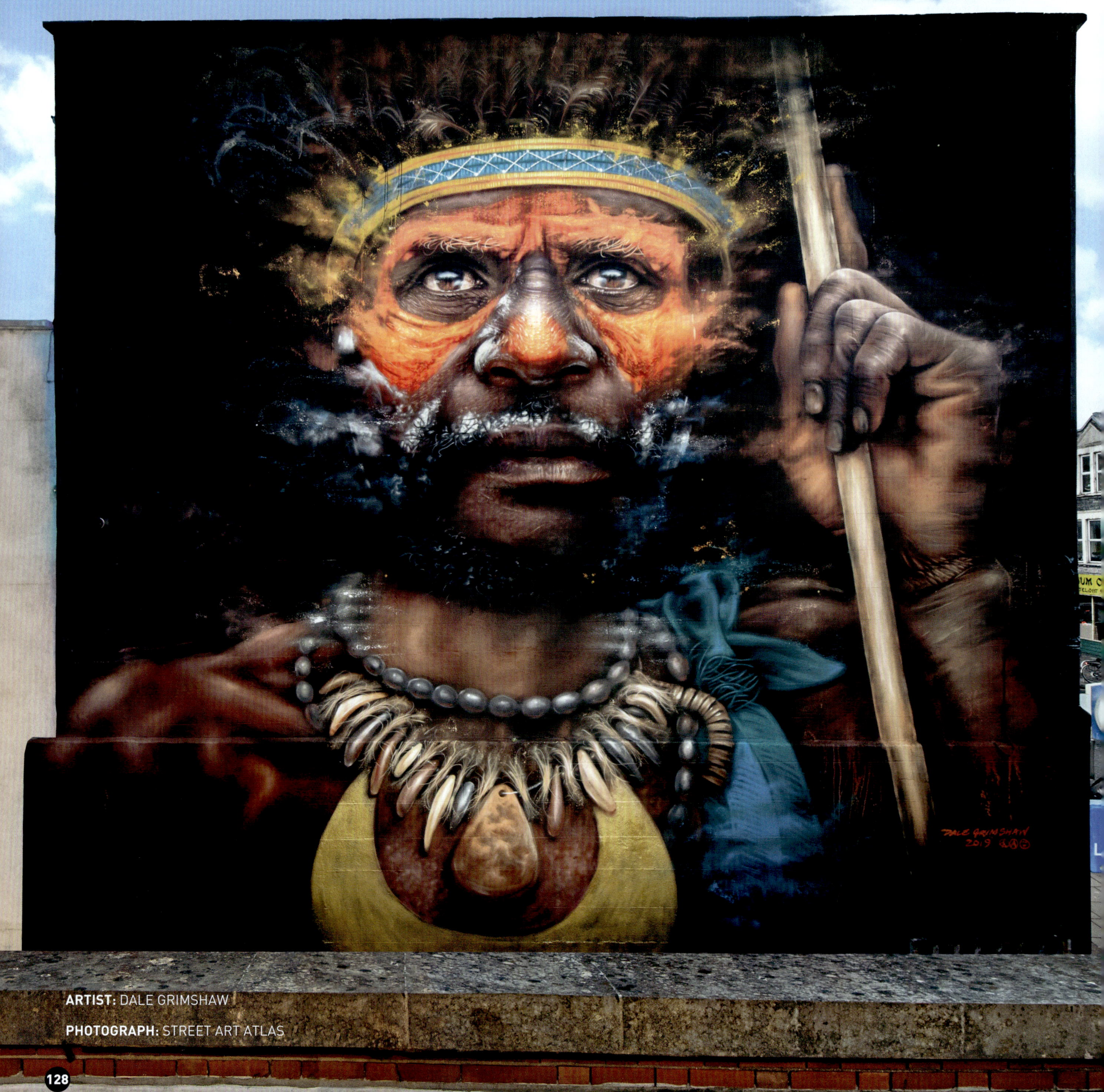

ARTIST: DALE GRIMSHAW

PHOTOGRAPH: STREET ART ATLAS

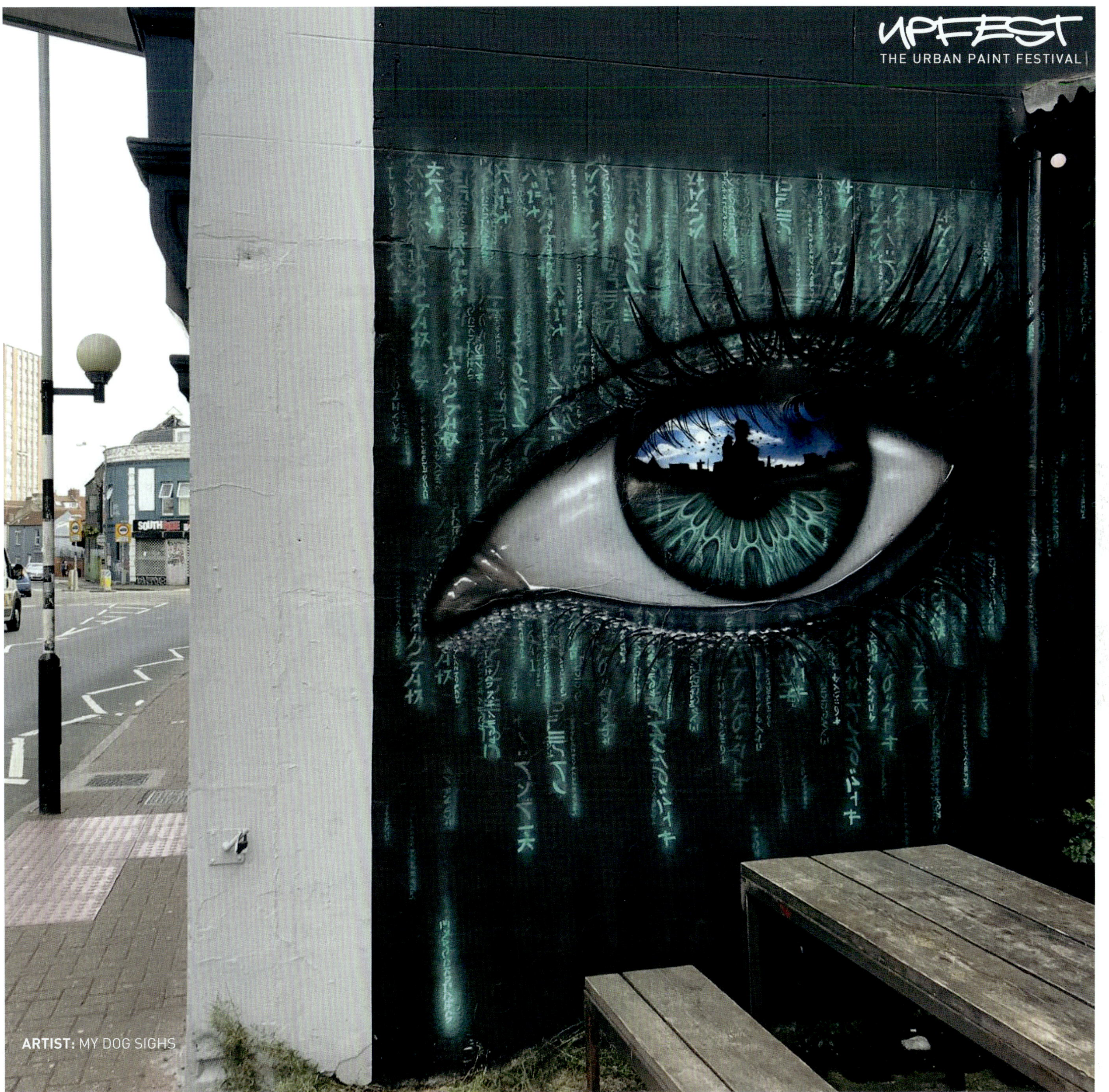

ARTIST: MY DOG SIGHS

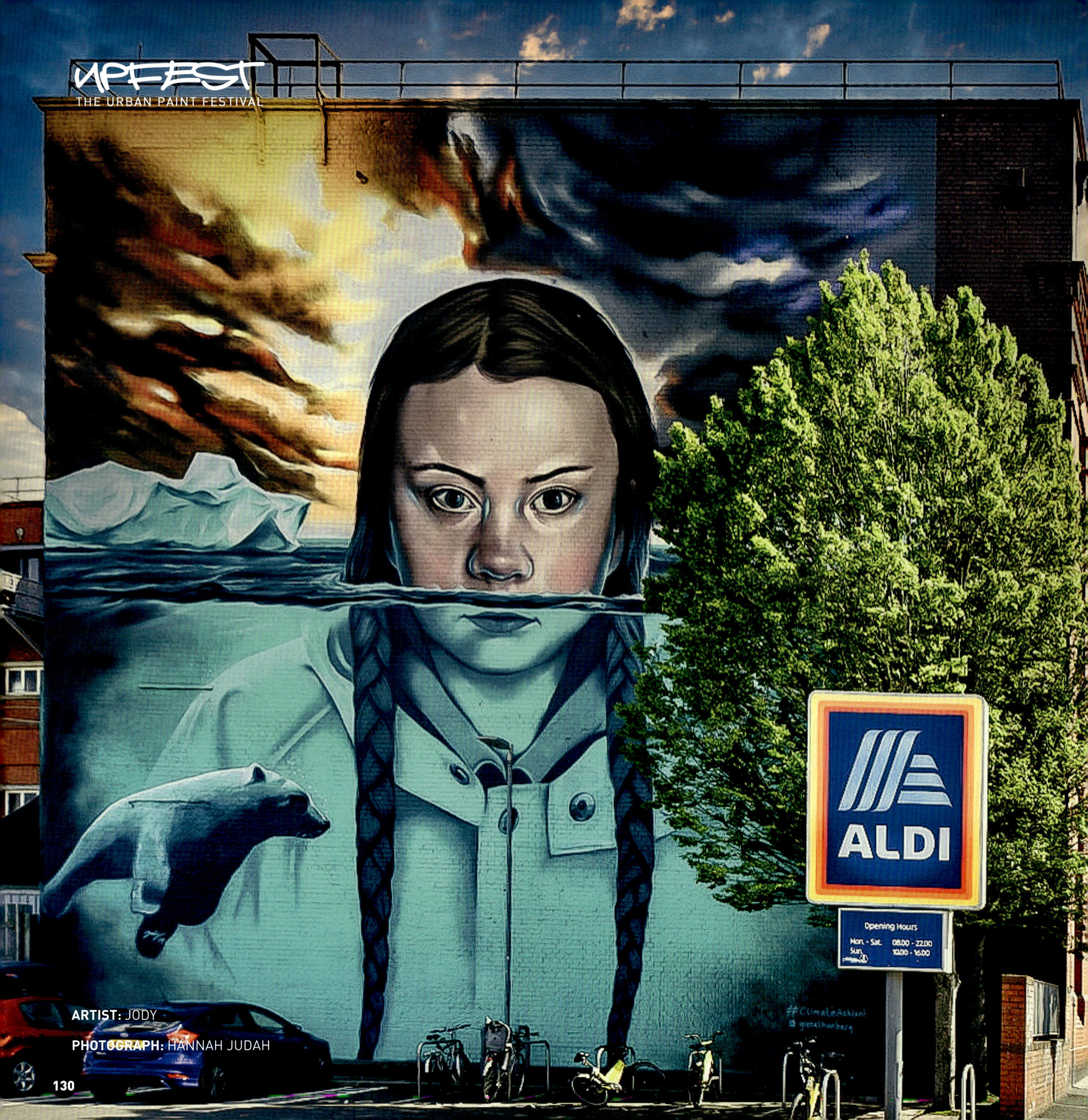

ARTIST: JODY

PHOTOGRAPH: HANNAH JUDAH

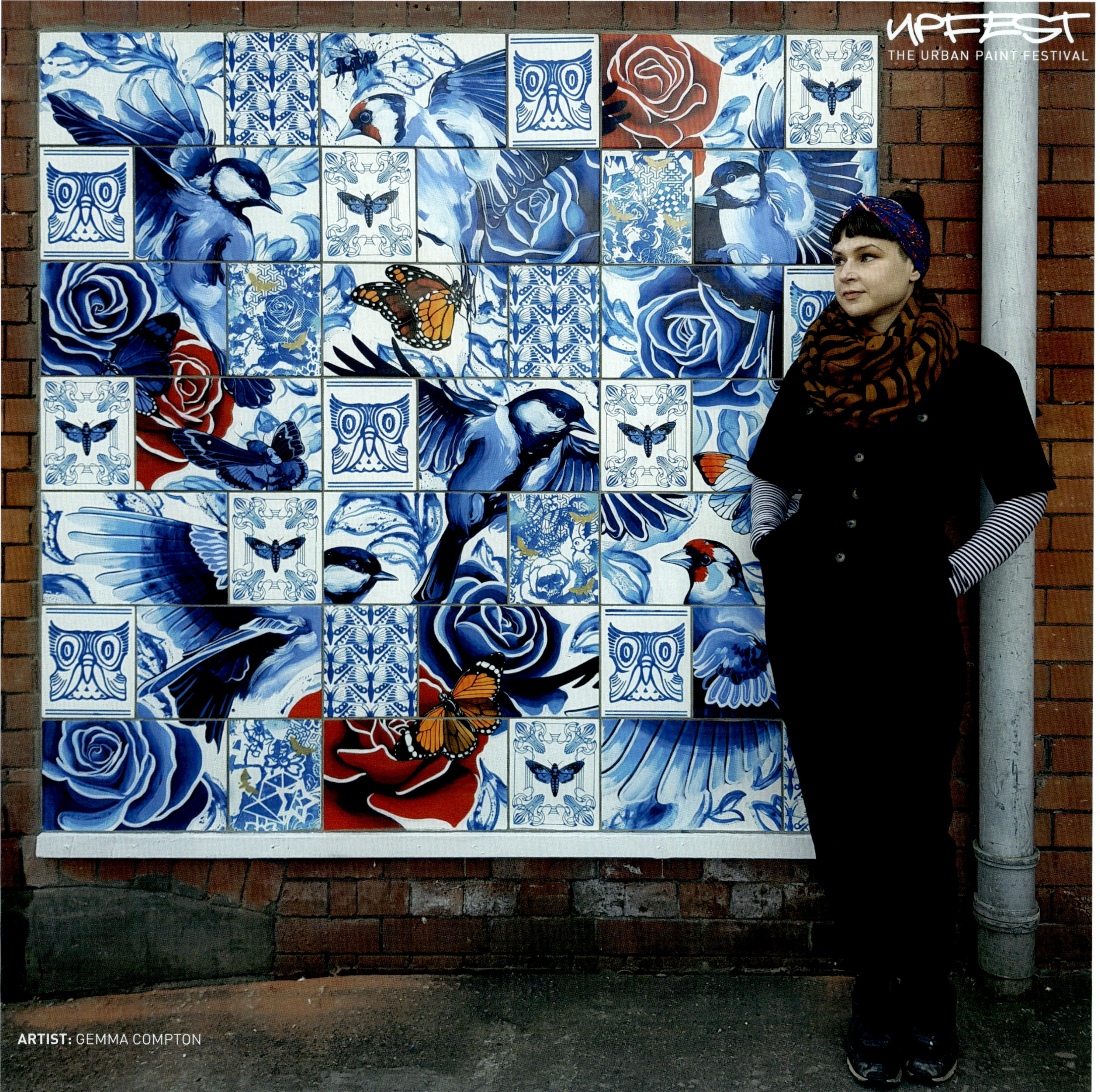
UPFEST
THE URBAN PAINT FESTIVAL
ARTIST: GEMMA COMPTON

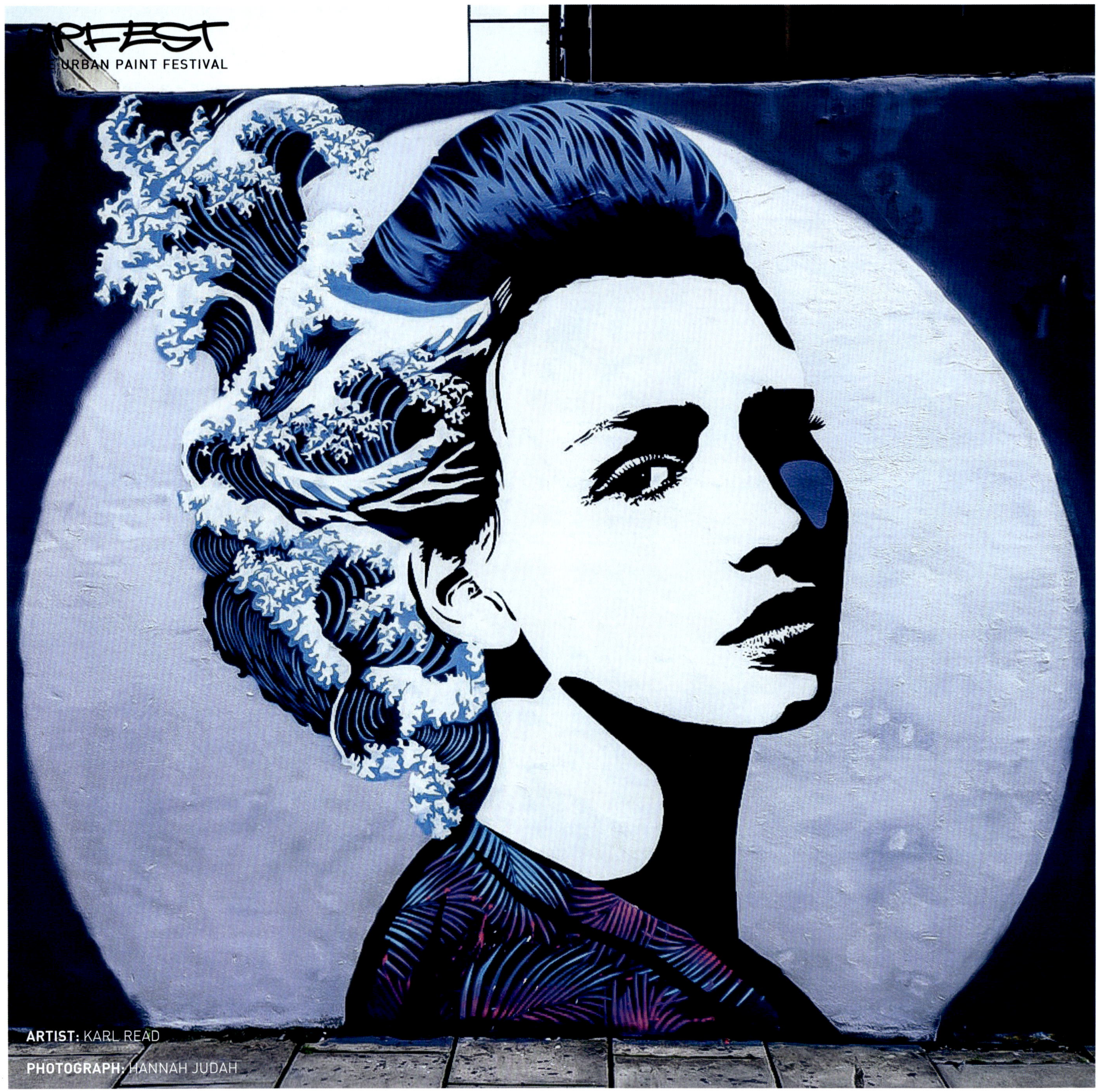
rFEST
URBAN PAINT FESTIVAL
ARTIST: KARL READ
PHOTOGRAPH: HANNAH JUDAH

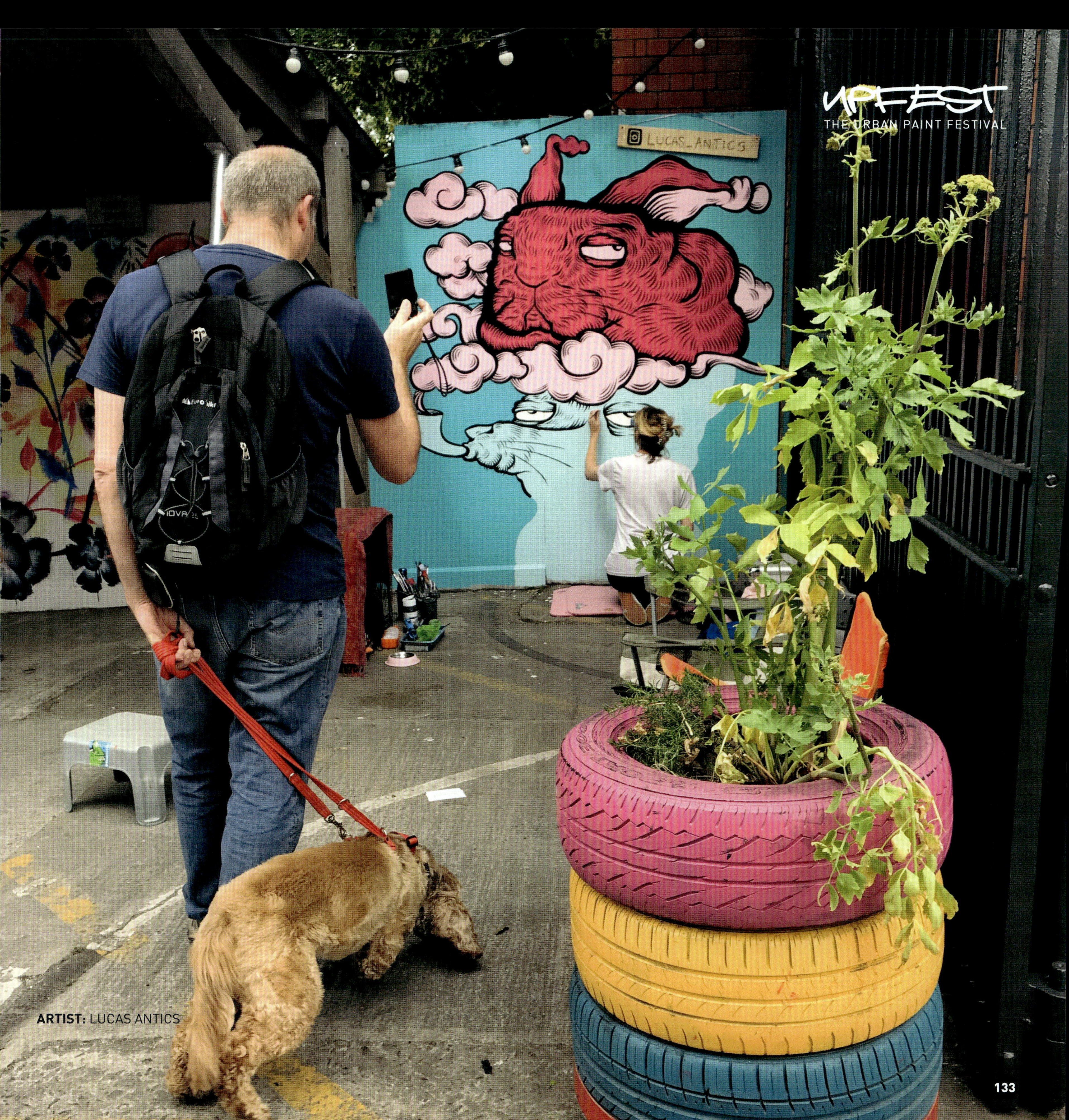

ARTIST: LUCAS ANTICS

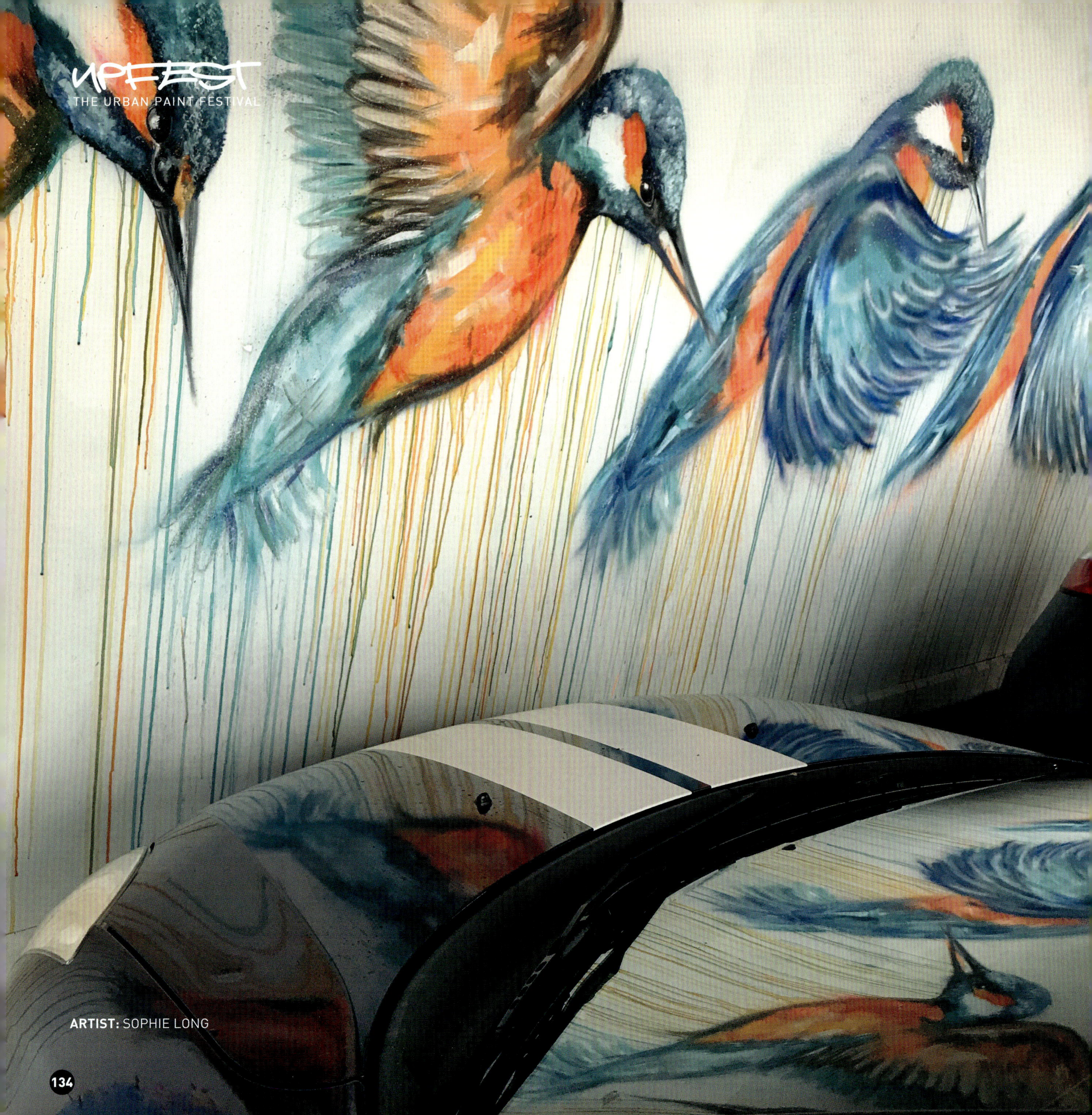
UPFEST
THE URBAN PAINT FESTIVAL

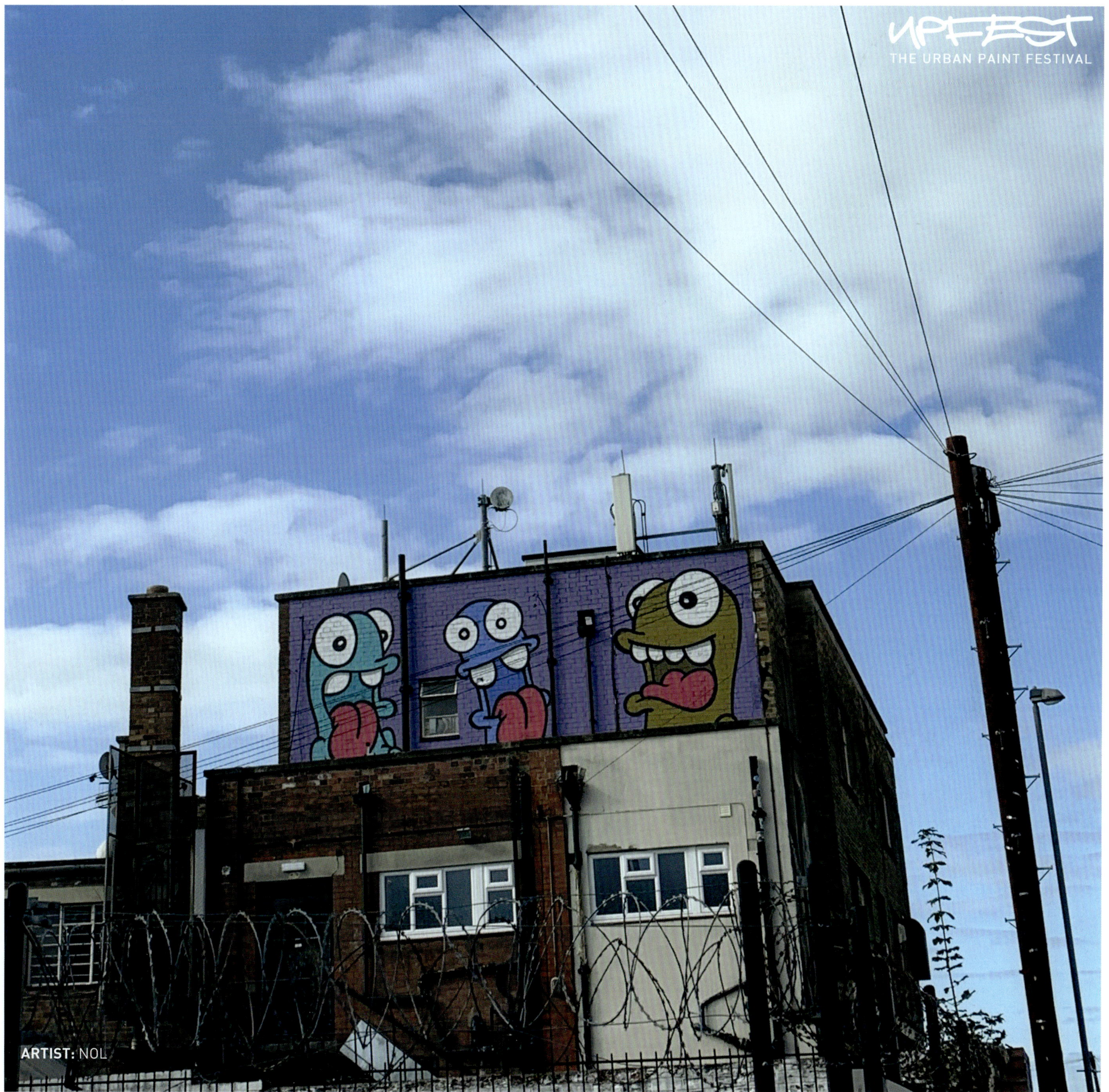

UPFEST
THE URBAN PAINT FESTIVAL

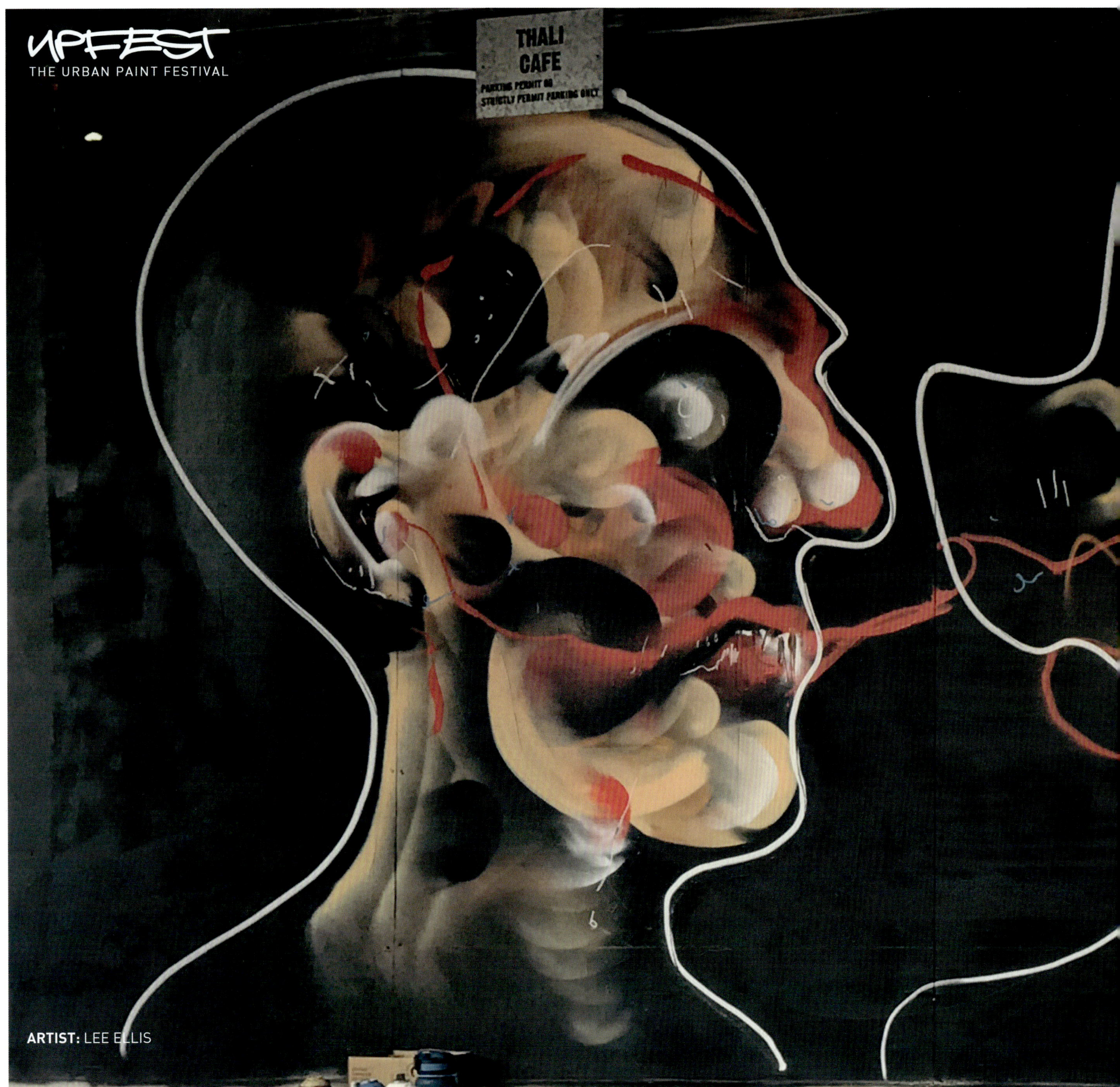
UPFEST
THE URBAN PAINT FESTIVAL
THALI
CAFE
PARKING PERMIT 00
STRICTLY PERMIT PARKING ONLY
ARTIST: LEE ELLIS

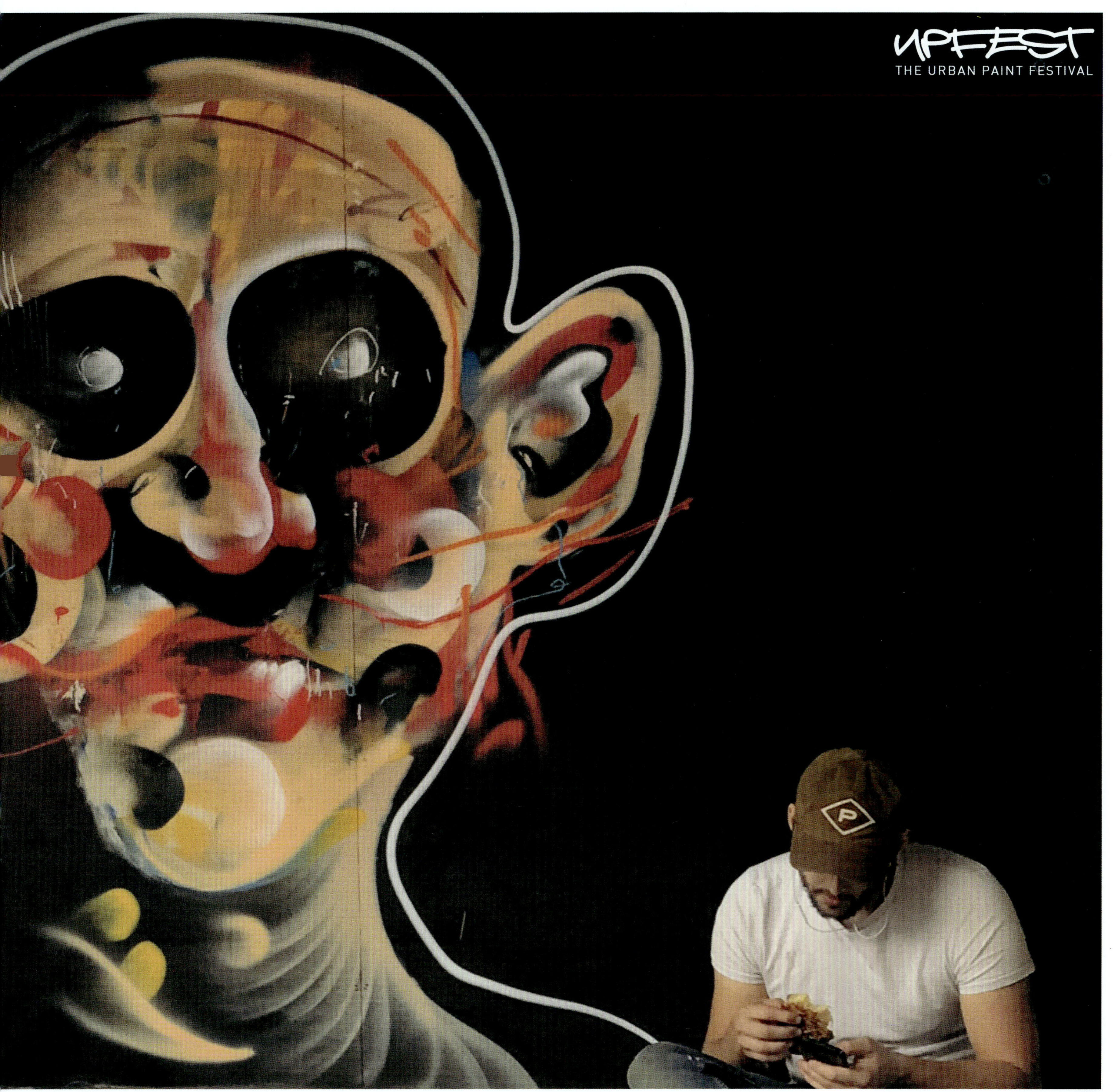

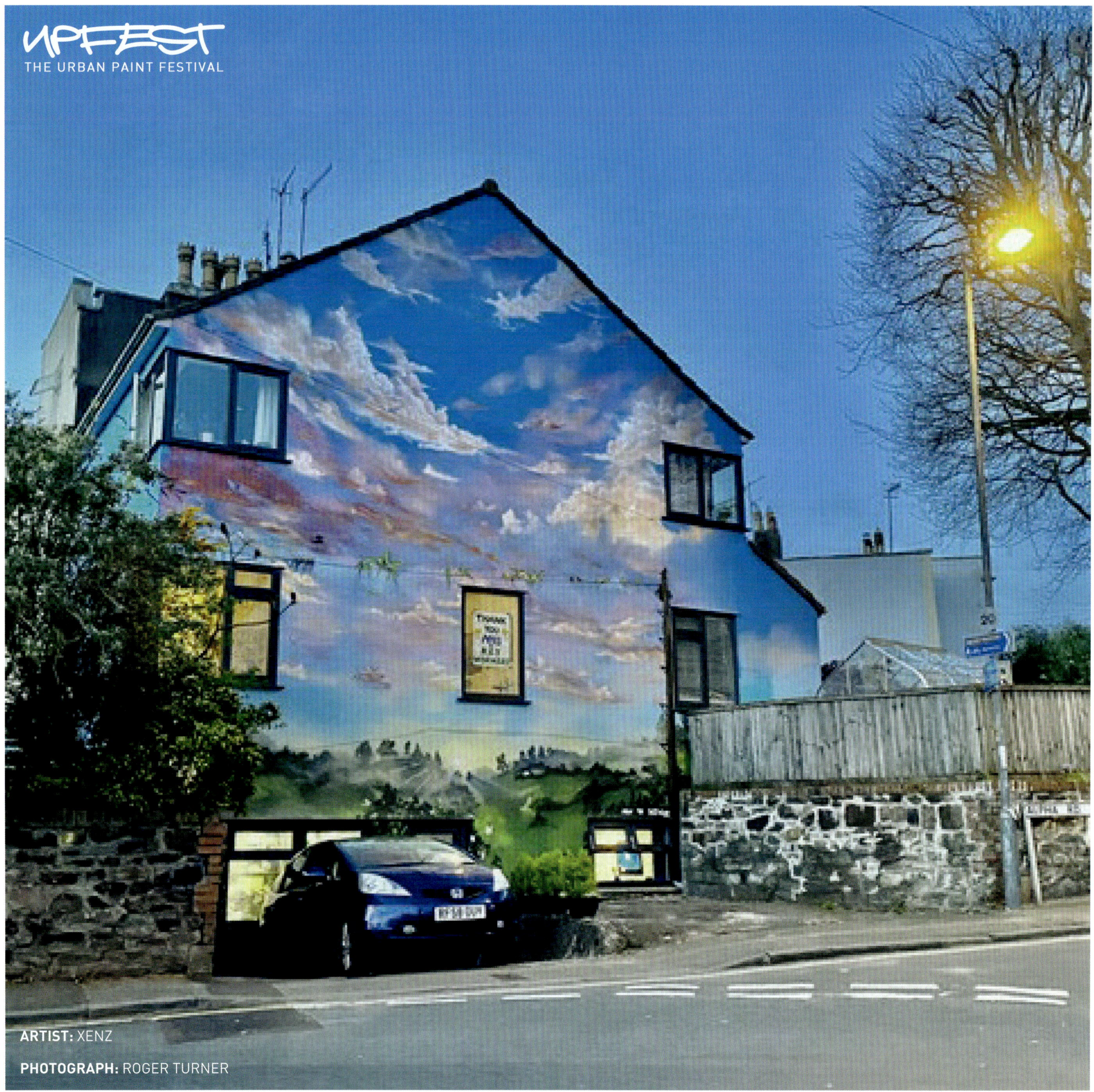

ARTIST: XENZ

PHOTOGRAPH: ROGER TURNER

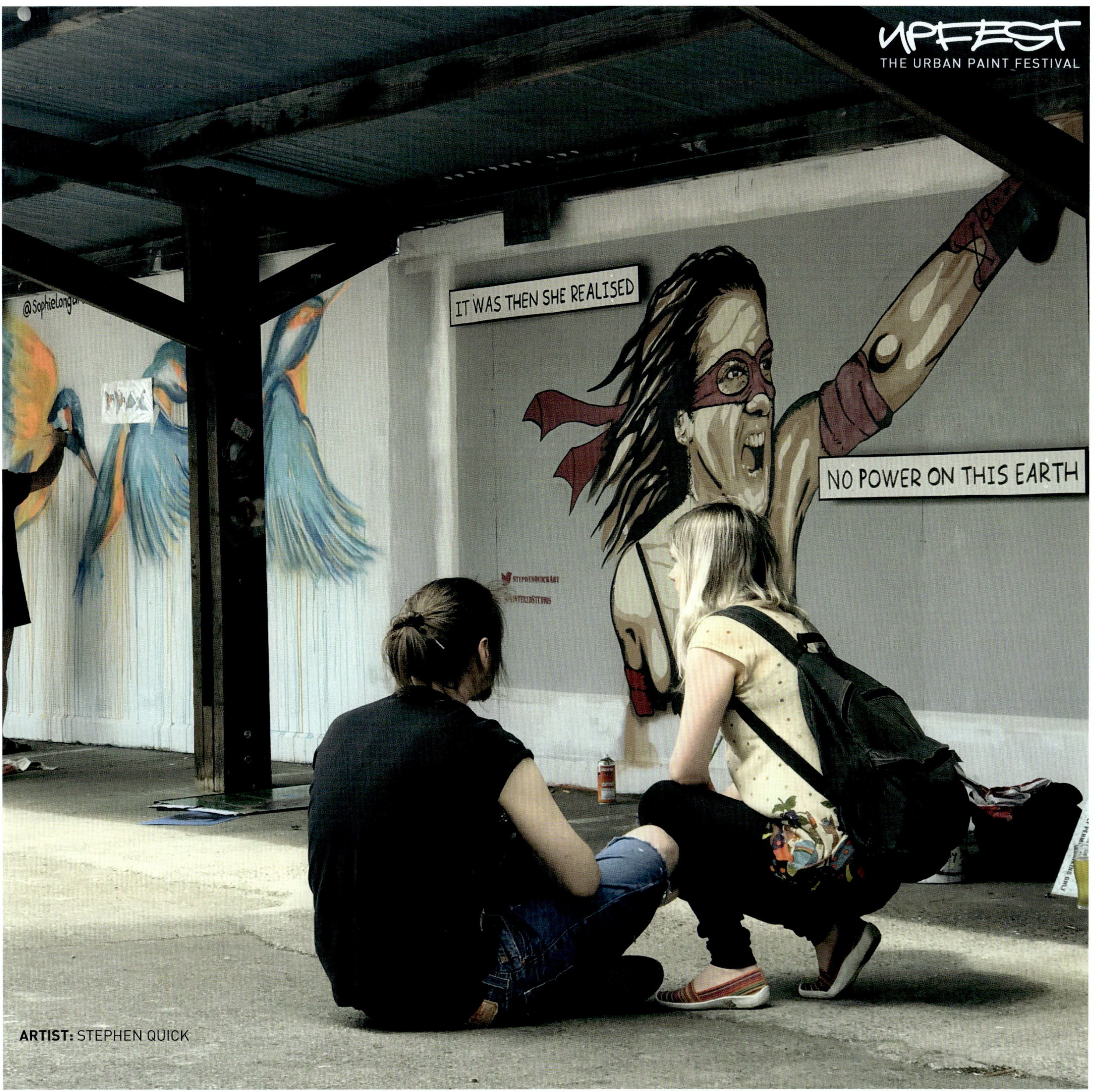

ARTIST: STEPHEN QUICK

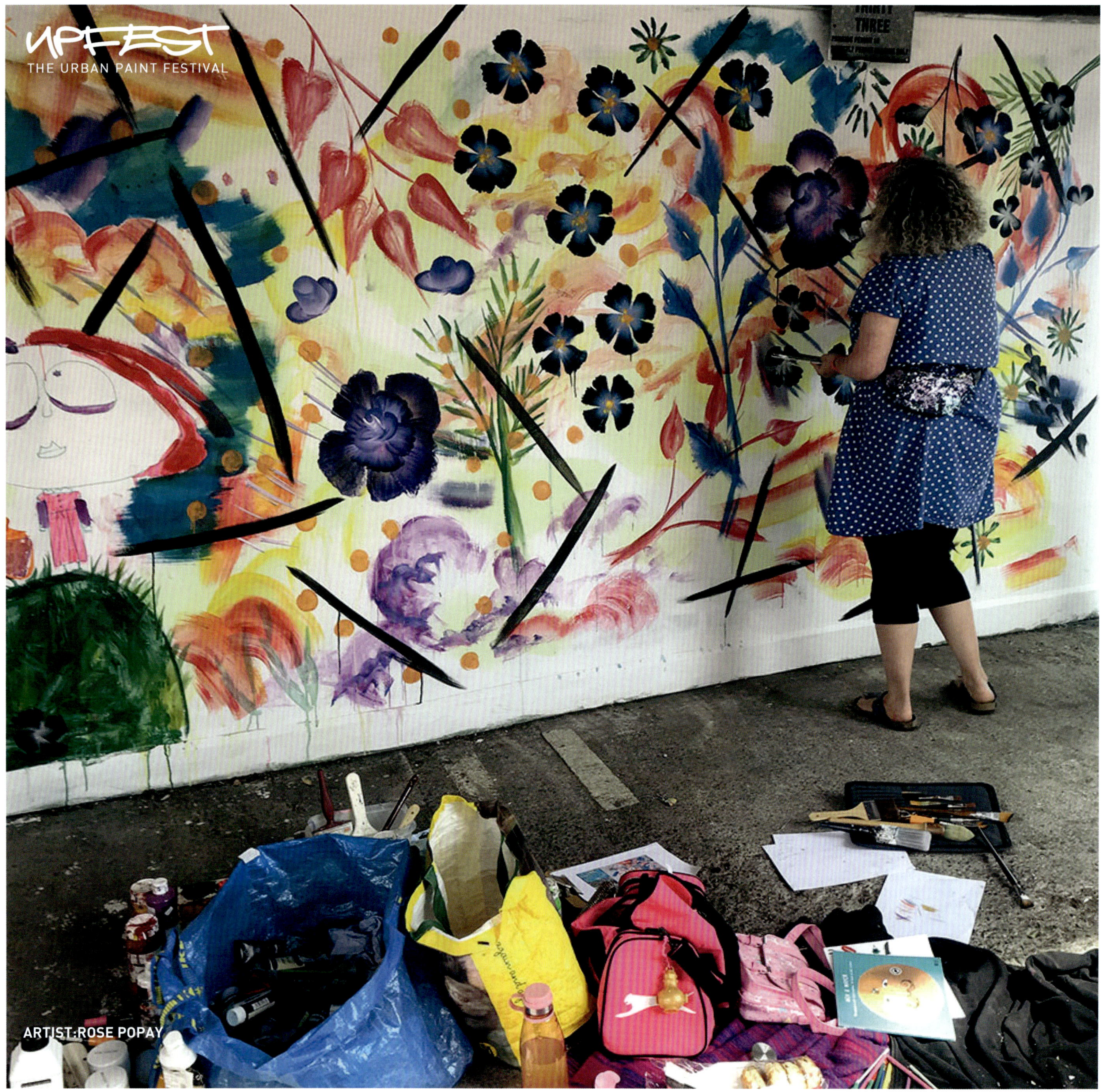

UPFEST
THE URBAN PAINT FESTIVAL
ARTIST·ROSE POPAY

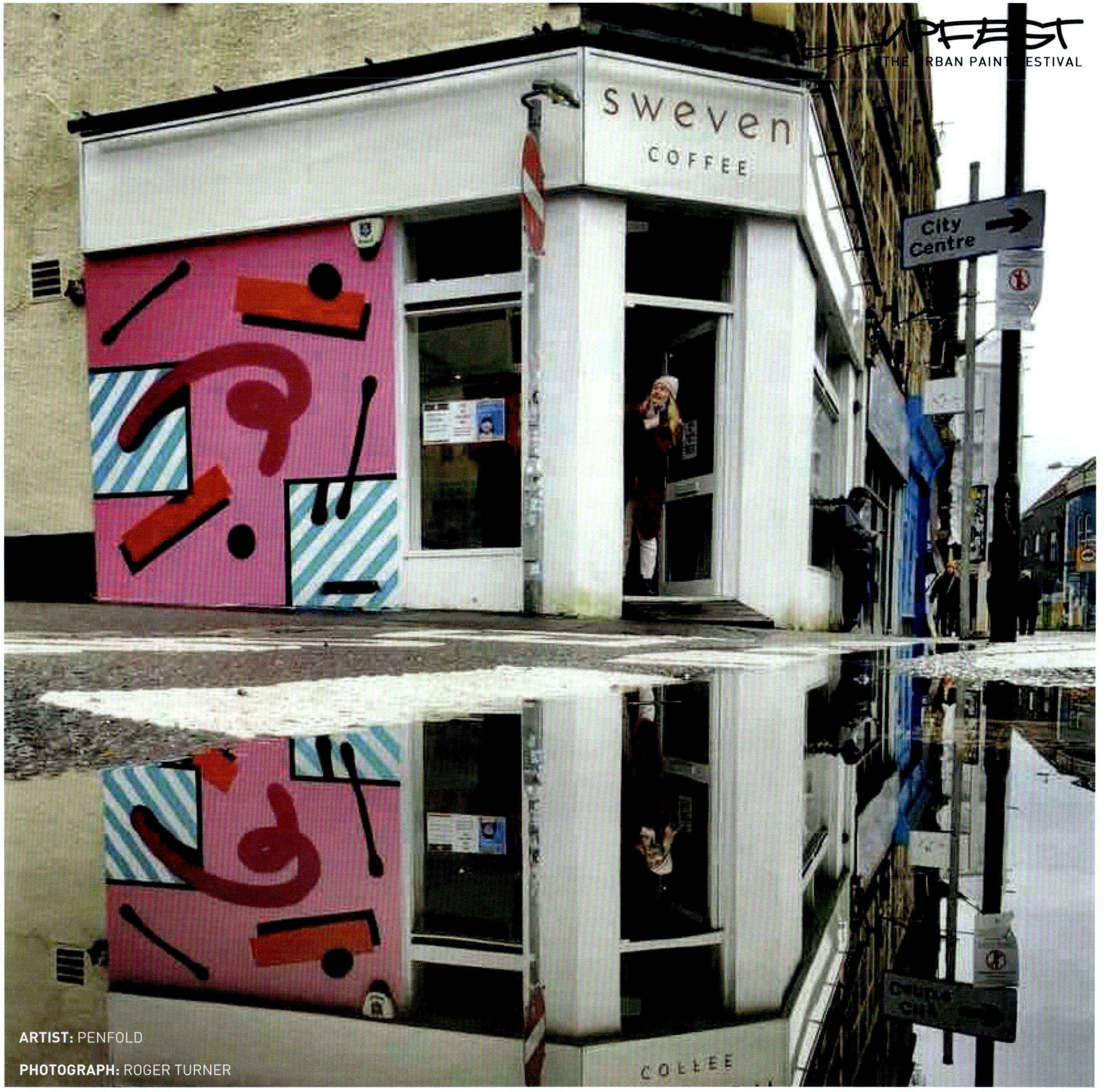

ARTIST: PENFOLD

PHOTOGRAPH: ROGER TURNER

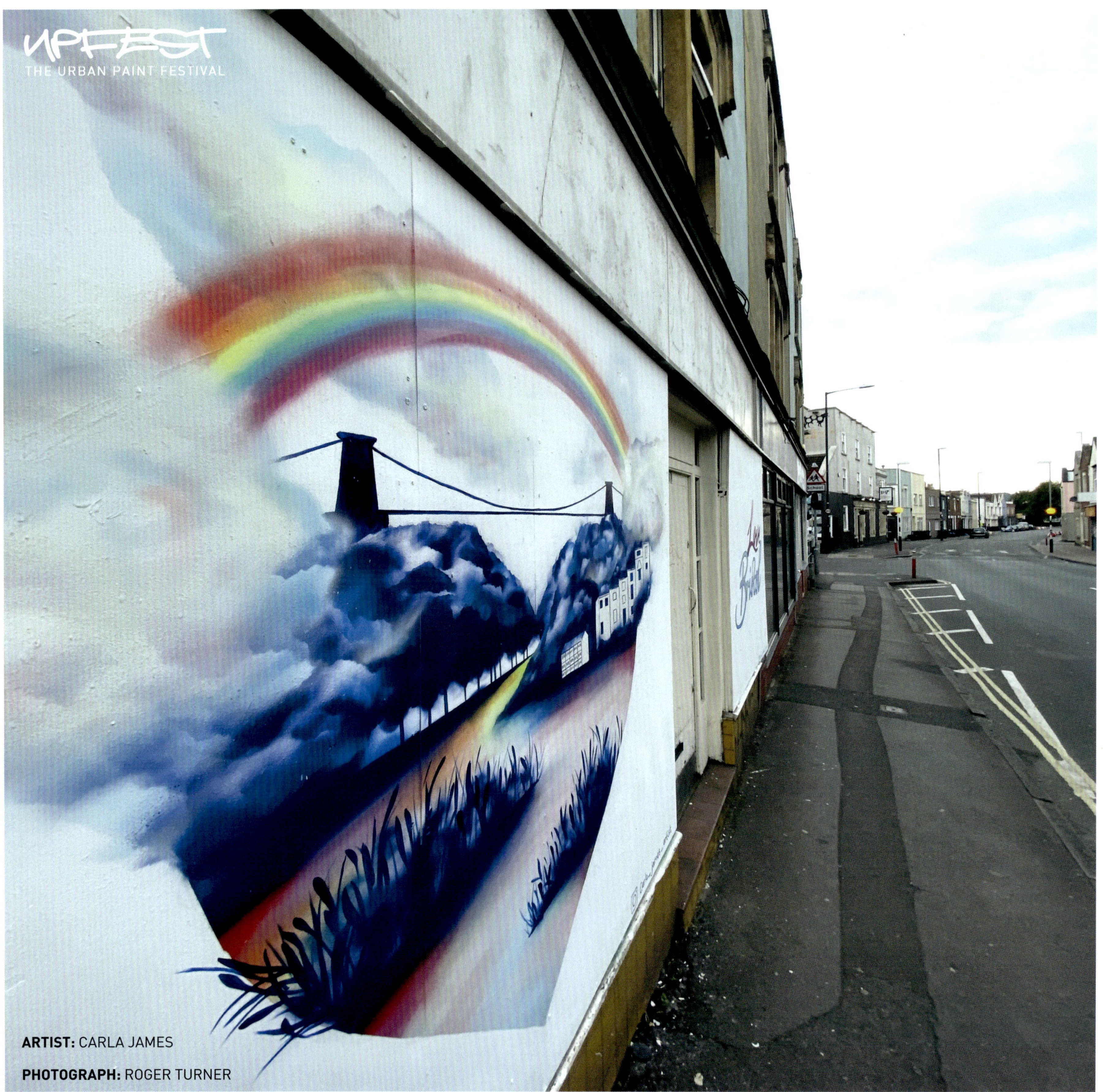

ARTIST: CARLA JAMES

PHOTOGRAPH: ROGER TURNER

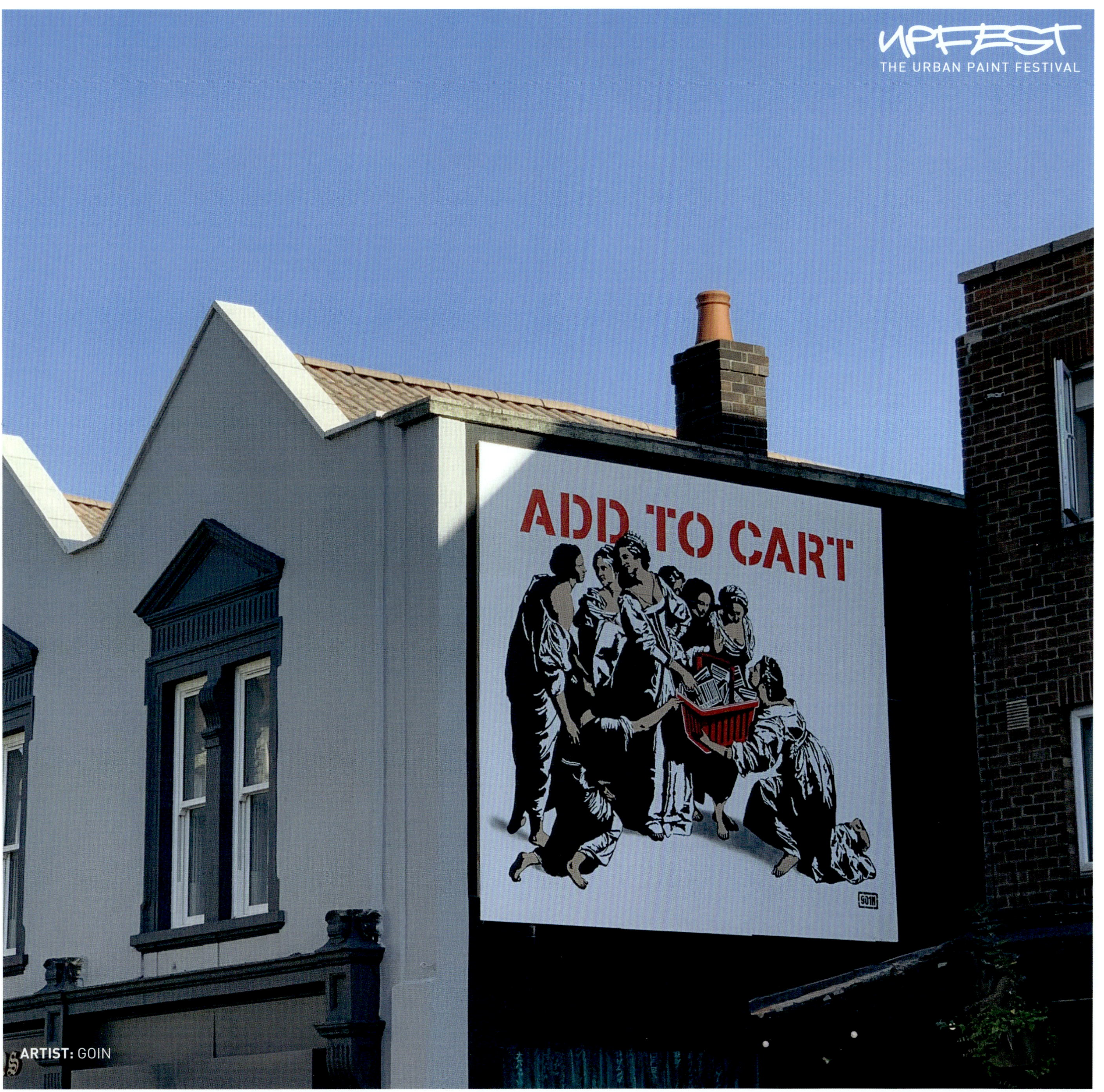

UPFEST
THE URBAN PAINT FESTIVAL
ADD TO CART
GOIN
ARTIST: GOIN

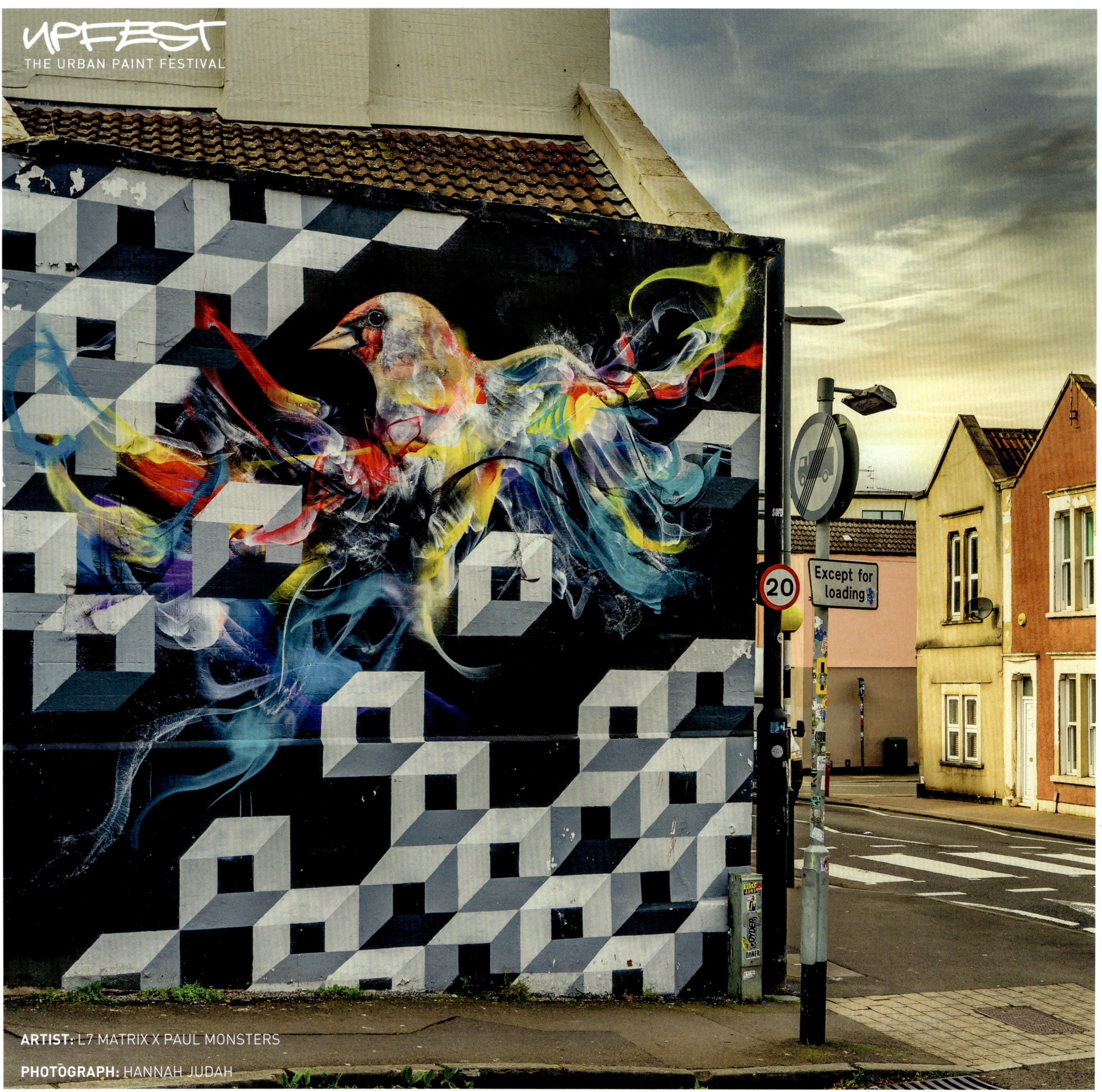
UPFEST
THE URBAN PAINT FESTIVAL
20
Except for loading
ARTIST: L7 MATRIX X PAUL MONSTERS
PHOTOGRAPH: HANNAH JUDAH